Praise for *Sandstorm*

"Hilsum's *Sandstorm: Libya in the Time of Revolution* . . . . measured account of why the battle for Libya happened . . . . . yed out, and
what may be yet to come. By hanging the distressi. . but often inspiring
stories of a group of Libyans around the central figure of the colonel, she
gives a rounded and readable snapshot of extraordinary change in a closed
country that few international journalists could claim to have known well
before last year's events."
—*Financial Times*

"Hilsum intersperses her well-researched and readable regional history
with on-the-ground portrayals and accounts that were gained by a reporter in a bulletproof vest getting her hands dirty. The effect is that the
book is more than the definitive document on the fate and future of a
nation—it is a history and a snapshot of a people."
—*The Daily Beast*

"*Sandstorm* is an impressive combination of vivid reporting and cool analysis from the veteran Channel 4 foreign correspondent. But what makes
her book so useful is that she zooms out from the day-to-day drama to explain how Libya was different: its tribal society, small population, vast oil
wealth, nonexistent or stunted institutions, routine repression, and, above
all, the wacky, capricious ruler who presided over it for so long."
—*The Guardian* (London)

"[Hilsum's] measured and sensible history of the . . . revolution, which
she covered on four separate trips, cannot be recommended enough. Well-
written, beautifully paced, with an understated command of the complex
background, plus a humor as dry as Libya's desert wind, the *ghibli*, it de-
serves to become the standard account."
—*The Telegraph* (UK)

"Hilsum's *Sandstorm* is a meticulously researched, finely crafted, and emi-
nently readable account not only of the revolution, but of the depravity of
the regime that triggered it. This is the most rounded account of Libya's
recent past that I have read."
—*The Times* (London)

"[Hilsum's] book brings together an account of the long months of the battle to overthrow him with an excellent replaying of Libya's history under Gaddafi, portraying previous generations of rebels and the failed attempts to unseat him. . . . Hilsum's account is essential (and accessible) reading for anyone who seeks to understand where Libya has come from and what the future might hold."   —*New Statesman* (London)

"Truer to the spirit of the messy, confused, and sometimes farcical character of the Gaddafi regime."   —*San Francisco Chronicle*

"A nearly incredible, fantastical tale of the rise and fall of the 'mad dog' of Libya . . . demonstrates not only the criminal megalomania of Gaddafi and his pernicious network of nepotism but also the venality and hypocrisy of the West that kept him in power until the bitter end. A fitting, clear-eyed send-off to an infamous dictator."   —*Kirkus Reviews*

"As well-paced and exciting as it is authoritative, *Sandstorm* is an epic account of the revolution that swept Muammar Gaddafi from power. Written by one of the finest war correspondents of our time, this is a must-read first draft of history."   —Jon Lee Anderson

"Lindsey Hilsum's powerful book is both a history of one of the world's most bizarre regimes and an unforgettable account of Gaddafi's rapid decline and fall. If only all revolutions had such intelligent and observant witnesses. Her prose is all the more effective for being restrained. She is also clear-eyed about the challenges facing Libyans after forty years of relentless repression by a corrupt family dictatorship. Essential reading."
     —Misha Glenny, author of *McMafia* and *The Balkans*

"No reporter was better placed than Lindsey Hilsum to tell the story of Libya's revolution, and she has not failed. She gives us both a compelling account of the rise and fall of one of Africa's most grotesque despots and a portrait of how ordinary citizens set about the task of toppling a regime. This is a kaleidoscopic, humane chronicle of how political convulsion is lived by real people. . . . Hilsum's writing is as lucid, nuanced, and intelligent as her pieces to camera, and the pages fly through one's hands."
     —Michela Wrong, author of *In the Footsteps of Mr. Kurtz*

PENGUIN BOOKS

SANDSTORM

Lindsey Hilsum is the international editor for Britain's Channel 4 News and appears regularly on PBS's *NewsHour*, CNN, and NBC. She has covered the major conflicts of the past two decades, including the wars in Iraq, Kosovo, and Afghanistan, as well as the Israeli-Palestinian conflict and the genocide in Rwanda. In 2011 she reported from Egypt and Bahrain as well as from Libya. Her journalism has won several prizes, including an Emmy, and recognition from One World Media and Amnesty International. Her writing has been featured in the *Sunday Times*, *The Guardian*, the *New Statesman*, and *Granta*, among other publications.

SANDSTORM

LIBYA IN THE TIME OF REVOLUTION

LINDSEY HILSUM

PENGUIN BOOKS

PENGUIN BOOKS
Published by the Penguin Group
Penguin Group (USA) Inc., 375 Hudson Street,
New York, New York 10014, USA

USA | Canada | UK | Ireland | Australia | New Zealand | India | South Africa | China
Penguin Books Ltd, Registered Offices: 80 Strand, London WC2R 0RL, England
For more information about the Penguin Group visit penguin.com

First published in Great Britain by Faber and Faber 2012
First published in the United States of America by The Penguin Press,
a member of Penguin Group (USA) Inc., 2012
Published in Penguin Books with a new epilogue 2013

Grateful acknowledgment is made for permission to reprint excerpts from the following copyrighted works:
"Epitaph on a Tyrant" and "Sonnets from China" from *Collected Poems of W. H. Auden.* "Epitaph on a Tyrant," copyright
1940 and renewed 1968 by W. H. Auden. "Sonnets from China," copyright 1945 by W. H. Auden, renewed 1973 by
The Estate of W. H. Auden. Used by permission of Random House, Inc. and Curtis Brown, Ltd.
"Mersa" from *Collected Poems* by Keith Douglas. Used by permission of Faber and Faber Ltd.
"Blood and Lead" from *Out of Danger* by James Fenton. Reprinted by permission
of Peters Fraser & Dunlop on behalf of James Fenton.

Map © William Donohoe. Used by arrangement with Faber and Faber Ltd.

THE LIBRARY OF CONGRESS HAS CATALOGED THE HARDCOVER EDITION AS FOLLOWS:
Hilsum, Lindsey.
Sandstorm : Libya in the time of revolution / Lindsey Hilsum.
p. cm.
Includes bibliographical references and index.
ISBN 978-1-59420-506-4 (hc.)
ISBN 978-0-14-312360-6 (pbk.)
1. Libya—History—Civil War, 2011–   2. Revolutions—Libya.   3. Qaddafi, Muammar.
4. Libya—History—1969–   I. Title.
DT236.H55 2012
961.204'2—dc23
2012005601

Printed in the United States of America
1 3 5 7 9 10 8 6 4 2

Designed by Marysarah Quinn

In memory of Tarek Ben Halim
1955–2009

The *Ghibli* is a hot, dry, usually south to southeasterly dust-bearing desert wind that occurs in Libya throughout the year, but most frequently in spring and early summer. . . . *El-ghibli* can have profound effect on the landscape by moving vast quantities of sand.

—WEATHER ONLINE

CONTENTS

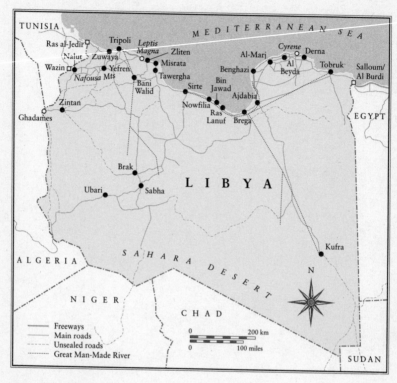

Map of Libya featuring major towns, significant places in the 2011 revolution and principal roads

SANDSTORM

PROLOGUE

There is no document of civilization which is not at the same time a document of barbarism.

—WALTER BENJAMIN, "ON THE CONCEPT OF HISTORY," *WALTER BENJAMIN: SELECTED WRITINGS, 1938–1940*

I will die as a martyr in the end.

—MUAMMAR GADDAFI, Tripoli, FEBRUARY 22, 2011

Colonel Muammar Gaddafi, Brother Leader, Universal Theorist, Falcon of Africa, King of Kings and Supreme Guide of the Great Socialist People's Libyan Arab Jamahiriya, met his end as he tried to reach his birthplace of Jahannam in the Libyan desert. One of the hottest places on earth, "Jahannam" translates as "hell," and that is what he went through. Dragged, wounded and bleeding, from a storm drain where he had been hiding under heavy fire, accompanied by his remaining bodyguards and fifth son, Mutassim, he was savagely kicked, punched, sodomized with a metal rod, and eventually shot in the chest and the head. Cheering fighters filmed using their cell phones as their comrades did to Gaddafi what they felt he had done to them for four decades. It was a cruel culmination of forty-two years of brutal and capricious rule and eight months of revolutionary conflict, an act of extreme violence from which a new state would be born, and from which a people who had grown used to dictatorship would have to learn to govern themselves.

The day after Gaddafi's death I drove east from the Libyan capital, Tripoli, to the town of Misrata to meet the men who had captured him. The fighters from Libya's third city were the most bitter of the country's revolutionaries, because they had endured months of siege in which thousands had been killed and wounded, women had been raped and constant bombardment had turned their most modern buildings into blackened skeletons. After Tripoli fell in August the Misrata brigades moved farther east, to Gaddafi's hometown of Sirte, which they destroyed as they hunted down the last of his supporters. Some people said the fighter who delivered the coup de grâce came from Benghazi, the town in eastern Libya where the revolution had started in February 2011, but it was the men from Misrata who seized and set upon the leader, and claimed his death as their victory.

In front of the mosque where they had celebrated Friday prayers they showed me the Thuraya satellite phone Gaddafi had been carrying, which he had used to call the Syrian TV station that broadcast his last defiant audio messages. It rang once, they said, and they heard the voice of a young woman they thought might be his daughter, Aisha, who had fled the country a few weeks earlier. I was handed a thumb-sized packet tightly wrapped in paper and Scotch tape that they said was an amulet, an African charm that he carried for good luck. Back at the barracks they displayed other artifacts. His boots—black, with a one-inch heel—an assault rifle and—prize of prizes—Gaddafi's golden pistol. I picked it up and turned it over. It was extremely heavy and oddly beautiful, embossed with a kind of fleur-de-lis pattern and engraved in Arabic with the words: "The sun will never set on Al Fattah Revolution."

It was a moment to reflect on the delusions of power. "Al Fattah"—he who opens the gate, just as Mohammed opened the gates to Mecca—was the name Gaddafi had given the revolution that brought him to power in 1969. The sun had set on it eight weeks earlier, when the fighters took Tripoli and he had fled. Libya was now emerging from the darkness. But

Gaddafi was deluded to the last. He was an old-style dictator, a ruthless megalomaniac, but he refused to call himself president, pretending that he had no formal role and that the Libyan people were in charge of their own destiny. His veteran bodyguard, Mansour Dao, hauled out of the drainage ditch with his boss, said Gaddafi had spent his final weeks moving from villa to villa in Sirte, sad and angry, alternating between rage and despair but convinced despite all evidence to the contrary that the Libyan people loved him still.

The brigade that caught Gaddafi said they were not the ones who had killed him. That had been the work of others, who had rushed to the scene as the news of his capture spread. Omran al Sheibani, a small, balding man in plain khaki fatigues, said he had been the first to recognize the wounded dictator as he emerged, bleeding and limping, his speech slurred, from the culvert where he had been hiding after a NATO air strike on his convoy.

"As soon as I saw him I started firing my Kalashnikov and praising God, saying, 'Allahu Akbhar!'" he told me. "This was the first time I had seen Muammar Gaddafi in the flesh. After eight months of fighting, all the people who were martyred, and all the children who perished in this war, he said—in the same way he speaks on television—'What's wrong with you? What's happening?'"

Those, then, were the last known words of the man who used to give interminable, rambling and often incomprehensible addresses to the Libyan people, and by extension, to the world. Sometimes he spoke from a balcony on the honey-colored walls of Tripoli Castle, overlooking cheering crowds in Green Square, the plaza he named after the color he had chosen to symbolize his rule. At others he would speak by the statue of a golden fist grasping a silver jet fighter, which he had erected in front of his house after it was destroyed in 1986 by an American bomb. In 2009, after his international rehabilitation as part of the "war on terror," he overran his allotted fifteen minutes at the UN General Assembly by an hour and a half, musing on topics ranging from the Palestinian question to who killed JFK and the possibility that swine flu was invented in a laboratory as a biological weapon. About halfway through, his interpreter, whom he had brought from Libya, suddenly cried out: "I've had enough! I can't take it anymore!" and a replacement had to be found in seconds. To the outside world Gaddafi had become a clown, a Botox-enhanced oddball in bizarre headgear who wanted to pitch his Bedouin tent in New Jersey while attending the UN, but to Libyans he remained a terrifying figure who could condemn anyone to death on a whim, with a single word or gesture.

Gaddafi's mutilated body was transferred to a refrigerated meat-storage facility in a Misrata supermarket, where people filed past filming on their cell phones in a macabre parody of a leader lying in state. The evening after he was killed, I went to the central square in Misrata, where thousands had gathered to celebrate. People kept thrusting their cell phones at me, as if showing me the footage would somehow make it more real. It was a way of convincing themselves that Gaddafi's rule was over. The National Transitional Council (NTC), the interim authority in Libya, tried to maintain that Gaddafi was a casualty of crossfire. Western governments, which had backed the revolution to overthrow him, expressed muffled outrage about the manner of his death but were privately relieved that he was gone, thus avoiding months of wrangling over where to try him and what punishment would be adequate. Human rights groups intoned warnings about the precedent the killing set. A few days later a plump elderly woman in a head scarf approached me in Benghazi, from where I was reporting on the official Liberation Day celebrations. "I want to tell you that we don't care how he died," she said, in flawless English. "If I'd been there I would have done worse. His family say they want his body. Well, where are the bodies of all our sons and husbands that he killed?"

In breach of Islamic law, which says that a body should be buried on the day of death, it was five days after his demise that Gaddafi's now stinking, rotting corpse was washed by an imam in the traditional way and prepared for burial. Before dawn it was taken in secret to an undisclosed location in the desert, where it was buried after a short ceremony. His son Mutassim and his defense minister, Abu Bakr Younis, who had been part of the original coup which brought him to power in 1969, were interred alongside him. The grave was covered with stones to stop wild dogs from digging up the bones. This time, Libya's transitional authorities made sure that no cell-phone footage would emerge. They were determined that the burial site would become neither a shrine for anyone who still saw Gaddafi as a savior nor a place to desecrate for those whose thirst for revenge had not been slaked. They wanted him simply to disappear.

In the days and weeks that followed, Libyans kept saying that now they could move forward, but they found themselves constantly pulled back to the past. Gaddafi had imprisoned and murdered their relatives; sponsored wars, coups and assassinations; and led a campaign of terror across the world. He had changed forever the relationship between oil producers and oil consumers and presided over an epoch of economic expansion in Libya, building housing, hospitals, schools and roads. He had confiscated private property, let the infrastructure he had built deteriorate and—in the boom years of capitalism at the turn of the century—allowed his children to steal the resources of the oil-rich state. He had defined their lives and the history of their country for four decades. Libya had been transformed from a sleepy desert outpost into one of the most controversial and notorious places on the planet. The Arab Spring uprisings of 2011 in neighboring Tunisia and Egypt removed the decrepit leaders but left the infrastructures of their governments more or less intact. Libya's, by contrast, was a true revolution, in which the entire apparatus of the state was turned upside down and routed. Nothing was certain, least of all what kind of country Libya would now become. Libyans needed to catch their breath, to congratulate themselves for a revolution that had succeeded in eight short months, but they also had to ask how this had ever come to pass, and why they had submitted to a whimsical despot for so long.

CHAPTER ONE

THE PEOPLE DEMAND THE FALL OF THE REGIME

Disobedience, in the eyes of anyone who has read history, is man's original virtue. It is through disobedience that progress has been made, through disobedience and through rebellion.

—OSCAR WILDE, *THE SOUL OF MAN UNDER SOCIALISM*

Walk like an Egyptian—Fight like a Libyan!

—LIBYAN JOKE, TOLD DURING THE REVOLUTION

I walked into the comfortable, middle-class living room in Benghazi and knew immediately that this would be a less than comfortable encounter. It was early March 2011, and the revolution wasn't yet a month old. There were some twenty people sitting on the plump sofas that lined the walls, men on one side of the room, women on the other, each silently holding up a portrait photograph pasted onto a board. These were the Abu Salim families, relatives of men who had been murdered in Colonel Gaddafi's most notorious prison. A stooped, elderly man, wearing a traditional dark red fez and huge black-rimmed glasses which dwarfed his thin face, came forward to speak. Fouad Assad Ben Omran described how every two months he used to make the long journey to Tripoli, taking food and clothing to his brother-in-law in Abu Salim.

"I used to go to Tripoli with his wife and children. His son was seven and his daughter five when we started," he said. "We took the basic things he needed and gave them to the guards. They told us he was there, but we weren't allowed to see him. We used to spend a day or two at the gate. We did this for fourteen years before we were told that he was dead."

That haunted me for days after the meeting; it haunts me still. A massacre is somehow an imaginable horror. But fourteen years of false hope, the deliberate not-telling, allowing the families to keep faith that one day their men will come home when in fact their bodies were lying in an unmarked pit, cemented over, possibly yards from where they queued up to deliver their baskets of food and piles of clean clothes, seemed to me cruelty of a different order. Repressive governments frequently make their opponents, or imagined opponents, "disappear," and families dwell in limbo for years, never knowing what happened to their sons and daughters. That is a particular kind of agony. Others live with the pain of knowing that someone they love is in prison, being tortured, maybe never to be released. Or they weep as they take delivery of a shabby parcel of belongings and learn that their relative has been executed or died under mysterious circumstances in custody. The Abu Salim families' not-knowing combined all of this into an extraordinary aggregation, wrought by a regime so callous that it encouraged its citizens to keep visiting the prison, to keep bringing comforts they could ill afford, which it knew would be stolen, long after it had murdered their husbands and sons.

On June 28, 1996, 1,270 men were killed in Abu Salim. No official list of the dead exists. The number has been gleaned from families who knew their son or brother was in the wing of the prison where the massacre took place, and from eyewitnesses. There may be more, because some families never knew that their relatives were in Abu Salim, or maybe fewer, because many men died of hunger, disease or torture before the massacre. In a country where families are large, and tribal connections bind together those separated by distance, such a massacre touches tens of thousands of people. In eastern Libya, where most of the victims came from, nearly everyone I met seemed to have a relative who was killed there. Some were Islamist fighters who had taken up arms against Colonel Gaddafi's regime while others were just religious men who went to the mosque too frequently, and so came under suspicion. Some had been arrested just a few weeks before the massacre while others had been inside for years.

It's hard to imagine the terror of that day. While protesting about their conditions the prisoners killed a guard they were trying to take hostage. The officials sent to negotiate agreed to improve conditions, and sick prisoners were loaded onto buses, apparently to go to the hospital. When they were led into the yard, the remaining prisoners believed that their demands had been met. What happened next was like canned hunting, in which big cats are caged so hunters have a better chance of making a kill. Soldiers positioned on the roof shot into the crowd in the yard until none was left alive. Blood splashed up the walls, and the noise of gunfire echoed across the neighborhood surrounding the prison. The smell of death lingered for days.

I knew none of this before I went to Libya. None of the people in that living room had spoken to a journalist before. Each held up their picture and pronounced the name of the person they had lost, followed by the word shahid, meaning martyr. A plump woman in a full black abaya stepped forward. "My brother was a normal person, practicing his religion, attending prayers and studying the teachings of Islam," said Faiza Ahmed Zubi. "He never did anything unacceptable or out of the ordinary. The day he was arrested, he was bringing the shopping home. They stopped him in the middle of the street on January 12, 1993, and from that moment on we didn't see or hear from him again." Everyone listened in silence as she told her story, even though they must have heard it a hundred times before. Faiza had heard rumors of the massacre four years after it happened, when released prisoners came to see her. "They told us that the walls were covered in bullet holes; they saw body parts and other proof that a massacre had taken place," she said. "They told me my brother was among the martyrs."

In 2009, the government presented the family with a piece of paper that said simply that her brother had died in Tripoli in 1996. No details, no cause of death, no admission of guilt. She had already joined others in approaching a young lawyer named Fathi Terbil, who encouraged the families to protest. "For more than four years we've been out there almost every Saturday demonstrating and demanding our rights. First, we want the bodies of our martyrs, and second, we want the criminals who killed our sons brought to justice."

I asked what kind of justice.

"I want Gaddafi, his sons, and all those who helped him to be killed," she replied, her face impassive, her voice steady.

"Kill them all?" I asked.

"Yes."

"Is there no other way?"

She shook her head.

"No."

As we said our good-byes another woman thrust a small blue envelope into my hand, the kind used by old-fashioned photography shops. I opened it in my hotel room and found a faded color passport picture of a round-faced boy with thick black hair in a cream shirt, and a similar-size photograph of an older man with white hair, wearing a black fez and a traditional black robe, a *jird*, fringed with gold brocade. A closer look reveals that he is sitting in a wheelchair. His legs, which are covered in white bandages, have been amputated at the knee. A father, a husband, an uncle? How did he lose his legs? Was he already disabled when they threw him in prison? I keep the pictures in my study. The boy and the old man stare out at me: people I never knew, victims of a crime I never heard about until long years after their killers tossed their bodies into an anonymous mass grave.

. . .

For years, anyone who mentioned the Abu Salim killings risked arrest or worse. But Seif al-Islam Gaddafi, the Brother Leader's second son, realized in 2007, when he was trying to open Libya up to the world, that the massacre could no longer be ignored. The families would never forgive and forget. Their pain and anger had to be acknowledged and diffused in some way, so he tried to engage with them, under the auspices of his Gaddafi International Charity and Development Foundation. The campaign of the Abu Salim families was personal for the lawyer Fathi Terbil. His brother, cousin and brother-in-law were killed in the massacre, so when other families asked him to represent them he couldn't say no. He had a plump figure and always wore a baseball cap and a black-and-white-checkered kaffiyeh; he had never married, devoting his time to unpopular and dangerous human rights cases. He knew he was taking a risk by championing the Abu Salim families, but it was his cause too.

Sometimes he would demonstrate alone, outside the Benghazi courthouse, sometimes with the families. He was arrested seven times. When the state finally admitted to the massacre—nearly a decade after it had taken place—most of the families rejected the paltry compensation offered. Terbil understood that they needed to know every detail: who had given the orders; who had carried them out; where the bodies were buried; who had decided to lie to them for so long about what had happened. As the regime tried to cauterize the running sore that was Abu Salim, it had no choice but to deal with him, but he remained, in its eyes, a dangerous agitator.

In February 2011, Libyans were looking west and east, to their immediate neighbors Tunisia and Egypt, hearts in their mouths. It was called the Arab Spring by those observing it, but the unrest was more like a fever, spreading from person to person, town to town, country to country across North Africa and the Middle East. It had started in Tunisia, where the government of Zine al-Abedine Ben Ali was toppled after twenty-eight days of ferment. In Egypt, it took just eighteen days to oust Hosni Mubarak. Both fell on a Friday. As Libyans planned their Day of Rage for Thursday, February 17, the joke went around the Middle East that Muammar Gaddafi had banned Fridays. They chose the seventeenth because it was the anniversary of demonstrations that had happened in Benghazi in 2006, when people protested against the Danish newspaper that had published cartoons of the Prophet Mohammed. As Muslims, many Libyans found the cartoons insulting to their religion, but when the demonstrators also started to shout slogans against Gaddafi, the police tried to stop the protest. The police shot into the crowd and eleven people were killed.

This time the authorities in Benghazi wanted to stop the protests before they started, so on the afternoon of February 15th, two days before the planned demonstration, twenty-four police officers arrived at Fathi Terbil's house and arrested him. Word quickly spread, and far from deterring the protesters, it spurred them on. The moment they heard the news, instead of waiting until the seventeenth the Abu Salim families immediately went to the police station where Terbil was being held to demand his release. Benghazi, in eastern Libya, had long been a center of resentment against Colonel Gaddafi's rule, but as the number of protesters grew, the authorities dithered. They were determined to stop an Egypt-style uprising, using force if necessary, but taking on the Abu Salim families was especially difficult. For a start, most of them were elderly women.

After midnight Terbil was taken to see an apparently nervous and confused Abdullah al Sanussi, Colonel Gaddafi's brother-in-law, who was not only the head of military intelligence but also widely regarded as responsible for the Abu Salim massacre, the man who had assured the prisoners that their demands would be met. He promised to release Fathi Terbil but requested that he tell people to stop protesting. But it was too late. By then the families had been joined by other lawyers, as well as by doctors, engineers and hundreds of other people. Even if Terbil had wanted to tell them to stop, no one would have listened.

I met Fathi Terbil a week after the uprising. He was brought to see me in my hotel room in Benghazi—smuggled in, because he feared that his life was still in danger from lingering Gadaffi loyalists in the town. By releasing him, the regime had revealed its vulnerability, but now Colonel Gaddafi's men were fighting for survival, and would show no restraint. Terbil had long thought this moment would come. He saw Abu Salim as just one of dozens of issues that made Libyans angry and ashamed. The list was long. Gaddafi had, for example, started a war in neighboring Chad, which most Libyans saw as futile and in which thousands of Libyan soldiers had perished. He had spent the country's money on schemes in sub-Saharan Africa while Libya's infrastructure crumbled. He had sponsored terrorist groups around the world in pursuit of his idea of worldwide revolution. Now the accumulation of grievances had toppled over, like a huge pile of documents. Fathi Terbil's arrest was the last file thrown on top, causing the whole lot to collapse.

"We, the Abu Salim families, ignited the revolution," he told me. "The Libyan people were ready to rise up because of the injustice they experienced in their lives, but they needed a cause. So calling for the release of people, including me, who had been arrested became the justification for their protest."

Throughout the sixteenth, after Terbil was released, the crowds in Benghazi kept growing, their chants swelling through the night. "Rise up oh Benghazi, the day you have been waiting for has come!" they shouted, and—in a persistent echo of Egypt and Tunisia—"The people demand the fall of the regime!" During the years they had been forced to demonstrate in praise of Gaddafi, the standard slogan was "God! Muammar! Libya! That's all we need!" Now they changed it, crying: "There is no god but God, and Muammar is the enemy of God!" Abdullah Sanussi met local

committees, Gaddafi's enforcers, to encourage them to crush the uprising. A video of a meeting shows a roomful of men each more eager than
the next to show loyalty to "our father," meaning Gaddafi. Sanussi is dis-
missive of the rebels. "They're mostly alcoholics and drug addicts who
have no family," he says. "We've described these recent events to The
Leader, and reassured him that 'Benghazi is your city, the people are up to
the task.'"

Unconvinced, The Leader sent his third son, Saadi, to sort out the
problem. It was a strange choice—Saadi was hated in Benghazi like
nowhere else because of what had become known as the Football Revolution eleven years earlier. Football was always a fraught issue in Libya—
people were passionate about it but fans were permitted to refer to players
only by number, never by name, in case any became stars whose popularity might exceed that of the Brother Leader, Gaddafi himself. All, that is,
apart from one player—Saadi.

Gaddafi's football-mad son fancied himself a great midfielder, and in
the late 1990s was appointed not only as captain of the national team, but
as owner, manager and captain of Tripoli Al-Ahly, a first-division team in
the capital. Unfortunately, Benghazi had a team by the same name. Saadi
decided that this situation could not continue—the team might have been
in existence since 1947, but Benghazi Al-Ahly must be no more. Fans of
the team say he set about destroying it by buying the best players and bribing referees, until it sank to the point where it was about to be relegated
from Libya's Premier League. Then, on a hot day in July 2000, when one
too many penalties had been awarded to the opposing side, the fans had
had enough. They booed. They shouted. They invaded the pitch. They
spilled out into the town, burning pictures of Gaddafi and—this being
what angered the Gaddafis most—parading a donkey dressed in a football
jersey bearing Saadi's number.

Punishment was swift and severe. About eighty fans were arrested,
some held for years and tortured in custody. That might have been the end

of it, but on September 1st, the thirty-first anniversary of the coup that brought his father to power, Saadi moved decisively against the team. Soldiers driving bulldozers were sent to destroy Benghazi Al-Ahly's clubhouse, while people were reportedly forced to watch and cheer. Saadi went on to play without distinction, and only very occasionally, for a couple of Italian teams, in a rare deal whereby the player pays the team rather than the other way round. The men of Benghazi nursed their resentment and bided their time.

What triggers the moment when people lose their fear? A sense of humiliation as much as anger drove people out onto the streets. For four decades they felt ashamed of having a leader who made them a laughingstock. Westerners might see Libyan religiosity and conservatism as a throwback to earlier times, but they saw themselves as modern people. In recent years an increasing number had traveled abroad to study or work, so they knew how other countries were developing economically and politically. Under the influence of satellite TV the society was gradually growing more open and cosmopolitan, but Libyan politics never changed. Gaddafi defined Libya, and Libyans began to feel like aliens in their own country.

Among the demonstrators in Benghazi on February 17th was businessman Ali Raslan and his fifteen-year-old son, Idris. He told me the story just after I arrived, when I was staying at his home in Benghazi—like others in those early days, he happily accommodated journalists in the belief that getting the news out was the best way to ensure that the revolution would not be reversed. His was a middle-class life, with a comfortable, large house full of marble and soft, ornate furnishings and frequent business trips abroad. At first he was reluctant to get too involved, but his son Idris insisted not only that they should demonstrate, but that they should go right to the front. Among Gaddafi's forces that day were a number of black men wearing yellow hard hats, who most demonstrators believed to be mercenaries from sub-Saharan Africa. It was the first time I had been told that Gaddafi was using foreign as well as homegrown fighters, something that fueled Libyans' anger and would store up trouble in the coming months. The crowd swelled, and the men in yellow hats began shooting. As everyone began to shriek and run, Ali ran too, and he lost sight of Idris. By the time he got home he was full of dread. He found his brother at the door and knew immediately that the worst had happened.

Ali's bottle-lens glasses misted up as he spoke. He looked bewildered.

"Idris was my favorite son. He used to come on private business trips with me—I took him to China and Turkey. I treated him like a friend. Now I will never hold him again."

He showed me a photograph of a handsome boy, with dark hair, in a smart blue shirt.

"Idris died in the defense of freedom, and for an end to Colonel Gaddafi," he said. "God is good."

When interviewed a few weeks after the uprising, Saadi Gaddafi denied that he had given the order to shoot into the crowd the day Idris was killed. His uncle, Abdullah al Sanussi, is believed to have been commanding the forces in Benghazi as they did their brutal best to quash the uprising. A cycle of funerals began, as more people turned out in mourning than had attended the original demonstration, and of them still more were killed, as Gaddafi's gunmen attacked those who were grieving. Four months later the prosecutor of the International Criminal Court, Luis Moreno-Ocampo, issued a warrant for Sanussi's arrest. There were reasonable grounds to believe, it said, that—once instructed by his brother-in-law, Colonel Gaddafi—he had directly ordered troops to attack civilians demonstrating in the city. If that could be proven, the prosecutor said, it was a crime against humanity.

It was no surprise that the revolution started in the east. Gaddafi's attempts to unite Libyans in support of his quasi-socialist, quasi-religious, idiosyncratic and shifting ideology had driven people back to older loyalties—family, tribe, town and region.

You could trust no one but those closest to you. The people of the east had never accepted Gaddafi; he had responded by neglecting Benghazi, the eastern capital. Its buildings were crumbling, and the streets were strewn with litter, rubble and sewage. Everything looked old and shabby, like a senile old man who can no longer dress himself when there's no one around to help him do up his buttons or replace his threadbare jacket. Easterners were nostalgic for the time when Benghazi was Libya's center of power, before Gaddafi's Al Fattah Revolution opened the gates to what they saw as chaos and ruin.

For centuries, Libya's three regions—Cyrenaica to the east, Tripolitania to the west and Fezzan, the desert south—were separate territories, but their histories are interwoven. Phoenicians, Greeks and Romans invaded Cyrenaica and Tripolitania, on the Mediterranean coast; the ruins of the Greco-Roman city of Lepcis Magna, which lies between Tripoli and Benghazi, and Cyrene, near Beyda in the east, are reminders of Libya's importance in the ancient world. The original inhabitants of Libya were the Berbers, or Amazigh, but the Cyrenaicans and Tripolitanians are primarily Arabs, descendants of those who brought Islam in the seventh century. Many, especially in Cyrenaica, have Bedouin roots and trace their ancestry to nomadic Arabs who herded goats and camels on the northern fringes of the desert. The people of Fezzan are more African than Arab, many of them nomadic Tuareg who roam across the unmarked borders of the Sahara into Algeria and Niger. There has been trade between the interior and the coast for centuries. History mixes people up, and no one's ethnicity is pure, so the definitions are approximate, and the country's geographical position makes a sense of identity even more ambiguous. Libya is both African and Arab, physically in North Africa but leaning culturally toward the Middle East. Libyans from Tripolitania and Cyrenaica frequently talk about Africa as if they had been born on another continent. Libya is often described as having "the highest standard of living in Africa" but to Cyrenaicans or Tripolitanians such a comparison is not only irrelevant but demeaning. They look east toward the Gulf or north toward Europe but never south toward the vast expanse of the Sahara. They want to compare themselves with Italy or the United Arab Emirates, not to Nigeria or Togo.

In the nineteenth century, the waters of the Mediterranean, north of what was known as the Barbary Coast, were full of pirates, who hijacked European and American ships. The U.S. Marines' official song, the "Marines' Hymn," that begins "From the Halls of Montezuma / To the shores of Tripoli" refers to the First Barbary War, which was fought in 1805 between the pirates and the Americans, who were fed up of having their ships hijacked. At that time Libya was part of the Ottoman Empire, as it had been since the sixteenth century, but toward the end of the Ottoman period, in 1911, Italy occupied all three territories. It was a particularly brutal form of colonialism, made harsher when Benito Mussolini and his Fascist government came to power in Rome. Much to the frustration of the Italians, the Bedouins of Cyrenaica resisted colonial rule. The Italians responded by herding about one hundred thousand of them into concentration camps, where conditions were cruel and starvation and disease were rife. Some estimates say most died, reducing the population of the east by one half. General Rodolfo Graziani, sent to quell the uprising, has long been a hated figure for Libyans, while his nemesis, the resistance fighter Omar Mukhtar, is a national hero.

I was to see a lot of Omar Mukhtar during the revolution in 2011; his distinctive profile, with a white beard and white cap, was ubiquitous on banners, stickers, key rings and other revolutionary merchandising across eastern Libya. He was born in Tobruk, Libya's easternmost city, and those now rebeling saw themselves as his heirs, fighting Gaddafi's government as if it were an occupying force like the Italians. Mukhtar was a Koranic scholar as well as a freedom fighter, revered for his expertise in desert warfare and his refusal to surrender. He led a band of guerrillas for twenty years, attacking Italian troops and sabotaging their supply lines. In 1931, he was captured, and within three days Graziani had him tried and publicly executed. His dignity in the face of death has become part of Libyan mythology. As he went to the gallows he is said to have recited a Koranic verse: "To God we belong and to Him we shall return." Gaddafi often tried to shore up his legitimacy by invoking the spirit of Omar Mukhtar. The Brother Leader was likewise standing up to the forces of imperialism; he too was defending Arabs against colonial powers. He funded the 1981 Hollywood film *Lion of the Desert*, an epic full of desert battles featuring noble resistance fighters and cruel Italian colonialists, and starring Anthony Quinn as Mukhtar and Oliver Reed as Graziani. A generation of Libyan children watched it again and again, as it was shown on Libyan TV almost nightly. The 2011 revolution was in part a fight over the legacy of Omar Mukhtar.

It was also about reclaiming the heritage of the Sanussis, the religious order to which Omar Mukhtar belonged. Sanussi was an Islamic sect founded by an Algerian Islamic scholar in Mecca in the midnineteenth century that took some of its spirituality from Sufism, a contemplative, mystical form of Islam, but that also encourages austere behavior, rather like the Salafis of Saudi Arabia. Theirs was a secret order that didn't reveal all of its religious practices to outsiders, but its austerity suited the harsh life of the Bedouin of Cyrenaica. The Sanussis resisted all forms of foreign occupation, including Ottoman rule in Libya, and garnered respect across North Africa in the early nineteenth century by resisting French colonialists. Their opposition to Italian occupation increased their authority and popularity in Cyrenaica. The Italians branded them as jihadis and religious fanatics, exactly as Gaddafi would define his enemies half a century later. During World War II the Sanussis's chief, Idris, fled to Egypt, where another colonial power, Britain, recognized him as the emir of Cyrenaica. At the end of the conflict the Italians had to surrender Libya to the British, who took control of Cyrenaica and Tripolitania, and to the French, who governed Fezzan.

Idris's ancestors had resisted occupation, but when he returned after the war he relied on the Great Powers, especially Britain, for support. In 1951, after independence negotiations at the United Nations, Tripolitania, Fezzan and Cyrenaica were united in a federal system, and Idris became king.

The years of neglect under Gaddafi made many easterners nostalgic for the eighteen years of the monarchy. King Idris was a product of Cyrenaica, and he kept his court in Benghazi, even though Tripoli was officially the capital. An old man, sitting in his shop doorway, told me how in the time of the kingdom window boxes of flowers decorated the balconies along the street. Easterners seemed to have forgotten the destructive intrigue of the court and the corruption among the elite. In 1963, the federal system was dropped, and Libya became a unitary state, but although he had extensive powers, King Idris failed to assert himself. A black-and-white photograph from May 1954 shows Idris with a young Queen Elizabeth, on what was only her second state visit since assuming the British throne. She is wearing a full-skirted summer dress with white elbow-length gloves, the epitome of 1950s chic. King Idris stands next to her, a serious-looking, tall, bearded man with round glasses, wearing traditional white robes and a dark fez. An unassuming and rather shy man, so diffident that he was known as the "reluctant monarch," he relied on the British and Americans for guidance and support.

Colonel Gaddafi seized power on September 1, 1969, while King Idris was having medical treatment in Turkey. The eastern families who owed their positions to their relationship with the king rapidly lost all power and influence. Gaddafi and the Free Officers who ousted the monarchy were angry young men resentful of royal privilege and of the king's reliance on Britain and America. Yet the new order in some ways resembled the old. King Idris had banned political parties as divisive. He had failed to create strong central institutions of government. Gaddafi frequently referred to his Bedouin roots, invoking the precolonial time as a kind of golden age when Bedouin values of equality and self-reliance prevailed. The heritage myth was different, but the outcome was the same: Libya had no strong, modern central state under King Idris, and it would have none under Colonel Gaddafi.

Libya's history of division gave credence to Gaddafi's February 2011 warnings that if he were ousted the country would disintegrate, tribe would fight tribe and Islamists would take over. But Libya had advantages too. With a population of just over six million, and considerable oil and gas reserves, it was rich—unlike Egypt, with its eighty million people, few natural resources and widespread poverty. Large numbers of Libyans had studied abroad, gaining the technocratic skills needed to build a modern economy. But there would be a long way to go. Before anything could be built, much had to be destroyed.

The first images of the Libyan revolution were blurred and shaky, but the scene was unmistakable. A group of youths was taking iron bars and hammers to the most potent symbol of Colonel Gaddafi's power: two concrete statues of his "Green Book," the treatise in which he had set out his eccentric political philosophy. The ugly blocks, painted bright green with white writing, were ubiquitous outside the headquarters of Gaddafi's revolutionary committees' buildings, where his thugs hung out in every town. On February 17th, as the protests took hold in Benghazi, the same was happening farther east, in Tobruk. Young men clambered on the debris as the ravaged blocks toppled over, while a swelling crowd sang and cheered, "The people demand the fall of the regime!" Smoke and flames swirled around as they set fire to the building. No one stopped them. The footage went viral. People watched on Internet sites and TV screens around the world as the previously quiescent population of Libya vented its fury.

Tawfik Othman al-Shohibiy didn't know the impact taking those pictures would have. A serious young man in a shabby duffle coat, he had just passed his twenty-fifth birthday and was looking forward to a year in America on an engineering scholarship. He thought of himself more as a computer nerd than a rebel. But as his friends were destroying the monumental books, he filmed it with his cell phone. His brother Seif emerged from the crowd.

"They'll cut the Internet soon," he said. "You'd better go and upload what you have."

The brothers had watched Egypt's revolution next door, and it had given them ideas. They had seen how the message of change had been spread on Facebook and YouTube, not only inspiring Egypt's youth but also alerting the world to the ferment in the country. Tawfik had his own reasons for hating Gaddafi. When he was born, his father was in prison. It was a time when hundreds of men were rounded up across the east on suspicion of plotting against the regime. Being related to someone suspected of plotting was crime enough, but it was known that the family did not support the Brother Leader. Although he was released after a year that time, he was imprisoned again when Tawfik was eight, this time for five years, again without trial. The members of his family kept their heads down, but Tawfik had nursed resentment and anger from those long childhood years never seeing his father and watching his mother struggle, dependent on the kindness and protection of his uncles.

Now, in February 2011, he locked himself inside Tobruk's sole Internet cafe for eleven hours. The line went up and down. It went dead, and then was somehow resuscitated. At the end of that long night, at 3:00 A.M., it was cut completely and would not work for another six months. But Tawfik had done what he needed to do. He uploaded the images on the Web site of the Arabic TV station Al Jazeera and onto his Facebook page, with a message asking anyone who found them to post them on YouTube. And he did something that would seal his fate: He added a message with his phone number and a request for anyone interested in revolution in Libya to call him.

That night he told his father there was no point in hiding any longer—what he had done ensured that Gaddafi's people would have him in their sights. "If you ride the camel, you can't keep your head down," he said.

Within hours his cell phone was buzzing. The first night it was mainly Egyptian journalists trying to find out what was happening and Egyptian revolutionaries offering salaams and support. By the next day he was getting calls from all over the world. Tawfik was scared; after his father's years in prison he understood the price of failure. But by Friday, February 18th, Libya's old red, black and green flag, with its white star and crescent moon in the center that had flown during the time of King Idris in the fifties and sixties, had replaced Gadaffi's solid green pennant in Tobruk. Their revolution had taken just over twenty-four hours. "Some people had kept the old flag hidden in their house since 1969," said Tawfik. "The old men had waited forty-two years to bring it out."

With Internet access cut off, Tawfik and his brother started a courier service. Tawfik went to collect cell phone footage from Beyda, Derna and all the nearby towns where demonstrations were continuing. Seif had crossed the border to the Egyptian town of Matruh, and every night a network of runners ensured the pictures reached him, so he could upload them onto YouTube and other sites. But if the revolution was to succeed beyond Tobruk they needed more than cell phones and flags, so their cousin started to smuggle Kalashnikovs over the Egyptian border and distribute them to fighters across eastern Libya. Others pulled out the weapons they had in their cupboards. Every Libyan boy learned how to use a Kalashnikov at school, and it was not uncommon to keep firearms at home. Tawfik laughed as he told the story. "Tobruk is full of guns," he said. "We don't respect the law in Tobruk. We have thousands of guns for shooting birds. The tribe controls everything."

Tribe and family, Tawfik explained, mattered more than anything else.

It was not dissimilar in other Arab countries, but in Libya tribe had grown more important as power was increasingly concentrated in the hands of one clan, one family. Many families had eight or ten children, so Tawfik numbered his cousins in the hundreds. He trusted them all. This was how the uprising gained momentum—networks of family members working together. Tawfik's Obeidi tribe had been split. Although the eastern tribes on the whole opposed Gaddafi, several important Obeidis were serving as senior officers in his military. Such division within the tribe could be bitter, but in other ways it was useful, because everyone had to deal with the regime that had held power for so long. In Gaddafi's Libya, revolutionary committees, People's Leadership Councils and any number of other groupings enforced arbitrary edicts as a substitute for government and policy. Even if you hated Gaddafi it was handy to have a cousin who worked in the system. You might be able to use your family network to get a job or a business contract, or even to be released from prison. The moment anyone was in trouble, a relative would look for another relative in a high position to plead the case. Tribe and family were the only way to survive.

As people began to stir in towns across Libya, loyalties were shifting. Gaddafi used the police and the army to put down protests, and sent envoys to try to secure the allegiance of tribal leaders, but he needed a backup plan. Worried that Libyans would not use sufficient force against their fellow Libyans, he decided he needed a third force, a group he could rely on to be loyal to him and him alone. He turned to mercenaries. Up to two million African migrant workers lived in Libya, many doing menial jobs that Libyans didn't want to do. When the uprising started, Gaddafi's men paid some to take up arms. Others were flown in from countries that Gaddafi had supported, like Niger and Mali. These were the men in yellow hard hats who Ali Raslan had seen shooting into the crowd in Benghazi. They weren't used in Tobruk, but reports of their deployment in other cities was enough to convince senior members of the Obeidi tribe that they could no longer support Gaddafi. It was the old Bedouin proverb: "Me against my brother, my brothers and me against my cousins, my cousins and me against strangers." Gaddafi had employed strangers to kill the brothers and cousins of his most loyal lieutenants. They could not stand by. The minister of the interior, General Al Fattah Younes, the most senior Obeidi in the regime, joined the revolution after his cousin was shot in the protests. Tawfik and his friends went to see another significant member of the tribe, retired general Suleiman Mahmoud Obeidi. "He loved Gaddafi, but he was shocked that he had used African mercenaries," Tawfik told me. The general joined the revolution. Family and tribe had won out.

For years the leaders of the Arab world had convinced Western politicians and many of their own citizens that there was no alternative to repression. Or rather, the alternative was chaos, Al Qaeda and war with Israel. The Americans pumped billions into Egypt, knowing full well how corrupt and sclerotic the government was but fearing what might happen if it fell. Even Colonel Gaddafi, excoriated by President Reagan as "this mad dog of the Middle East," had become a valued ally after 9/11 in the war on terror. Gradually, as protests spread from one country to the next, Western governments began to realize that they could not sit it out, waiting for this moment of madness in the Middle East to pass. This wasn't a gentle wind of change but a hurricane.

It was tempting to compare the Arab world of 2011 to Eastern Europe of 1989, when one by one the countries of that region rejected communism until the Berlin Wall fell, and the Soviet era came to a close. But while the governments of Tunisia, Egypt, Bahrain, Yemen, Libya and Syria might be similar to each other in corruption and nepotism, and might employ the same brutal tactics to keep control, there had been no single ideology or dominant power uniting the Middle East. Every country was unhappy in its own way.

In Egypt, the demonstrators made a distinction between the police and the army. The police were regarded as corrupt and brutal but the army was widely regarded as a patriotic force. Much of the prestige of the Egyptian military derived from the widely held delusion, promoted by heroic dramas and documentaries on state TV, that Egypt had won the 1973 war with Israel. Egyptian soldiers are mostly conscripts, so nearly every family has someone in the military. In February 2011, as the youth filled Tahrir Square in Cairo calling for change, most Egyptians seemed to believe that the army stood apart from the regime. It wasn't true—demonstrators who returned to Tahrir Square a few months later were beaten and shot by soldiers—but it enabled the military to retain its position even as their protégé, President Hosni Mubarak, lost power. He could no longer trade on his background in the air force. But as his thirty-year rule crumbled, the men who had shored him up were undiminished. President Zine al-Abedine Ben Ali had been forced out in Tunisia the previous month, but that didn't herald the collapse of all organs of state. He had hijacked the infrastructure of government for the duration of his rule, but after he had taken off for exile in Saudi Arabia, the integrity of the Tunisian state remained intact.

In Libya, it would be different. This would not be an uprising in which cameras rolled as smiling young women put flowers into gun barrels. Libya had no institutions of state. It had no unified army, just brigades, which were under Colonel Gaddafi's handpicked officers, and tribal allies carefully divided up so they would not unite to overthrow him. It had no parliament ("Parliament is a misrepresentation of the people," Colonel Gaddafi famously wrote in his Green Book), just the *lijan thawriya*, self-selecting revolutionary committees under his command that tyrannized their neighborhoods. The ministries were parallel, and at times overlapping, centers of power. Multiple intelligence services reported directly to Gaddafi and operated independently from the police. Gaddafi had destroyed the private sector in the 1970s, and now the businesses that thrived were monopolies owned by his sons and other relatives, and by cronies. Libya didn't even have a president with defined powers—Gaddafi denied that he held any official position at all, pretending that power resided with the people. He ruled by an unwritten personal decree.

If Colonel Gaddafi were overthrown, the state—such as it was—would collapse with him. This would be the first real revolution of the Arab Spring.

I crossed from Egypt into Libya on February 23rd. Revolution had not damp-ened the Egyptian ardor for bureaucracy. Their side of the border had checkpoint after checkpoint manned by functionaries whose writ ran for the next twenty yards, where others demanded passports, press cards and a cursory glance into the glove compartment. The Libyan side was marked by a white wall on which someone had sprayed, in English, "Free Libya!" A few young men dressed in jeans and wearing bandanas around their heads, armed with Kalashnikovs, glanced into the car and, on establishing that my companions and I were journalists, happily let us through with no visa, no stamp in the passport—no procedure at all.

I was to hear many times the complaint that Gaddafi had neglected the east, and the road from the border was a testament to that. Low mud-colored buildings in the villages we passed didn't look like the kinds of dwellings you might expect to see in the world's ninth-largest oil pro-ducer. The few shops and occasional gas station were shuttered. There was no one about. The landscape was scrubby and featureless, with only tufts of rough grass pushing through the sandy soil. The desert winter had not yet passed, and the air was cold. I noticed that the window frames and doors in every village were green. No one, it seemed, had dared stock any other paint as Gaddafi had decreed that all other colors stood for depres-sion and decay; only green represented hope. We passed a pile of green rubble, all that remained of the Green Book statues at some desert outpost. Graffiti, in English, read: "Down with the System." Every few miles we came across a checkpoint made of scrap iron, or chairs, each flying the tricolor flag from an oil drum and manned by smiling young men with Kalashnikovs and sashes of bullets draped across their chests, who would shout, "Welcome, welcome, Libya!" as they waved us through.

For those who have read Michael Ondaatje's *The English Patient,* or about the heroic siege of the town in 1941, the name Tobruk may have some romance. Today, however, there is little in the center of the city to remind a visitor of the World War II desert campaign when the armies of Europe battled for control of the area around the port. Concrete is the construction material of choice, and in places it is hard to tell if the town is half built or half destroyed. The road sweeps around the port, where in normal times tankers would call to collect oil piped from the refinery on the hill overlooking the bay. A squat fortress sits beside the oil terminal—the German war memorial built around a courtyard with romantic bas-reliefs representing War and Suffering. Whereas the Commonwealth cemeteries are carefully tended, the modern town is not, and when we arrived it looked more ramshackle than ever, because demonstrators had set fire to the police station and other buildings they regarded as emblems of Colonel Gaddafi's rule.

Tawfik, who was not only providing translation but also accommodating reporters in his family home, a two-story building in the center of Tobruk, took me to see the central square where he had filmed the destruction of the Green Book statues. As we drove through the streets of the city we heard a deafening cacophony of car horns. Hundreds of families were racing around town, waving tricolor flags and banners and leaning out of their windows flashing the V for victory sign. When they saw a foreigner they honked and shouted more loudly. As we roared along the esplanade, past the port, we could see that the charred walls of government buildings had been covered in graffiti. "February 17: Libya wrote history in the blood of her sons," read one.

Normal life had been suspended until further notice, and no one was going to work. It was joyous chaos. Their revolution was less than a week old, and they gathered every afternoon at the Green Book rubble as if they had to see it again to believe what they had done. But the revolution was not cost-free. In the hospital we met a man with a ruptured spleen and a fractured pelvis who had been crushed between two tanks. Another had been shot in the eye. The doctors told us of at least four who had been killed in Tobruk, and they had no idea what we would find farther west, in Benghazi.

The next morning I drove along the coast road, the pale beaches of the bright blue Mediterranean to my right. It was cold, despite the sun. Beyond Beyda, the desert gave way to the Green Mountain, where Omar Mukhtar had fought the Italians; orchards and wild flower meadows replaced the scrub. No wonder the Italians felt at home when they colonized Libya in the 1920s—in places it looked like Tuscany. This was where the Greeks built Cyrene, the Athens of Africa, next to the port of Appollonia and facing toward Malta. It was later occupied by the Romans, until in decline it became, in the words of the fourth-century bishop Synesius, "a vast ruin at the mercy of nomads."

While driving into Benghazi under a series of concrete overpasses, I felt I was entering a Luis Buñuel film: judges, in black gowns with white collars, were directing the traffic. It was, I was told, part of the collective spirit of revolution. The traffic wardens had disappeared, so everyone was pitching in. A few days later the judges were replaced with twelve-year-olds, who seemed even less qualified for the job.

That night I stayed with Ali Raslan, the man who had lost his son Idris on the first day of the revolution. I assumed that he was an old friend of Tawfik, but it turned out that they had only just met. "From the vagina of revolution, true heroes are born!" said Tawfik. I didn't have the heart to tell him that that didn't sound quite right in English. He was going to see his sister, who had given birth on February 17th to a daughter whom she had named Libya, in honor of the moment. The revolution would free up the country's intellectuals, Tawfik told me. "My brother-in-law wasted ten years of his life under Gaddafi," he said. "He's frustrated and hopeless. He thought up a new kind of string theory. You must meet him—he's awesome in quantum physics!"

I went to the Katiba, the barracks that had been the center of Colonel Gaddafi's power in Benghazi. The previous Sunday, day four of the revolution, Mahdi Ziu, a manager at the Arabian Gulf Oil Company, had loaded his black Kia sedan with gas canisters and driven straight at the *Katiba* gate. If Ziu had hated the regime for a long time, he seems to have kept his feelings to himself, but according to his family, something snapped when he saw a protester killed in front of his door. The explosion that ended his life also killed several of the guards and punched a hole through the massive concrete walls. Within a few hours young men had driven bulldozers into the Katiba, and crowds of protesters—many of them fans of the ill-fated Al-Ahly Benghazi football team, some wearing the club colors—had stormed the compound. The soldiers cast off their uniforms and fled. By the time I got there a few days later what remained of the walls had been decorated with graffiti and cartoons, the most arresting being an anguished-looking Colonel Gaddafi with a huge boot up his backside. Families posed next to it—Mum, Dad and the kids, smiling into cell phone cameras. A week before they would have averted their eyes, such was the terror this place held. Now it was a tourist attraction.

I watched a group of rebels driving at a furious pace in a tank they had commandeered, waving flags, yelling slogans, scattering onlookers and cheering as they tore around the compound. A few yards away was a "guesthouse," where Saadi Gaddafi and other members of the family used to stay when they came to Benghazi. It was impossible to tell whether it had been luxurious or plain, because while the structure was intact, the inside had been burned to ashes. On the outside wall someone had written in felt-tip a list of names. These, I was told, were people who had supported Gaddafi. The revolutionaries told me there would be no revenge, but this was not encouraging. No one seemed to know how many people had died. The hospitals had reported hundreds of bodies after Gaddafi's forces opened fire indiscriminately at funerals and protests. For several days snipers had picked off individuals at will. Yet everyone I met was thrilled with their revolution. Those who had died were martyrs, honored and loved for their sacrifice.

That day they uncovered a prison underneath the Katiba. I felt my way down the stairs on the heels of a group of curious Benghazi residents, lighting the way with a flashlight. A round-faced, middle-aged man standing with his young son approached me. His name, he said, was Khaled Kwafi, and at the age of seventeen he and two friends had been held in that very cell for the crime of questioning Colonel Gaddafi's Green Book at school. The teenagers had been held without a glimpse of daylight for three months, often blindfolded and beaten. "They kept saying they were going to hang us, they were just waiting for Colonel Gaddafi to give the order," he recalled.

Khaled had never before been able to talk of what had happened. He had kept the secret of his detention for half a lifetime. He and his friends were given daily indoctrination sessions, accompanied by slaps and kicks, and on several occasions were taken outside blindfolded for a mock execution. Eventually they were released, without really knowing why. The misdemeanor threatened to blight his career, but he had kept quiet and managed to get back on track, training as an oil engineer.

I wondered how many Khaleds there were in Libya. No one seemed to know how many had been imprisoned, tortured and killed during Gaddafi's forty-two-year rule. The east had been a center of dissent. Tawfik was brought up on stories his father told of seeing dozens hanged in public. Salwa Bughaigis, one of the few prominent women on the council that was running Benghazi after the uprising, recalled seeing an activist's body hanging in front of Benghazi's biggest church when she was going to the university in the 1980s. Others were hanged in basketball stadiums. She was lucky that her punishment for criticizing the regime was only a one-year suspension from the university. "They tried to frighten us all," she said.

The revolution centered on the area around the port, near North Benghazi Courthouse, and Salwa and her colleagues made it their headquarters. Tents and makeshift marquees appeared on the square in front, as did stalls selling revolutionary T-shirts, ribbons and flags. Every day relatives posted more photographs of those who had been killed in the Abu Salim massacre or had disappeared in more recent years. Graffiti in Arabic and bad English covered the walls: "Gadafi is Anemel," "Now I Am Free Human." There was no security—anyone could go in and out—so the new council members sometimes had to hide in their offices to avoid well-wishers in order to get anything done.

They were for the most part lawyers, doctors, engineers and other middle-class, educated people. Many spoke English. Their leader was Hafiz Ghoga, a lawyer from a prominent family. On the first Friday after the revolution I stood with him on the courthouse roof looking out over the thousands who had gathered to pray. Three coffins of people who had just died in the hospital after being shot during the protests were borne shoulder-high through the crowd. People waved when they saw Ghoga, and he waved tentatively back. I asked if he had ever thought it would be like this, and he silently shook his head. It was as if he were in shock. When they went out on the streets on the sixteenth and seventeenth they had no idea that they would end up as leaders of a revolution that now might spread across the country.

They had started as reformists, hoping for gradual change. In 2004, after Seif al-Islam Gaddafi had started gradually opening Libya up to the outside world, after years of isolation, fifteen Benghazi lawyers, including Hafiz Ghoga and Salwa Bughaigis, formed a group to campaign for political prisoners. "Seif wanted to open the door a little bit, so we just went straight through," said Salwa, a lawyer in her midforties wearing a slash of dark lipstick applied not entirely accurately and—unusual for a Libyan woman—no head scarf. They had also campaigned for the Palestinians, and in 2010 demonstrated for the right to form a lawyers' union. The regime wavered over whether to arrest them, but in the end just watched and waited. Two weeks before the revolution, Gaddafi called Hafiz Ghoga to meet him, and he offered to appoint him head of all the country's unions, which had until then been under strict government control. Ghoga refused. The uprising in Egypt was already under way, and he knew it was a trap.

Salwa's sister, Iman, was an orthodontist. The two women represented the educated elite of Benghazi, repressed and marginalized under Gaddafi. Their father, Saad Bughaigis, a political dissident, had been exiled to the United States for thirty years, so they were brought up largely by their mother, and had become far more independent than many Libyan women. They were sure that the revolution would usher in democracy and deal humanely with African migrants who tried to use Libya as a way station to get into Europe. Aware that European countries were watching with alarm, worried that unrest in Libya would trigger a wave of African refugees, Iman was making the case for foreign intervention. "It will benefit the international community to support us," she told me. "We will be a democratic country which respects minorities and human rights. We will respect the rights of immigrants, and try to return them home [to] invest in their own countries, so they can live in dignity."

She said that women and men, who had been working side by side, would be equal in the new Libya, and that even imams had praised her and her sister. I wondered if her optimism would prove misplaced. In Benghazi I saw far fewer women on the streets than in Egypt, and the Bughaigis sisters were the only ones I met who went out bareheaded. They had the support of their families: Salwa's husband, Issam, acted as her unofficial aide, and their mother looked after Iman's young daughter. I asked about

Salwa's three sons, and she laughed. One was proud of her, she said. Another was scared. And the third? "He's just annoyed that his school trip to Greece has been canceled!"

The Bughaigis sisters seemed to epitomize what Western journalists and governments wanted Libya to be—modern, liberal, secular. But there was a dark side to the revolution, a violent undertow to the tide toward freedom. At night I would hear shooting—sometimes it was celebratory gunfire, but there were also disturbing reports of vigilantes carrying out revenge killings against people who had supported Colonel Gaddafi. The anger about mercenaries had exacerbated the racism that already existed in Libyan society. Many Libyans from Tripolitania or Cyrenaica saw themselves as a cut above those from Fezzan, and now any black person was suspect. One of the most horrific acts of the revolution came in the first week, when a crowd of men chanting "Libya—freedom!" crowded around Benghazi's North Courthouse, where the revolutionaries gathered every day, to witness the lynching of a man accused of being a mercenary. Footage posted on YouTube shows two young men stringing up the victim by his feet from a window, while another, down below, decapitates him with a knife. Blood pours down the wall, but what is most disturbing is the mounting excitement of the crowd, all holding up cell phones to film the horror. Salwa's husband, Issam, told me that he had tried to stop the killing but found himself powerless among the mob. "I cried," he said. "My friends and I tried to surround the man to protect him, but we couldn't." Issam was a psychologist. "One product of the Gaddafi regime is that we have a tendency to resort to violence to sort out any differences," he said. "That's what I'm most afraid of in this revolution."

The first stone had been cast and the ripples were spreading across Libya. On February 19th the people of Misrata came out to protest about the killings in Benghazi. They threw stones and Molotov cocktails at the riot police, and the first local martyr was created——Khaled Abu Shahma, who was gunned down by Gaddafi's forces near the main square. His funeral turned into another protest, and soldiers, who had now been brought in, fired antiaircraft weapons at buildings near the crowds. On February 24th, Gaddafi flew in reinforcements, so Misrata Airport became a battleground, as the men of the town fought to keep the troops out. The fighting in Misrata turned into fierce house-to-house combat, with many deaths. The men of Misrata were initially armed only with old hunting rifles and homemade grenades, but they seized weapons from Gaddafi's forces, and the fiercest fighting of the revolution was under way. Gaddafi's snipers installed themselves in the office and apartment blocks along Tripoli Street, the main road in from the capital. The insurance building, the tallest structure in the town, gave Gaddafi's snipers an excellent vantage point.

Gaddafi's forces were joined by volunteers from the Tawergha community, who lived in a shabby neighborhood in Misrata called El Goush. The Tawergha, a much darker people than the Mediterranean Misratans, were descended from slaves, and they did many of the menial jobs in the port city. Gaddafi favored them as part of his project to integrate Libya with the rest of Africa, buying their loyalty with jobs, subsidies and a new town near Misrata that they called, simply, Tawergha. They repaid the debt by fighting for him and hosting his armored brigades as they fired artillery into Misrata during the siege. But the people of Misrata accused the Tawergha workers who had lived in their city of a far greater crime, saying that the men used rape as a way of terrorizing the population. There is no question that rape occurred——Marie Colvin of the *Sunday Times* saw cell phone footage documenting it——but whether it was as widespread as Misrata men say, and whether the Tawergha rather than regular troops were the main culprits, is unconfirmed. In Libyan culture, where rape brings shame on a family, women are reluctant to talk to outsiders. Some of the incidents reported may have been molestation——the tearing off of head scarves and clothes rather than what would be called rape in a Western court of law. But the horror of those weeks of hand-to-hand combat remained one of the most bitter legacies of the revolution in Libya, and the people of Misrata would not forgive the Tawergha.

In the Nafousa Mountains, southwest of Tripoli, revolution rolled like mist along the ridge. The indigenous Berber people, who had settled the area centuries before the Arabs and are found in much of north and west Africa, had reason to resent Gaddafi. For a start, they didn't like being called Berber, preferring their traditional name, Amazigh. In his quest for unity and a single Libyan identity, Gaddafi had forced them to give their children Arabic names and to speak only Arabic in public. In 2008 he had visited the area and warned, "You can call yourselves whatever you want inside your homes—Berbers, Children of Satan, whatever—but you are only Libyans when you leave your homes."

The region had produced several army officers who spearheaded a failed coup attempt in 1993. When I visited, Khaled Omar Al Azabi, a young Amazigh teacher, showed me the football stadium in his home-town, Nalut, where at the age of fourteen he was brought with the rest of his class to watch five local men hung. The noose was looped around the horizontal bar of the goal they used for football matches as the men were brought out, hooded, and everyone was told to cheer. Soldiers stood around the stadium watching the crowd. These, it was said, were the coup plotters. We stood on the roadside looking down. "I can still remember how frightened I was," he said. "I suppose that's why I'm here now."

It wasn't just the Amazigh. The town of Zintan, which was largely Arab, went over to the rebel side right at the beginning and never looked back. Zintan people hadn't been great enemies of Gaddafi, but unemployment was increasing and resentment of the regime had been on the rise. As Egypt burned, Gaddafi dispatched envoys to buy fighters from towns he thought might be loyal should revolution start in Libya. On February 12th, every Zintani family was offered 250,000 dinars ($200,000) to provide a son. The elders gathered to discuss the offer. "Why does he only want us now?" they said. "Zintan is not for sale." On February 18th, Mohammed Madani, a revered elder and former military commander, addressed a crowd outside the main mosque. "Gaddafi is a coward!" he cried. "No negotiation, no surrender!" The people of Zintan roared their assent. A week later, the Zintan Friday prayer imam, Taher Ejdea, addressed a similar crowd in the main square, delivering a series of insults about Gaddafi that was received with cheers and laughter. "He is like a peacock who thinks the sun only rises for him. He sees himself as a cockerel, but in fact he is nothing. He is a chicken," he said. "He is despicable. He only loves himself. He is arrogant and condescending. . . . He is a suffocated mouse."

The capital, Gaddafi's seat of power, was also rising against him. On Sunday, February 20th, as demonstrators massed in Green Square to show their solidarity with the people of Benghazi, Seif al-Islam Gaddafi spoke on state TV. If this didn't stop, he said, Libya would split along tribal lines and descend into civil war. It would be occupied by Britain and the United States. Bread would become more expensive than gold. He accused the protesters of being drug addicts and fundamentalists led astray by Egyptian Facebook pages. "Gaddafi is not Mubarak or Ben Ali, a classical ruler; he is a leader of a people. Tens of thousands of Libyans are coming to defend him," he said. Under threat, Seif the reformer retreated instantly to the laager of family power. He wagged his finger at the camera. "We will fight to the last man and woman and bullet," he said, and every Libyan understood what he meant. Within hours, armored vehicles approached the square and fired large-caliber rounds, some from antiaircraft guns. Scores of people were killed, hundreds arrested.

Nizar Mhani watched Seif's speech at home in Cardiff on the Al Jazeera network. Age thirty, he was on the brink of a promotion as an oral surgeon at the University Hospital of Wales. His parents were both Libyan, but the family had moved to Europe after their businesses were confiscated during Gaddafi's socialist phase in the 1970s. Niz, as he was known, had done his medical training in Cardiff and, although his parents and sisters were in Tripoli, his life was in Britain. Niz had the calm personality a successful surgeon needs, but when he heard Seif's speech, anger engulfed him. "It was Seif's condescending manner, the way he wrote off the revolution as a conspiracy," he recalled. "I went upstairs, packed a bag and took the train straight to Gatwick." He e-mailed his employers to say he would be gone a couple of weeks, and got on a plane the next day.

At Tripoli Airport Niz battled his way through the throngs desperately trying to leave the country, eventually finding his cousin, who had come to pick him up. "It was a scene from a movie," recalled Niz. "Tires burning, barricades, graffiti everywhere saying 'Down with Gaddafi.' It was surreal. I could hear gunshots and see four-by-fours mounted with soldiers." Protesters gathering on street corners beckoned them into side streets, saying the main roads were full of soldiers, so they wove their way to Niz's parents' house, a half-hour journey taking two hours. Still, Niz didn't understand what he was taking on: "I thought it would be like Tahrir Square in Egypt, that we'd protest and then he'd fall."

Nizar's older sister, Mervat, knew better. She wanted to protest too. "I could have bitten off Seif's wagging finger," she said, but her husband said this was not the time for women to be on the streets. She grabbed her children, ages three years and eighteen months, and went to her younger sister's place. Mervat didn't share Nizar's optimism that this would be over soon. "I knew Gaddafi would come out with guns straightaway," she said. Mervat was born a month after the coup that brought Gaddafi to power—she was a child of his revolution. Like most Libyans of her generation, from her childhood she remembered seeing hangings on TV during Ramadan. She couldn't forget watching the chairman of the cigarette factory where their father worked being tried on television—she had no idea for what. "I remember he had a black eye," she recalled. Mervat had returned to Libya in 1989, studied dentistry, married a doctor and started a family. She began to wear a head scarf, because it felt right; in the end, she was Libyan, more comfortable in Tripoli than anywhere else. Until February 20, 2011, she believed that Seif Gaddafi might bring reform, as he promised. "Now I think that speech was a gift from God," she said. "If it had been about reform and going forward, people would have believed him and backed down."

Two days later Mervat and Niz watched on TV as Gaddafi himself appeared in Green Square, attired in a brown woolen *jird*, a Bedouin robe, in front of a crowd of supporters jumping up and down and waving green flags. He made an hour-and-a-half-long speech that revealed the extent of his delusions, and his ruthlessness. Slamming his fist into the podium, his voice emotional and trembling, he repeated his son's invective against the "drug addicts, jihadis and rats" who dared oppose him. As the speech wore on, the threats against the demonstrators grew more dire. Any act of insurrection, he said, would be punishable by execution. But it was a statement at the end of the speech that would go down in history, when he said that he and "millions from the Sahara . . . will cleanse Libya inch by inch, house by house, home by home, alleyway by alleyway, person by person, until the country is cleansed of dirt and scum."

The phrase "alleyway by alleyway"—in Arabic, "*zenga zenga*"—became a rallying cry for the revolution. As a foreigner in the east, all you had to say was *zenga zenga* and everyone would laugh, shake your hand and clap you on the back. It was a threat, but Libyans turned it into a joke. Then it went worldwide. An Israeli rapper, Noy Alooshe, from the techno group Chovevei Tzion, posted on YouTube a mash-up of Gaddafi's *zenga zenga* speech and the hip-hop song "Hey Baby." Some Arabs objected to it because it was made by an Israeli, but it was too funny for most to care. By August more than four million people had watched the clip; after requests from around the Muslim world, Alooshe had removed the section featuring half-naked, gyrating women, and nearly 1.5 million had seen this more demure version. Colonel Gaddafi, King of Kings, defender of the Arab world against the Zionist enemy, was being undermined not just by armed, rebellious youth and the desperate fury of Libyans across the country, but by a hip-hop artist from Tel Aviv.

That Friday, February 25th, Niz went with his cousins to pray at a mosque near Algeria Square. Benghazi had already fallen—now, they thought, it was Tripoli's turn. The imam condemned the revolution in his sermon, saying it was un-Islamic to challenge a country's leader. Niz and most of the rest of the congregation stood up and left. This was not what they had come to hear. As they finished their prayers in a friend's house nearby, the sound of gunfire grew louder and more continuous, and they could hear the cries of "Allahu Akbhar!"—"God is Great"—from the streets. An elderly man came rushing in. "Boys, it's started," he said. Someone was shouting through a megaphone: "With our blood and our spirit we will redeem you, oh Benghazi!" They ran out to join the demonstration.

For fifteen minutes the protesters walked and chanted, the crowd swelling as more people joined. No one stopped them. Then suddenly they saw a truckload of uniformed men driving up the road toward them, and Niz's heart began to race. "In all my time in Tripoli I never saw tear gas or water cannon, and there were no police," he recalled. "They were military, and I will never forget their behavior. They were so controlled." The soldiers disembarked and took up positions, some at ground level, others on walls. They raised their rifles and shot straight into the crowd. "I saw people falling," said Niz. "We dragged away those we could, but in the end we just had to escape." Among the gunfire and screaming, women, some veiled, were rushing out of their front doors and inviting the protesters to hide in their houses—unheard-of in conservative Libya, where for a woman to allow an unknown man into her home is to invite dishonor. Crouching inside, every few minutes the protesters would hear more shooting as the soldiers went past, and then they would venture out onto the streets again, chanting anti-Gaddafi slogans, until they dared do it no longer. The soldiers had taken Gaddafi at his word; they were hunting protesters down *zenga zenga*.

How many died that day? We may never know. Niz saw dozens, maybe more, lying on the streets. He watched in horror as a man leaning over a wounded friend was shot in the head by a soldier. Another soldier pointed his rifle at a man bleeding profusely, so no one could save him. The soldiers would shoot directly at anyone trying to salvage a body. "That day it dawned on me that it would not be like Egypt or Tunisia," he said. "Gaddafi wouldn't stop. Those countries had had pseudo-democracies, but we had nothing. We had never had demonstrations or strikes. We were a society void of activism or protest. So we quickly took the route of armed conflict."

Not, however, Niz himself. Maybe it was his peaceful upbringing in Wales. Maybe it was his conscience as a doctor. Maybe it was the determination of his sisters to be involved. But Niz knew he would not pick up a gun. The crackdown had been murderous and successful, so if they were to do anything, it would have to be underground, secret and highly risky. For a few days they met and discussed what to do next—cousins, brothers, sisters, friends, about twenty young men and women who didn't want to fight but would not submit. So the Free Generation Movement was born, a group of young people who would madden the authorities for the next seven months with their stunts and staged "happenings," many of which mysteriously appeared almost instantaneously on YouTube and international TV channels long after the Internet had been cut off.

Back in Benghazi, those who had started the uprising now believed it to be irreversible. The young men of the east had decided to push on toward

Tripoli. At first it was easy. They mounted antiaircraft guns and rocket-propelled grenades on the back of their pickups and careered, honking horns and flashing V signs, through the town of Ajdabia to the oil centers of Brega and Ras Lanuf, shooting their Kalashnikovs into the air in celebration. Gaddafi sent bombers, but the rebels had a lucky shot bringing one down, and two pilots discharged their munitions into the sea before flying into exile in Malta. The rebels roared up and down the road waving flags and cheering. War was fun.

Most had no experience of fighting at all. I met a twenty-one-year-old economics student at the roadside leaning on a shoulder-launched rocket that, he said, had "a bit missing." He said he wouldn't go to the front until the bit arrived but seemed vague about when or how that might be. His friend, a twenty-three-year-old civil engineering student, had no weapon at all, and when asked if it was not foolhardy to plunge into battle unarmed, replied, "As Shakespeare says, the question is: to be or not to be." They were a mixture of unemployed youth and frustrated graduates, all fighting together, carried on a wave of idealism and hope. An armed English teacher tried to explain in words a foreigner might understand, or at least recognize: "Why should I think myself better than my brothers?" he said. "I believe that you shouldn't ask what your country does for you, but what you can do for your country."

It couldn't last. In the first week of March Colonel Gaddafi's forces started to hit back in earnest. The rebels found themselves under mortar fire. Unprepared and untrained, with no tactics, let alone a strategy, they leaped into their vehicles and tore back along the road toward Ajdabia, relinquishing all the ground they had just taken. Every time they ventured forward, they were pushed back. They began to fight among themselves about what to do next. No one was in charge. Ambulances screeched along the road to the front line, hurtling back full of injured. Every day more young men were killed, sometimes by their own weapons, over which they had such little control. Maybe war was not such fun after all.

In Benghazi, the lawyers and other professionals who had emerged as leaders of the revolution in the first few days formed a national transitional council, which would—according to Hafiz Ghoga, who was its spokesman—provide "a political face for the revolution." Some of the members were well-known activists—Fathi Terbil was named as the representative for the youth—but others were scarcely known to the fighters or to the throngs gathering outside the North Courthouse every day. "The council derives its legitimacy from the city councils who run the liberated cities," said their founding declaration, but the problem was that key Libyan cities, including Tripoli, were still in Gaddafi's hands. The NTC was determined that the revolution would bring change to the whole country and not lead to the secession of the east, so they appointed five representatives for each town, keeping secret the names of those in places still under Gaddafi's control. They appointed an executive board to run the part of the country it now controlled. Banks were closed, civil service salaries were going unpaid, and there was no oil revenue coming in, so it was hard to set up any kind of administration, but people in the east were willing to put up with a few months of confusion. The head of the executive council, Mahmoud Jibril, a smooth, American-trained economist who had once headed Libya's National Economic Development Board, was appointed chairman, and he embarked on a world tour to get international recognition.

I went to Beyda, between Tobruk and Benghazi, to see the man who had emerged as the leader of the National Transitional Council. Mustafa Abdel Jalil seemed an unlikely revolutionary. A small, quiet man wearing a traditional dark red fez, he had resigned after four years as Colonel Gaddafi's justice minister, finding his attempts to gain the release of political prisoners frustrated. Most Libyans seemed to respect him as an honorable man who had tried but failed to make things better. When his hometown of Beyda, between Tobruk and Benghazi, fell to the revolutionaries on February 17th, Gaddafi had summoned Jalil, instructing him to rein in his rebellious townsfolk. Instead, he too joined the revolution, along with the local police, who had refused to fire on the demonstrators. He was a universally respected figure, but despite his new position, he only visited Benghazi from time to time, preferring to stay in Beyda, curiously distant from the turbulent events unfolding. The day I went to see him he was addressing those assembled for Friday prayers, the strength of his rhetoric belied by his mild, almost mousy, manner.

"We're not going back until we liberate the whole country—victory or death!" he said, his voice so quiet it could scarcely be heard. "The enemy controlled and humiliated your fathers for forty years. All the wealth of our country has gone with the wind. Gaddafi created chaos." He was known to be a religious man, and that was part of his appeal, but he had no history as an extremist, or of using Islam as a political platform. Maybe Libyans liked him because he was the opposite of Gaddafi: self-effacing, not flamboyant; pragmatic, not ideological; quiet, not verbose. He had no charisma, and—as far as one could tell from his few public statements—no plan for the country's future. After his address I caught a few words with him before his security detail bundled him away from the jostling crowd. He said that Libya needed the Americans and Europeans to impose a "no-fly zone" to protect civilians from Gaddafi's helicopter gunships and fighter jets. It was a line he had clearly worked out in conversation with European politicians who were starting to talk about supporting the rebels. Libyans, it seemed, couldn't do this alone, and the new leadership had been consulting those they believed could help.

They needed foreign military support because their own war effort was a shambles.

The rebels trying to advance west from Benghazi toward Tripoli were a mixture of Islamists, young professionals, unemployed youth and

tribe-based militia. General Al Fattah Younes, the former interior minister, was supposedly in charge of a rebel army, but no one seemed to know
how many soldiers he had under his command, and if he issued any orders,
the militia ignored them.

Every day a stream of injured men were ferried to Ajdabia and Benghazi hospitals, where harried doctors did their best with minimal resources
to patch them up. Over one long night in Ajdabia we watched from a roof-
top as hundreds of families picked up what belongings they could stuff
into cars and pickups and started to retreat down the road to the east.
What had been unthinkable in late February, after Gaddafi's forces had
been pushed out of the east in days, now looked possible, even likely—
Gaddafi might retake Benghazi. He might make good on his threat to hunt
people down *zenga zenga*, alleyway by alleyway. If he did that, not only
would Libya's revolution be quashed, it would send a message to all other
governments in the Arab world: If you ignore all diplomatic entreaties and
crush an uprising by force, nothing will happen to you. The more people
you kill, the more likely that you will prevail.

Every morning I would drive to the front line, where Gaddafi's forces
were confronting the rebels along the coast road, to see whether the fighters from the east had advanced—or been pushed back again. Every evening, as I returned, a sandstorm would be blowing along the desert road
between Ajdabia and Benghazi. The Libyans called it *el ghibli,* the wind
that comes from the direction in which you must pray. The Italians had
called it *sirocco,* blowing sand from the Sahara to the Mediterranean,
scouring Libya and southern Europe. Clouds of dust whipped across the
tarmac and up into the air, where they swirled in rapidly changing patterns, rising and falling with every gust. It was hard to tell which way the
wind was blowing. Dust devils, twirling towers of air and sand, spiraled
on either side of the road, and the light gained a reddish hue as the sun
went down. You could see neither ahead nor to the side, and if you got out
of the car dust would clog your eyes and nose. It was impossible to film or

photograph *el ghibli,* but in the morning a light blanket of sand would cover the road, proof that it had blown through. Grain by grain, the desert was shifting. Each day the wind seemed fiercer; it just wasn't yet clear how much the landscape would have changed when the season of *el ghibli* was over.

CHAPTER TWO

THE STRANGE WORLD OF MUAMMAR GADDAFI

Perfection, of a kind, is what he was after,

And the poetry he invented was easy to understand;

He knew human folly like the back of his hand,

And was greatly interested in armies and fleets;

When he laughed, respectable senators burst with
   laughter,

And when he cried the little children died in the streets.

—W. H. AUDEN, "EPITAPH ON A TYRANT"

Gaddafi—You are the Weakest Link. Goodbye.

—GRAFFITI IN BENGHAZI

Colonel Gaddafi was a man out of time. By 2011 he seemed like a character from an old movie that no one wanted to see again. He had come to power in the era of the Vietnam War, the moon landings, Woodstock and Richard Nixon. The United States had elected seven presidents since then, and the UK eight prime ministers—although the same queen reigned, as Gaddafi frequently pointed out. "She has been a queen for fifty-seven years, and the king of Thailand has been there for sixty-eight years," he said in his first speech after the uprising began, when every news report mentioned his forty-two-year rule. He was the last of his generation of Arab dictators—Hafez el Assad of Syria, Gamal Nasser of Egypt, Saddam Hussein in Iraq were all dead, but Gaddafi saw no reason that he shouldn't rule indefinitely. Except that he said he didn't rule. The people ruled; he just guided them.

That wasn't how people I met in Benghazi saw it. Satellite TV and the Internet had ended the regime's ability to control their reading and viewing, so they knew how anachronistic Libya's political system was. It wasn't just the news; they watched the same quizzes and reality shows as everyone else in the world. As I was picking my way through the charred remains of the Gaddafi house in the Benghazi Katiba, a young man came over to tell me a joke: Gaddafi is on *Who Wants to Be a Millionaire?*, and he can't answer the question, so he asks if he can phone a friend. He calls the devil, who hangs up on him. Even the devil won't help Gaddafi anymore!

Sometimes the Brother Leader appeared dressed as a Bedouin sheikh, in earth-colored robes and a turban or a black fez. Or as a Ruritanian army officer, in pale gray and scarlet, a raft of medals across his chest and golden fringes hanging from his epaulettes. For a while he favored a royal blue jumpsuit, then a smart dark, serge naval uniform decorated with gold brocade and even more medals. One of his favorite outfits was a shimmering purple *jird* with a matching embroidered waistcoat and hat. He rarely appeared without sunglasses and liked high-heeled leather boots or lizard-skin slippers. He went to a meeting of the African Union draped in a purple-and-green sash that featured a map of the continent, a gold chain around his neck, a huge jeweled ring on his right hand and a golden headband encircling his collar-length hair that looked like something a little girl might wear to a Christmas party. His dyed black hair grew longer and wilder as the years went by, while his face grew more distorted by Botox, like a sinister, Middle Eastern Michael Jackson. He appeared on state television just after the uprising started to disprove rumors that he had fled to Venezuela. The evidence was that it was raining in Tripoli (and presumably not in Caracas). He sat in the front seat of a beige-colored minibus wearing a black felt hat with ear flaps, his face strangely impassive, his eyes narrow, as the rain fell on his silver umbrella, which he thrust out of the half-open door and waved at the camera. An Italian comedian dubbed the theatrical appearance, "I'm Killing in the Rain."

He had long ceased to draw any distinction between himself and the country. In his *zenga zenga* speech he drifted into a peroration about how Libyans should be grateful because he had made them famous. "In the past, Libyans lacked an identity," he said. "When you said Libyan, they would respond 'Libya? Liberia? Lebanon?'—they didn't know Libya. But today you say Libya, they say 'Oh, Libya—Gaddafi!'" That was true, but the association brought embarrassment, not pride. A week later, when challenged by British and American journalists in an interview, he responded in his characteristic rasping voice, in English, "My people—they love me all! All of them they love me!" Over the four decades of his rule, he had, like most dictators, become isolated, in touch only with close family and aides whose fabulous lifestyles depended on his survival, and who dared not tell him what was going on, or had no interest in doing so.

The September 1, 1969, coup was not unexpected. Many Libyans were frustrated with King Idris's lackluster rule and with what they saw as his kowtowing to British and American interests. Until 1959, when oil was discovered, Libya had been one of the poorest countries in the world, its biggest export being scrap iron from tanks and other armor littering the desert after the World War II campaign. In exchange for aid, the king agreed to let Britain continue to use the World War II Al-Adem air base near Tobruk and leased the Wheelus base in Tripoli to the Americans. Both armies used the Libyan desert for training and testing new weapons. Relations became even closer after 1959, as British and American companies, including British Petroleum, Esso, Texaco, Hunt Oil and Shell, were granted concessions alongside Italian oil companies. Small expatriate communities settled in oil towns along the coast. There were still twenty thousand Italians in Libya, mainly farmers, left over from the colonial era. Yet Libyans remained poor, some 40 percent living in tents or huts. They began to ask if the king ruled for himself and his foreign friends, or for them.

Gaddafi and his fellow Free Officers overthrew the monarchy with remarkable ease, despite being ill prepared. One of the coup plotters left his gun and ammunition in the Tripoli taxi that he hailed to get to the barracks to meet the others, only managing to reclaim it when the revolution was over. Bashir Hawadi, another of the original coup plotters, went to the radio station in Benghazi where a co-conspirator accidentally blew himself up with a grenade and the staff fled. Hawadi says he found himself alone in the studio facing the microphone. "I wasn't quite sure what to do," he recalled, when I met him shortly after Gaddafi's death. He claims to have announced the revolution; no one else remembers anyone but Gaddafi speaking. Within a few years, the original group split; after Gaddafi emerged as the leader, Hawadi was involved in a coup attempt against him. Gaddafi threatened him with death, but in the end put him under house arrest for two years and then sent him to the town of Jufra, deep in the desert, where he remained for more than three decades, banned from moving beyond the town limits until someone involved in the 2011 revolution remembered him and sent a car to bring the old man and his family to the port of Misrata.

I asked when he had last seen Gaddafi. "He sent an officer to invite me to dinner in 1982, when he came to Jufra," he said. "We had an hour and a half together. We just chitchatted, really. I told Muammar he should help the Libyan people more, give them money, free the prisoners."

"How did he react?" I asked.

"He laughed."

It was not only young officers who loved Gaddafi in the beginning.

Mohammed Mustafa Saudi worked in Souq al-Ghizhir, the metal foundry section of the souk. He'd left school at twelve; at twenty his hands were already rough and calloused from beating out brass trays and copper crescent moons for the tops of minarets. He enjoyed the camaraderie of the craftsmen and the atmosphere of the souk, with its narrow alleyways, and the constant noise of metal hammering and sewing machines, but he was discontented nonetheless. He and his friends often chatted about how weak and distant King Idris was—such a contrast to Egypt, next door, where the leader made you proud to be an Arab. Mohammed worshipped the Egyptian president, Gamal Abdel Nasser, because of his success in nationalizing the Suez Canal in 1956. The contrast was painful—Nasser had triumphed over the French and British while King Idris did their bidding. In 1967, Nasser led Egypt to defeat in the Six-Day War against Israel. His military were routed after Israeli fighter bombs wiped out the Egyptian air force and seized part of Sinai, but Nasser presented the story for Arab consumption as a victory, and as evidence of Zionist aggression. Mohammed was ashamed that while the leaders of Jordan and Syria had provided troops to fight the Israelis, King Idris had done nothing. He had been to school with some of the Jews who lived in the medina, but when a mob started attacking their houses and synagogues and setting fire to their cars, he joined in, ending up in prison for three days. Several Jews were killed. Accounts from those who fled to Israel, fearing that worse was to come, say they left each carrying just one suitcase of clothes and a maximum of twenty pounds sterling.

Two years later, on September 1, 1969, while Mohammed was having breakfast in the café where he ate every morning, he noticed hundreds of soldiers on the streets. Someone arrived with a message from his father telling him to come home. They had no TV, so they stayed at home and listened to the radio. A young officer they had never heard of before addressed the people of Libya, promising freedom and a better life. "Your armed forces have destroyed the reactionary, backward and decadent regime whose putrid odor assailed one's nose," said Gaddafi. "With one blow from your heroic army, the idols collapsed and the graven images shattered. In one terrible moment of fate, the darkness of ages—from the rule of the Turks to the tyranny of the Italians and the era of reaction, bribery, intercession, favoritism, treason and treachery—was dispersed." Mohammed, then twenty-two, rushed to Martyrs' Square—which Gaddafi would later call Green Square—to celebrate with his friends. At last, Libya had a leader like Nasser. "Everyone was with him," recalled Mohammed. "That's why his revolution succeeded."

Gaddafi was twenty-seven. The black-and-white pictures from the early years show him as a handsome, charismatic, dashing, dynamic young officer. Here he is, grinning, at the center of a group shot with the Revolutionary Command Council, the political core of the Free Officers Movement, which had mounted the coup alongside him. Another shows him standing upright in an open-top vehicle alongside Gaafar Numeiri of Sudan, waving at the crowd; here he is with Nasser, smiling and shaking hands with a young woman in a short skirt, who covers her face with the other hand, as if overcome by excitement. He has thick eyebrows, clear skin, short hair and perfect teeth. He is already revealing a predilection for varied headgear and garb—sporting variously a garrison cap tilted to one side French-style, a beret, a peaked military cap. At different times he is pictured in uniform, in an open-necked shirt, a leather jacket, even a pinstripe suit. He is a shape-shifter; he would be whatever you wanted him to be. It's not hard to understand the appeal he had for a generation of Libyans fed up with the old monarchy, obsessed as it was with noble lineages, doing the bidding of its powerful friends and passively watching the world move ahead while the country stagnated.

It was the era of pan-Arabism, anticolonialism, Marxism, socialism, Third Worldism, any new ideology that promised to get rid of the hated vestiges of colonialism, imperialism and capitalism. Nasser had been Gaddafi's hero since adolescence. The young Muammar was born to a nomadic family in Jahannam in the burning desert southeast of Sirte and spent his early years herding goats and camels. He and his fellow young officers saw themselves as representatives of Libyans who had been neglected by King Idris. "We are not propertied people," he said in an interview with *Le Figaro* one month after seizing power. "The parents of many of us live in huts. My parents still live in a tent in the Sirte area." It was true—his family were deprived, especially compared to the aristocracy in Benghazi. They were from a small tribe, the Gaddafa, and his father regularly had to work for men from more powerful tribes, herding their animals across the inhospitable scrub and sand. It was a harsh way of life, with no electricity, no sanitation and no running water, but later Gaddafi would hark back to his childhood as a kind of prelapsarian paradise, seeing desert and rural people as somehow more noble than those who lived in the city. In *Escape to Hell*, a book of essays he allegedly authored while meditating in his Bedouin tent, he wrote: "Flee, flee the city and get away from the smoke! In complete happiness, go to the village and the countryside, where physical labor has meaning, necessity, usefulness, and is a pleasure besides. There, life is social, and human; families and tribes are close. There is stability and belief." Nonetheless, he built a modern city in Sirte, which was scarcely more than a village when he was born, enabling many Bedouin to settle down and live an easier urban life.

The young Muammar's father, who was illiterate, wanted his only son to have an education, so he was sent to school first in Sirte and then in Sabha, in southern Libya near the border with Niger. It was there, at age fourteen, that he first read about Nasser, which inspired him to mount an unauthorized pro-Nasser demonstration for which he was expelled from school. After finishing his secondary education in the coastal city of Misrata, he enrolled in the military academy in Benghazi. In 1966, as part of the military cooperation between Libya and the UK, Gaddafi and a group of fellow officers were sent on a short signals course at the Royal Army Education Corps Center in Beaconsfield, in the English countryside.

Gaddafi told Musa Koussa, a Libyan master's student in sociology at the University of Michigan who wrote a thesis about his leadership, that the first foreigner he had met in his life was an English teacher who visited his school in Misrata and whom he hated on sight because he thought of him as a colonialist. In Beaconsfield, his loathing only increased, because—he said—he "sustained oppression and insults." He took pride in refusing to speak English and in wearing the Libyan robe, the *jird*, at all times. "I put on *al-jird* and went to Piccadilly," he said. "I was prompted by a feeling of challenge and a desire to assert myself."

A few months after the coup Gaddafi promoted himself from captain to colonel, the same rank as Nasser when he seized power in Egypt in 1952, and started to make speeches about "freedom, socialism and unity," glorifying Arab history and culture as Nasser had done. The king had banned political parties in 1952, and Gaddafi reinforced the ruling. "Henceforth, after the first of September, he who engages in party activities commits treason," he announced. He banned alcohol and insisted that all official documents should be in Arabic alone, with no English. Workers were ordered to paint out any English on road signs. Islam, he said, was a socialist religion. It was also going to be the only one in Libya—he ordered that the Catholic Cathedral of the Sacred Heart of Jesus be turned into a mosque, named after Nasser. The remaining Jews and Italians were expelled, and the British and American air force bases closed. These were popular moves, a sign of the times, applauded across the Middle East and Africa and by people like Mohammed in the medina. Gaddafi championed the Palestinian cause, which also garnered support both in Libya and the region. Arabs should not be divided by tribe, he said. His disapproval of the traditional structures of Libyan society was partly ideological—tribes weren't part of a pan-Arabist, modern consciousness—and partly pragmatic: He wanted no alternative leadership to his own. Gaddafi adopted the color green, the color of Islam, which was also supposed to represent hope and a "green revolution" in agriculture, making the desert bloom.

Everything was painted green for the next four decades, to the point where, after the 2011 revolution, Libyans joked that they were going to paint the trees another color.

In April 1973, Gaddafi went to Zuwara, near the border with Tunisia, to make the speech that would define his rule. He announced the repeal of all laws, threatened "perverts and deviants"—meaning his political opponents—said he would get rid of "all forms of bourgeoisie and bureaucracy," replacing the organs of government with the revolutionary committees known as *lijan thawriya*. Libya, he said, would now embark on a "cultural revolution" modeled on Mao Tse-tung's purges, which were still under way in China. Bashir Hawadi says that Gaddafi consulted no one, and even his colleagues in the Revolutionary Command Council were taken aback at the scope and ruthlessness of his ambition. Local *lijan thawriya* were established to judge landlords, intellectuals, civil servants— anyone who could be regarded as a remnant of the old ways, when Libya had been a bastion of capitalism and a friend of the West. Thousands were arrested, scores hanged. Any vestige of a professional civil service was undermined by the committees, which answered only to Gaddafi. Security services multiplied and divided like invasive cells, and people began to fear their neighbors.

A few years later, frustrated that the society was not transforming itself quickly enough, he decided that—as the French anarchist Pierre-Joseph Proudhon had said sometime earlier—property was theft, so he abruptly confiscated houses, lands and anything else that he thought was held in excess by private individuals. Overnight, anyone who rented a house had more rights to it than the landlord. Private businesspeople, Gaddafi announced, were parasites, so shops and factories closed down, since the owners could no longer raise credit or pay wages. He introduced a new currency, so people put whatever they had left into gold. Wage labor was slavery, he said, and encouraged workers to oust their employers or leave their jobs. Revolutionary committees were inserted in publicly owned companies as an alternative management structure while private companies were nationalized or collapsed. Educated Libyans, many of whom had lost all their property, left the country for new lives in Britain, America and the Gulf.

If this had been anywhere but the Middle East in the 1970s, the Libyan economy would have quickly collapsed, but Gaddafi made one shrewd move—he used what he called "the oil weapon." Libya has vast energy reserves, and at that time a population of less than three million, so he knew that whatever he did, the country would be rich. He jump-started the global oil boom of the 1970s by raising the price of oil and the taxes charged to foreign companies. The American company Occidental Petroleum got 97 percent of its oil from Libya, so when Gaddafi's government cut its production by half, it faced ruin. The condition for increasing production back up to the previous level was to pay an extra thirty cents a barrel. Occidental had little choice but to agree. With that move, Gaddafi forced other Middle Eastern leaders to realize how powerful oil had made them. They rapidly followed the Libyan lead, each outdoing the other by revising the price, demanding compensation for a weakening dollar and threatening to withhold supply. Gaddafi announced that producer countries would from now on dictate the price of oil, and prices in Europe shot up 35 percent overnight.

In 1971, Gaddafi went a stage further by nationalizing British Petroleum's assets after the company refused to accept a 49 percent reduction in its share. Two years later the remaining oil companies were given a choice: Accept that the Libyan state will take control of 51 percent of your assets or leave the country. Gaddafi's decision to nationalize Libya's oil was not unlike the policies of the Iranian nationalist Prime Minister Mohammad Mossadeq in the 1950s, but—unlike Mossadeq—he managed to avoid attempts by the West to overthrow him, and he carried his policies through. At the outbreak of the Yom Kippur War in 1973, the Arab countries en bloc withheld supply in protest against U.S. and European backing for Israel. By 1974, the oil price had reached unprecedented heights.

The strategy was popular, and it benefited the Libyan economy. He never forced his revolutionary committees into the National Oil Corporation, which was always professionally run, and throughout his rule Libyans went abroad to train as engineers and managers for the oil sector. Although a glut would later reduce the price of oil, and sanctions would erode his ability to make the most of the country's energy resources, Gaddafi could claim credit for changing the relationship between Western oil companies and producer countries forever.

It became a struggle to keep afloat for those in other sectors: in the case of Morajea Karim, literally, as he was a first mate in Libya's merchant navy, the General National Maritime Transport Company. He was at sea when five men, all toting guns, walked into the company administration block and said they were now in charge. One came onboard, so Morajea took him onto the bridge, showing him the derricks and cranes to the fore of the ship and the accommodation wing in the aft. "Which way does it go?" asked his new revolutionary boss. The man in charge of Libya's merchant navy didn't know the front from the back of a ship. A long-standing contract for the oil tanker fleet to be maintained in Liverpool was abandoned within a week—Britain might have the expertise, but it was a colonial oppressor. Orders became whimsical. "You could receive a phone call from the management saying 'We want a vessel for a special trip,'" recalls Morajea, a short, dapper man now in his sixties, easily imaginable as he must have been at the time in his crisp, naval uniform. Crew, insurance and fuel would all be organized, only for the ship to sit in port doing nothing for days or even weeks. Sometimes they would be sent on spying missions. "I remember a vessel, fully loaded with oil products, was heading to northern Europe when the call came to go to Gibraltar, because there was a target north of Crete. But there was nothing there." The "targets" might be U.S. aircraft carriers or other "enemy" vessels, but the merchant navy crew often had no idea what they were supposed to be looking for on their special missions, let alone why.

In the early years, resources were put into health and education, to good effect. Libya trained engineers, doctors and other professionals, and the people got free health care and schooling. But with the *lijan thawriya*, the revolutionary committees, in charge of hospitals and universities, standards declined, and the infrastructure built in the early seventies began to deteriorate. The new hospitals were not maintained, let alone modernized, and those who could afford it started to go abroad for treatment. Salaries were pitiable. Libyan doctors went to work in the UK and America, where conditions were better. Gaddafi filled the gap with foreigners on expatriate salaries—a Filipino nurse could be paid ten times more than a Libyan doctor.

Building in Tripoli was unregulated, so no two pavements were the same height, and ugly concrete blocks sprang up among the fading Italianate architecture. Grandiose schemes were dreamed up and abandoned: half-finished apartment complexes littered Tripoli and Benghazi; the plan for a railway from the Tunisian to the Egyptian border was derailed before it started. One project he did carry through. The Great Man Made River was a scheme to pump water from deep under the desert in southern Libya and channel it through massive pipes to the north. No thought was given to the environmental impact, which is still undetermined. It remains the largest irrigation project in the world, at an estimated cost of $20 billion, much of it paid to British and American engineering companies that carried out the work. Gaddafi called it "the eighth wonder of the world," and in many ways it was, because everyone wondered why you would choose such a complex, untested and expensive way of bringing water to your cities instead of using desalination or other solutions adopted by neighboring countries. So extraordinary was the concept, so unlikely the engineering, so enormous the cost that Western intelligence agencies couldn't accept that this was really a water channel and believed it must be some strange system of tunnels for hiding weapons. But it really was simply a giant system of water pipes, half a million of which were transported to the project, the distance traveled by the trucks being "the equivalent of going to the sun and back," according to the Great Man Made River Web site. Thirty million tons of sand and gravel were used, enough to build the Great Pyramid at Giza twenty times over. It was one man's extravagant dream, come true because no one dared counter him and too many were profiting from his grandiose visions.

Literacy rates increased, but the education system turned more idiosyncratic after the publication of the Green Book, which became the basis of the school curriculum. Mukhtar Nagasa, the son of one of Gaddafi's diplomats, had no idea that what he was learning at school while growing up in Tripoli might be regarded as outlandish elsewhere in the world. He was part of the elite, attending the same school as the Gaddafi boys Seif al-Islam, Saadi and Mutassim. Thanks to the Guide he got to fly in an airplane. It was 1981, he was nine years old, and the trip to Sabha, deep in the Sahara, was a prize for ten students who had excelled in the study of what was called national discipline. They had written essays showing how Gaddafi was not only like Nasser, the late Egyptian leader, but also like Saladin, the great twelfth-century Muslim warrior who vanquished the Crusaders. (Saddam Hussein in Iraq also used to like being compared to Saladin—it seemed to be a standard delusion of Arab dictators in the late twentieth century.) The essay encompassed the evils of the Ottoman Empire and the Italian occupation. The young Mukhtar was taken into the cockpit as they soared through the cloudless sky, the desert rolling seamlessly beneath their wings. The pilot was his hero. So was Gaddafi. And Nasser. "They were like rock stars to us," he recalled. "I loved Gaddafi. It was personal." Years later, after living abroad, he looked back on his younger self in amazement. How could he have been taken in for so long? But there were hundreds of thousands of boys like Mukhtar in the 1970s and 1980s, who had known nothing but Gaddafi, to whom it all made sense.

The Green Book, translated into more than thirty languages, including Esperanto and Hebrew, was a discourse on politics ("The party is the contemporary dictatorship. It is the modern dictatorial instrument of governing"), economics ("Labor in return for wages is virtually the same as enslaving a human being"), social behavior ("It is unreasonable for crowds to enter places of worship just to view a person or group of people praying without taking part. It is equally unreasonable for crowds to enter playgrounds and arenas to watch a player or team without participating themselves") and much else besides. It was in places nonsensical and in others a fairly standard old-style socialism. Gaddafi, the Universal Theorist, was styling himself as a philosopher king, but many of his ideas were both derivative and discredited. By the late 1970s, when he was nationalizing the economy, other countries were already starting to reverse socialist economic policies that had brought ruin. While he had appeared as the man of the moment in 1969, ten years later he was still harking back to the Nasser of the 1950s. But his declaration in 1977 that Libya was a Jamahiriya was truly original. He made up the word, which translates as a "state of the masses," and elaborated on it in the Green Book. Having rejected parliamentary democracy, because in his view it marginalized those who did not vote for the winner and created a form of dictatorship, he invented a permanently changing system of what he called "direct democracy." As well as the revolutionary committees there were basic people's congresses, the General People's Congress, people's social leadership committees, purification committees, people's guard and other ad hoc committees, all of which were theoretically in charge, under his benign guidance. A more conventional system of ministries and ministers ran in parallel, but Gaddafi would frequently issue unwritten orders through the committees that contradicted ministerial policy. Yet the

masses were always something of a disappointment to the Guide, participating only in small numbers in his grand political experiment. He frequently berated them for their apathy, to little effect, as most Libyans
were too busy trying to survive or looking for a way out.

In each of Libya's main towns there was a Green Book center, a conical
structure with green-tinted windows that looked like nothing so much as
a spacecraft that had landed from above. In August 2011, a few days after
the fall of Tripoli, I walked through shards of broken glass into a cavernous
hallway of eerie green light and looked down into a pool of greenish water
that had a globe in the center. Around the circular central hall there were
rooms, upholstered in green, for the study of the book, hundreds of copies
of which had been strewn around by furious rebels. I picked up a muddied
version in Italian as a souvenir. The young men who escorted me explained
that this had been the headquarters of the *lijan thawriya*, who had spied and
fought for Gaddafi. During the revolution, snipers had shot at passersby
and the apartment blocks opposite from inside the flying saucer. We went
to a sports center next door, which also had been under the control of the
revolutionary committee. Dried brown blood stains on the concrete and
an unmistakable putrid stench told their own story. Fifteen bodies had
been found stuffed into a refrigerated truck around the back, victims of
Gaddafi's committeemen's desperate struggle to retain power.

Gaddafi saw himself as the natural heir to Nasser, who had died in 1970. He
looked hungrily around the region: Libya was not big enough for one with
such expansive ideas. Moreover, the monarchs of the Middle East, notably
King Hussein of Jordan and King Hassan of Morocco, were resistant to his
radical views. In the early 1970s, he supported plots to assassinate them,
which failed but—unsurprisingly—made neighboring governments suspicious of his motives. He saw himself as the great champion of the Palestinian cause, arming and funding militant groups; he proposed that

instead of two states, one each for Jews and Arabs, only one should be created, called Isratine, where they could live together. Such views were popular in the Arab world, except among Arab leaders who were trying to tread a line between satisfying their own populations and keeping on the right side of the United States. No Arab League summit was complete without a theatrical gesture from Gaddafi. At one he wore a white glove to avoid shaking the "bloodstained hands" of his fellow leaders; at another he blew cigar smoke into the face of the late King Fahd of Saudi Arabia. Kings, sheikhs and presidents saw his hand in every plot to unseat or kill them.

Gaddafi saw himself, however, as a leader for a pan-Arab federation like the United States or the USSR. He tried to merge Libya variously with Egypt, Tunisia, Syria, Sudan, Morocco, Algeria and Chad. Treaties were signed, brotherly love was declared, but no other leader ever allowed Gaddafi to realize his dream, because they knew he wanted to grab rather than share power. The Sudanese leader, Gaafar Numeiri, who had ridden with him so triumphantly in the open-topped vehicle some years earlier, said Gaddafi had "a split personality—both of them evil."

In 1973, Gaddafi organized the Green March, a motorcade of twenty thousand vehicles that drove seven hundred miles east from Tripoli, along the Mediterranean coast to the Egyptian border, where the authorities stopped it in its tracks. Gaddafi loathed Nasser's successor, President Anwar Sadat, who later returned the compliment by describing Gaddafi as "100 percent mad." The convoy was meant to be a provocation. It was billed as a manifestation of the will of the masses, the idea being that the Libyan people wanted their country to be united with Egypt. After all, as Gaddafi frequently pointed out, he wasn't a president, just a guide. The masses were in charge.

In March 2011, when the revolution to oust him had taken root in eastern Libya, he organized a similar Green March: Buses of his supporters would drive the same coastal road from Tripoli to show their solidarity, and retake Benghazi in an echo of his former project. Among the loyalists and those press-ganged into taking the trip was a group of Benghazi residents who had been stranded in Tripoli and were now trying to get home to join the revolution. At Gaddafi's stronghold of Sirte, halfway along the route, Ali Mufta, a young rebel who had been taken prisoner on the front line, imprisoned in Sirte and then released, hopped onboard. Twelve buses were reduced to four, as those who genuinely supported Gaddafi realized they were entering rebel-held territory and executed a swift U-turn, heading back to the capital. Soon the four were down to one bus, but just outside Bin Jawad—at that time, the front line—the bus driver refused to go any farther. Ali, who once worked as a truck driver, took the wheel and drove toward the rebel lines. "They started shooting us, but we were on their side!" he recalled, when I met him a few days later in Benghazi. Eventually, the cheering young men onboard the bus managed to convince the rebels that they wanted to join the revolution, and they were allowed to proceed by car. A dark blue bus, the last vestige of the Green March, was left, drunkenly tilted in a ditch, full of bullet holes, at the side of the road, a symbol not only of Gaddafi's doomed attempts to reverse the revolt against him but of his delusions about Arab unity in previous decades.

Many Libyans have childhood and teenage memories of turning on the TV and seeing men walking to the gallows to be hanged. Mervat Mhani recalls her parents trying to stop her watching a man called Sadeq Shweidi, who had taken part in an attempt to overthrow the Brother Leader, dangling from the gibbet in Benghazi's basketball stadium. She was fifteen. "I remember him screaming, 'Mother have mercy,'" she says. "The trial, verdict and execution were all on TV. I cry every time I think of that guy." Grainy, jumpy footage of it, found during the 2011 uprising, shows a young man with curly dark hair kneeling in front of four men from the *lijan thawriya*, who will be his judge and jury. When they announce that he is guilty of "terrorist activities," a great cheer goes up from the audience, many of whom are children. A young woman in green fatigues can be seen waving her arms, whipping up the crowd. The case became notorious because, on seeing he was not yet quite dead, that young woman, Huda Ben Amr, leaped out of the audience and swung on Shweidi's legs to finish him off. She is reported to have said, "We don't want talk, we want hangings in the public square." She went on to become mayor of Benghazi, known popularly as Huda the Executioner, one of Muammar Gaddafi's most trusted aides.

"It was one Ramadan that Muammar started hanging people," recalls Mohammed Mustafa Saudi, the copper beater in the souk. "We would see it on TV after we had broken fast in the evening, when everyone was at home watching." Sometimes he would be walking home and people would warn him not to go down such-and-such street, because the gallows had been brought out, or he would hear cheering and shouting from the plaza outside the souk, now called Green Square, and realize that someone was about to be hanged. "I think Muammar would just decide he didn't like someone, so he'd get rid of them," he said. "He was hanging people for any small thing."

One day in 1978 Mohammed was out buying supplies for his metal workshop when he heard that the young worker he employed had been arrested. He rushed back to the souk to find that it had been surrounded by police and what he thought were soldiers wearing civilian clothes. They had beaten up the young man and thrown him on the ground. When Mohammed asked why, they seized him as well, and took him to prison for two days. Then they sent him to an air force base in Tripoli for medical checks and declared him fit. Suddenly Mohammed was a soldier. The men surrounding the souk composed the press-gang. He would remain in the military for eleven years.

The first nine months of training were not so bad, but in January the following year he found himself on an airplane heading into the unknown. He was being sent for further training in Turkmenistan, then part of the Soviet Union. "It was minus-five degrees," he recalls. "We had never experienced anything like it." He learned how to fire a rocket and a SAM-6 Antiaircraft Missile. There were Iraqis being trained at the same base, but they were not allowed to talk to the Libyans. Life was monotonous. "We weren't allowed to leave the base—all we could do was walk around a bit." He worried about his family back in Tripoli—by then he had four children, and although his wages had been paid to his wife in advance, he could make no plans for the future, because he had no idea how long he would have to spend in the army.

Within a few months of his return, he found himself on the Tunisian border. "We were very scared there would be war with Tunisia," he said. "We didn't want that, but we were soldiers and had to obey orders. Then suddenly we were taken to Beyda, near the Egyptian border. There was trouble between Muammar and Sadat." Tensions with Tunisia and Egypt ebbed, but now there was war with Libya's southern neighbor, Chad, and Mohammed was sent to the Aouzo Strip, a slice of desert that Mussolini had claimed from the French as part of Italian North Africa and which Gaddafi had decided should be reincorporated into Libya. It was a long, disastrous, pointless war, which sputtered on through most of the 1980s and would reduce the Libyan army from a reasonably professional force into a broken, fragmented, loose grouping of militiamen. Mohammed sat in the desert and waited for it all to be over. Every four months he was allowed to go home for a month. After three years he was reassigned to a radar facility in Tripoli. Little did he know what kind of action he would soon see.

Muammar Gaddafi was a great expert on women. "It is an undisputed fact that both man and woman are human beings," he wrote in the Green Book. He goes on to explain in some detail the purpose of menstruation—citing "gynecologists" as his source—and breast-feeding, which he thinks should continue for two years. He is a big fan of children being raised by their mothers at home. "Nurseries are similar to poultry farms into which chicks are crammed after they are hatched," he says, and meanders down a small detour about how the meat of wild birds is tastier than the meat of factory chickens to prove his point. In the world according to Muammar, a woman does physical work only because "a harsh materialistic society" forces her to, and he rails against anything "which stains her beauty and detracts from her femininity." Women, he believes, "are like blossoms which are created to attract pollen and to produce seeds."

He was certainly attracted to women like a bee to a flower. He always preferred to talk to female journalists, and a not very subtle seduction attempt was part of the drill. The late Marie Colvin of the *Sunday Times* (London) interviewed him on numerous occasions and probably knew him better than any other reporter. She recalled an occasion when he tried to make her put on little green shoes before starting an interview. Others were subjected to groping and kissing. His female bodyguards, with their tight uniforms, high-heeled shoes and nail polish, were the subject of endless speculation in the European and American media. They graduated from the only women's military academy in the Muslim world and were allegedly selected for their "quick reflexes." They had to have a "certificate of morality" and adhere to the Guide's ideology, but many Libyans regarded them as prostitutes, there for the pleasure of the Brother Leader. Abdelsalam Abu Zitaya, a distant relative of Gaddafi's who worked as a guard at Bab al Aziziyah, Gaddafi's compound in Tripoli, made the mistake of starting a relationship with a female guard who had caught Gaddafi's eye. When his superiors found out, he was initially instructed to marry her, which he refused, and he was then dismissed. The storm passed, and after a month he was allowed back. "Gaddafi didn't want any of us sleeping with his women, because he feared HIV," he said, when I met him after the 2011 revolution. "He loved women," he said. "There was an office with a bedroom in it. We were never allowed inside, but nearly every day cars would arrive with young girls, and they would be taken into that office. They were very beautiful, usually about eighteen or twenty years old. I don't know who they were."

He was fascinated by powerful women. When he told Marie that he had a message for Madeleine Albright, then U.S. secretary of state, she wondered if she was about to be privy to some important political move. Far from it. Instead, he told Marie that he loved Albright. "He watched her every move on television and was annoyed that sometimes the cameras didn't show her full face," Marie recalled. "Could I get her special phone number for him, preferably for the phone next to her bed? Would I also communicate to her that if she felt the same as he did, she should wear green in her next television appearance?"

He was equally struck by Condoleezza Rice, President George W. Bush's secretary of state, whom he referred to as "my African Princess." In 2007, he said to *Al Jazeera:* "I admire and am very proud of the way she leans back and gives orders to the Arab leaders . . . Leezza, Leezza, Leezza. I love her very much. I admire her, and I'm proud of her, because she's a black woman of African origin." In her memoir, Rice recalls that when she visited Tripoli in 2008, he revealed "a slightly eerie fascination with me." She refused to meet him in his tent, instead going to his formal residence, where he showed her a "quite innocent collection of photos of me with world leaders . . . set to the music of a song called 'Black Flower in the White House.'" She called it one of the more unusual encounters of her career. "It was weird, but at least it wasn't raunchy," she writes.

Gaddafi's compulsion, if that is what it was, only grew as he became older and ever stranger looking. The U.S. ambassador, Gene Cretz, in a 2009 diplomatic cable uncovered by WikiLeaks, writes of Gaddafi's reliance on a Ukrainian nurse, Galyna Kolotnytska, "a voluptuous blonde," suspected of being his lover. Abdelsalam told me that one of a team of

Ukrainian nurses would appear at ten every morning carrying bags of creams, to administer some kind of medicine. "The nurses had a very good life," he said, with some jealousy. They were reported to be earning a high salary, but their tasks were onerous. The Guide insisted that everything be sterilized, as he was phobic about germs. His chair had to be sprayed with disinfectant, and the microphone had to be sterilized before he would speak into it.

Wherever Gaddafi went, young women went too. According to the guard, a Tuareg woman called Mabrouka Targi, who was close to both the Brother Leader and his second wife, Safia, was in charge of organizing the harem. Gaddafi's reputation was well known, and Libyan women lived in fear of his gaze lighting upon them. I met female medical students who had trained alongside his adopted daughter, who said they were careful never to make friends with her, not because they disliked her, but because they feared being invited back to Bab al Aziziyah and being spotted by her father. In Western society, coercion would be the crime. In Libya, dishonor was an additional and dangerous complication. Both boys and girls were supposed to be virgins when they married, but if girls were "sullied," that was a far greater disgrace for the family. Honor killings were rare, but a woman's reputation was critical if she was to make a good marriage into a respectable family. This was a collective culture, in which marriage was still a contract between families, not just an individual choice. You couldn't say no to Muammar—What might happen to your father? Your brothers?—but if you said yes, your honor would be ruined and a rapid wedding to one of his relatives or minions would be the only option.

Under his saccharine words about blossoms and chickens lay contempt for women, whom he regarded as decoration and forced to submit to his will. Yet during the four decades of his rule, in contrast to many Arab and African countries, women made progress in Libya. Less than a quarter of all girls went to primary school under the king, but Gaddafi increased compulsory education for all from six to nine years, which boosted female literacy from one of the lowest to one of the highest in the region. By the time he was ousted there were more women than men attending universities. He encouraged women to take jobs such as teaching, nursing and doing administrative work, but they also became pharmacists, doctors, dentists and sometimes engineers. Traditionally, a Libyan woman joined a man's family on marriage, after the payment of a bride price, and she was then largely restricted to the home, but through the 1970s and 1980s the old ways started to break down. By the end of Gaddafi's rule there were more women in the workforce in Libya than in most Arab countries. The harsh life of the desert, which had always required both men and women to work outside, meant that Bedouin women had traditionally enjoyed more freedom than urban women, so perhaps that was why Gaddafi didn't think women should be confined to the private sphere. The age of marriage was equalized for men and women, polygamy restricted, and a wife could sue for divorce. Libyans even started to have smaller families; older Libyan women tend to have six or more children, but now—as in all countries where girls are educated—the desire is for smaller families. There was social change across the Middle East, but Gaddafi encouraged it. A few Libyan women started to go outside the house unveiled, and some adopted Western dress. Gaddafi's daughter Aisha frequently went unveiled, her long hair loose, earning her the nickname "the Claudia Schiffer of North Africa."

As the Guide invoked Islam less, religion became a vehicle for dissent. You couldn't oppose Gaddafi, but it was well known that the clergy saw him as a heretic, partly because of his views on women and marriage, but more because he set himself up as an alternative religious authority, once even describing himself as the "imam of the Muslims." Religious devotion became a form of resistance. Educated women, many of whom had traveled, didn't want to give up their gains, but the veil came back as a political fashion statement. It was happening across the Muslim world, especially in neighboring Egypt, as people looked for a way to show their disgust for corrupt and dictatorial secular governments that were regarded as serving Western interests. While Western women might see the head scarf as a sign of oppression, many Arab women saw it as an expression of identity. A photograph of a young woman shaking Gaddafi's hand as he sits next to Nasser, taken in 1970, shocks, because you would never see a woman in either Egypt or Libya today with her hair loose or wearing such a short dress in public. Modern Libyan women like Mervat Mhani wear tight jeans covered by a loose, thigh-length tunic. They pin their scarfs tightly around their heads, so the neck and hair are completely covered, the face, often lightly made up, framed in cloth. Others, like Salwa and Iman Bughaigis, go bareheaded. Those who choose to be veiled see that as an expression of their political and religious identity—those who choose not to feel the same.

Oil had made Libya rich, so Gaddafi decided to go on the world's most extravagant shopping spree for weapons. At one point he was devoting nearly a quarter of the national budget to arms. During his first decade in power he spent $22 billion on armaments—$890 per year for every Libyan citizen. No one could match him in spending. Israel was the nearest, at $480 per person per year. Only the Iranians spent more in total, and they had ten times the population. The Russians were by far his biggest supplier, and from them he bought four thousand tanks, 350 fighter aircraft, six submarines and two frigates. Libya became the best client in the world for French arms companies after then president Georges Pompidou clinched a deal with Gaddafi for 150 Mirage fighters—Libya, a country at that time of less than three million people, ended up with an air force as big as that of France, totaling 500 combat aircraft. Italy scrambled to keep up, selling the Libyans transport planes, helicopters, naval ships and missiles. It was a bonanza, missed by the British and Americans, who had supplied King Idris and so were out of favor.

In March 2011, I came across dozens of warehouses and bunkers dug into the desert outside Ajdabia, in eastern Libya. Unused weapons, some still in their boxes with dates going back to the 1970s, were piled high. It was as if a compulsive shopper had put their purchases in the garage, forgotten what they'd bought and gone out to buy more again and again. Some bunkers had recently been ransacked by the rebels, and the contents were in use on the eastern front—Gaddafi had unwittingly provided plenty for his adversaries. The designs might have been outdated, and the choice wasn't necessarily ideal for guerrilla warfare, but there was enough here to provide for dozens of small armies. A box of warheads for antitank missiles, manufactured in France, was marked FROM AEROSPATIALE FOR LIBYAN AIR FORCE. I saw rocket-propelled grenades, rockets and ammunition for illuminating projectiles, but I didn't hang around to identify more. A few days earlier one of Colonel Gaddafi's warplanes had crashed in the desert nearby, and others were bombing just up the road—if they had hit one of the warehouses, the blast would have killed people for miles around.

Gaddafi's problem was that he didn't have enough trained manpower, so in the 1970s and 1980s he imported Soviet, Pakistani and even North Korean pilots. Baffled foreign military analysts said the acquisitions were devoid of strategic rationale, and without personnel trained in their use, could do little to protect Libya's borders. It did, however, make for splendid military parades. An African diplomat told me how, at one of the annual celebrations marking the September 1st Al Fattah Revolution, he and other guests had to sit in Green Square from dawn until dusk. It took nine hours for all the tanks, antiaircraft weapons and other hardware to file past.

The weapons, Gaddafi said, were for the fight against Zionism, and he gave Egypt $1 billion worth in 1973 to fight the Yom Kippur War. That year, a Libyan passenger aircraft lost its way in a sandstorm and ended up flying across the Israeli-occupied Sinai. The Israelis shot it down, more proof for Gaddafi that he was right to build up his armed forces. Yet, he knew, however many tanks and fighter jets he bought, he couldn't beat Israel in a conventional war, so he started to fund militant and terror groups across the globe. "I am against terrorism, but I support the just causes of liberation. I am ready to fight," he said. "If you say I am a terrorist, then George Washington was a terrorist." America was the prime enemy, and in 1986 came the attack that would turn Gaddafi, in the eyes of the Western world, from an irritant into a disruptive force that must be stopped.

On April 5th, two young East German women entered La Belle discothèque in West Berlin, a favorite haunt of U.S. servicemen. They had a drink and walked out, one leaving her handbag behind. A few minutes later an explosion tore through the crowd of dancers, leaving 3 people dead and 230 injured, some permanently. The handbag had contained not only explosives but iron nails designed to kill and maim as many as possible. American soldiers comprised 2 of the dead and 79 of the injured. The American government had been monitoring the radio traffic between Tripoli and the Libyan People's Bureau in East Berlin. Within hours they knew that this was a Libyan operation, backed by the East German secret service, the Stasi.

U.S. president Ronald Reagan, who had been reelected in 1984, believed there was only one way to stop Gaddafi. His ally, the British prime minister Margaret Thatcher, agreed. Ten days after the Berlin discothèque attack, U.S. fighter jets dropped sixty tons of munitions on targets in Tripoli and Benghazi, including Colonel Gaddafi's Bab al Aziziyah compound. The raid, which lasted eleven minutes, killed sixty people; Gaddafi himself narrowly escaped injury. Tripoli was unprepared. There were no sirens, and by the time the antiaircraft batteries were in action the planes were back over the Mediterranean. Colonel Gaddafi was in his bunker at the time, which was not unusual, as he spent a lot of time underground. When he failed to appear in public for several days, Libyans speculated that he had been injured, but he emerged, unscathed, to say that he had no response for Reagan. "I have nothing to say to him, because he is mad," he said. "He is foolish. He is an Israeli dog."

"I thought it was thunder, but it was so loud," recalled Mukhtar Nagasa, the diplomat's son who lived not far from Gaddafi's compound. "I woke up, and my mother rushed in. I saw her face, and she was really scared. She said, 'Americans, Americans!' and we ran downstairs." Mukhtar's father handed him a hunting rifle and went out, saying, "Mukhtar, you're the only man in the house now. Don't open the door to anyone." Age fourteen, he was left to guard his mother and eight sisters. "I was so scared," said Mukhtar. "I sat in the chair in the living room with the rifle across my knees. I really didn't know what to do." Luckily he didn't have to do anything, as his father returned the next morning, and after a few days the whole family went to stay with relatives in Zintan. Others were not so lucky. A school friend, whose family lived in Bab al Aziziyah because his father worked for Gaddafi's intelligence network, was killed alongside his sister. The TV showed gruesome hospital scenes of those who had been injured. When Gaddafi was shown on TV again it was to mourn his adopted baby daughter, Hana, who he said had been killed in the bombing.

Mohammed Mustafa Saudi, the metalworker conscripted into the military, was stationed at an air force base when the United States attacked. "When the planes came in we didn't know at first if they were friend or foe," he recalled. "Then we could see on the radar that we had been targeted. We released two rockets, but I never saw any plane come down." The following day a man dressed as a U.S. serviceman was paraded on TV, the announcer claiming victory because Libya had captured an enemy combatant. "It was obvious he wasn't American," says

Mohammed. One plane had in fact been hit by a rocket, but it crashed in the Gulf of Sirte and the crew was rescued by the Americans. "We'd known for ages then that Muammar was a liar," said Mohammed, "but there was nothing we could do. I was fighting for my country and for Libyans, not for him."

The faces of the enemy were everywhere: Margaret Thatcher and Ronald Reagan, the evil twins, determined to destroy the Brother Leader and his adoring people. Gaddafi became a hero across the Arab world, and to some fringe sections of the Left in Europe and the United States. Gaddafi gave money to Arabs and Africans afflicted by poverty, and talked of Arab unity. He railed against Zionism and donated billions to the Palestinian cause. He refused to accept the hypocrisy of the time, which saw Arab leaders championing the Palestinians in theory only to betray them in practice. To many it seemed that Gaddafi, alone, told it like it was, challenging sheikhs and potentates whose pusillanimous actions belied their anti-American rhetoric.

But for Libyans, life was getting tougher. The Guide's failing economic policies and foreign adventures were bringing the economy to the point of collapse. As long as the oil price remained high, his attempts at redistributing wealth had some success, but by the mid-1980s the price of oil had crashed—Libya's annual oil income dropped from $22 billion in 1980 to $9 billion five years later. Sanctions exacerbated the problems. The shelves of the "People's Stores" were bare. There were shortages of meat, matches, soap and toilet paper. Twice in 1986 people stampeded after the arrival of boats from Nicaragua that brought a coveted cargo of bananas. Two women were reported crushed in the melée. Those Libyans who didn't accept the Brother Leader's version of reality were restless, but the penalty for opposing it would become harsher than ever.

CHAPTER THREE

SUBVERSIVES AND STRAY DOGS

Death is the solution to all problems. No man—no problem.

—JOSEPH STALIN

We do not surrender. We win or we die.

—OMAR MUKHTAR

The Guide lived in constant fear that he would be assassinated. Sometimes he would prepare as if he was about to fly somewhere in his official jet—the one with the Jacuzzi and the silver leather armchairs—but would then travel in an unmarked car instead. Nonetheless, it wasn't difficult to predict that he was planning to visit your town. For a start, they would cut down the trees near any possible route for his convoy, to stop people from hiding in the branches and taking a potshot. Whenever he was scheduled to give a speech in Al Kish Square in Benghazi, the residents of apartment blocks and shops overlooking the area would be forced to move out for a few days.

He was right to be afraid—a lot of people wanted to kill Gaddafi. The first conspiracy, ascribed to a group of fellow army officers close to the Revolutionary Command Council, was hatched within a few months of the 1969 coup. The plotters were tried and imprisoned, their original sentences extended for several years by popular demand, according to

Gaddafi. The following year, King Idris's nephew, known as the Black Prince, plotted to bring five thousand mercenaries across the desert from Chad with the aim of arming tribes still loyal to the monarchy, but the plan was aborted after a reconnaissance unit was caught by Gaddafi's troops. When that was uncovered, one of the king's former counselors approached David Stirling, the founder of Britain's Special Air Service, the SAS, who was at the time running a private military company called Watchguard. The idea was for twenty-five British mercenaries to land by boat from Italy, free hundreds of political prisoners from a notorious jail in Tripoli that they code-named the Hilton, provide them with arms, get them to storm Colonel Gaddafi's headquarters at Bab al Aziziyah and then restore the monarchy. The British secret service, MI6, vetoed what became known as the Hilton assignment, not because it was a lunatic enterprise with no chance of success, but allegedly because the Americans were not yet convinced that Gaddafi was sufficiently troublesome. Although he had closed their military base he had not as yet touched their economic assets, and Libya was a significant source of oil. Subsequent coups were plotted by the French, but they too were aborted, confirming Colonel Gaddafi's view that Western powers were unlikely to move against him, despite his anticapitalist rhetoric.

After his famous Zuwara speech in 1973, which marked the start of his cultural revolution, Gaddafi unleashed his Green Terror: purges, mass arrests, summary trials by *lijan thawriya* and executions. Communist East Germany provided agents of the Stasi secret police to train and work with the *mukhabarat*, Gaddafi's internal intelligence agency, tracking down anyone who might speak against the colonel, at home or abroad. The twelve-man Revolutionary Command Council split, after several members attempted a coup against Gaddafi in 1975. Different sectors of society were targeted: members of underground political parties, royalists, soldiers suspected of plotting, and in 1976—in what would become the most notorious purge—university students.

For Wanise Elisawi there was no choice but to oppose Gaddafi. As a relative of the king's first wife, he was automatically suspected of disloyalty; in a Marxist state he would have been called a class enemy. Wanise's father was put under house arrest when Gaddafi and his group seized power in 1969, in their hometown of Al Marj, near Benghazi, and accused of being a traitor. Soldiers arrived at a second family house, where Wanise was staying near his school in Tobruk, and made him pack up and leave. It was the new regime's house now. In 1973, he started a degree in architecture at the University of Tripoli. He was a studious young man, but like many of his peers became obsessed with political ideas. "Islamists, Marxists, nationalists, everyone was fighting to control the student union," he recalls. In another country youthful ideological clashes might not merit much attention, but in Libya in the 1970s the stakes were much higher. Gaddafi knew that his ideas and increasingly autocratic rule were being challenged at the universities in Tripoli and Benghazi, and he resolved to stop it. The *lijan thawriya*, the revolutionary committees, infiltrated the campuses and struggled with other groups for control of the student unions.

Libya's intellectual life had always been influenced by Egypt, its bigger and more developed eastern neighbor. Gaddafi had Nasser as his model, so those who opposed him naturally looked to Nasser's political and ideological enemy, the *ikhwan*, the Muslim Brotherhood, with its slogan "Islam is the solution." Sayyid Qutb, the brotherhood's most radical theorist, had been hanged by Nasser in 1966. Wanise was among the students who debated Qutb's radical ideas: Could violent struggle against bad government be justified? Was the West the source of spiritual and material corruption? The influence of the Sanussis remained strong, especially among easterners like Wanise, and in the mid-1970s Libyan society was still very traditional, with few women attending university and arranged marriages between cousins the norm. Gaddafi had tried to co-opt some of the same ideas, condemning Western materialism and citing Islam as central to his political thought, but he was frustrated by the conservatism of Libyan society. The Muslim Brotherhood was vague on ideology and ambiguous on the use of violence, and it only ever gained adherents among intellectuals in Libya. Nonetheless, the Libyan leader saw organized political Islam as a threat to his power, so the brotherhood was banned. Wanise describes himself as a "moderate," but as a young man he was attracted to the brotherhood's ideal of an Islamic state based on the *sharia*. Islamic law, with its clear moral strictures and defined code of conduct and punishment, appealed to his conservative nature and seemed to hold the line against what he saw as Gaddafi's dangerously radical ideas. In time, his generation would split between those—like him—who moved to a more secular position and others who took a more radical Islamist line.

In January 1976 the struggle for control of the student union turned violent, with clashes between pro- and anti-Gaddafi students at the university in Benghazi leaving several dead and others injured. In April, Gaddafi went to the Benghazi campus and called for "reactionary" students to be "cleansed," both there and in Tripoli. Wanise found his name on a list of twenty-five posted on the faculty wall: expelled. On April 7th—a date that would become feared and famous in subsequent years—pro-Gaddafi students attacked those like Wanise who were regarded as enemies, and Gaddafi's deputy, Major Abdul Salam Jalloud, appeared on the Tripoli campus shooting his pistol in the air and declaring that a popular revolution had started at the university. Hit on the head by a stone in the commotion, Wanise passed out and ended up first in a hospital, then in prison for a month. About eight hundred of his fellow students were also jailed. Torture was routine—he was starved and beaten on the soles of his feet. Release was contingent on signing a document agreeing not to return to the university, so he went to work for the Italian oil company, Agip, in the desert. After the turbulence of his youth he rather liked the calm atmosphere of the desert camp. It gave him time to think. He organized a sports team and a library, and in 1978 got a civil engineering scholarship to Ohio University.

The universities he left behind were in turmoil. On April 7, 1977, the anniversary of the purge, a gallows was erected in the main square in Benghazi and four people, two of them students, were publicly hanged. Other students were forced to watch, chanting: "Down with the enemies of the revolution! We will liquidate the enemies! We will not fear blood!" Twenty-two army officers convicted of involvement in the 1975 coup attempt were executed the same week. It was the beginning of a period of severe repression in which thousands would be executed and even more imprisoned and tortured. Gallows were erected on the campuses of the universities, and students were forced to watch their comrades being hanged. April 7th became one of Gaddafi's favorite days for public hangings, an annual reminder of the cost of arguing with the Universal Theorist.

Ali Abuzeid was an expansive, sociable man who loved to talk politics. In his youth, he too had been attracted to the Muslim Brotherhood, which he spent long hours debating with friends in his hometown of Roujban, in the Nafousa Mountains. After qualifying as an accountant, he had started a small business in Tripoli and built up a little capital so that he and his young wife, Amina, could move out of the flat they were renting and into a villa they were building on the outskirts of town. He was looking forward to starting a family when he, like many others who moved in opposition circles, was arrested. He was released after a year in jail, but now that his opposition to Gaddafi was public, he knew that he could be rearrested at any time, so he immediately fled to London, followed by Amina with his baby daughter, Huda.

Within a few years, Huda and her mother—pregnant with a second child—were back in Tripoli. The half-finished villa had been confiscated under a decree that unoccupied property reverted to the government, or was given to any tenant who fancied it, so Amina was keen to see if they could get it back. The idea had been to spend just a few weeks in Libya, but the authorities confiscated their passports, so they couldn't go anywhere. A year sped by. Amina gave birth to a baby boy; Huda went to school in Tripoli. One day her uncle in Roujban told them to pack their things. Huda dressed in her best new jeans and waited. The following night a man she had never seen before arrived in a pickup and told them to climb in and hide under blankets. After a few miles, he said they must walk through a shallow river. Up to her knees in water, new jeans ruined, seven-year-old Huda kept going as long as she could, but in the end the man who had brought them carried her on his back. Her mother cuddled her baby brother to stop him from crying and alerting anyone to their presence. They walked all night, until they had crossed the border into Tunisia, where Ali was waiting for his wife and daughter, and for the son he had never seen. The strange man was a people smuggler, paid to get them out. It was the only way. The family returned to London, where Ali took a job with an accounting firm. They had two more children, and Amina tried to settle into life in Britain, where she had no relatives and didn't speak the language. Their sole aim was to go back home, but scores of people were being executed and hundreds arrested in Libya in the early 1980s; at least they thought they would be safe in London.

One sunny April afternoon in 1980, Mohammed Mustafa Ramadan, a journalist based in London with the BBC Arabic Service, walked out of the Regent's Park Mosque where he had been attending Friday prayers. Two men were waiting for him; one shot him with a pistol. At their trial it came out that they had been sent from Tripoli. Ramadan had written several open letters to Colonel Gaddafi, criticizing his policies; this was Gaddafi's reply. Two weeks later a Libyan lawyer, Mahmoud Nafa, was shot outside his office in Kensington. He was not a prominent opponent of the regime, but had defended members of King Idris's government, so that was enough for the *lijan thawriya*, who had taken over the Libyan embassy in London, renaming it the Libyan People's Bureau. The new ambassador was Gaddafi's friend Musa Koussa—the former graduate student who had written the fawning master's thesis about the Brother Leader. His job was to carry out the policy known as the liquidation of stray dogs, which had been announced at the revolutionary committees' annual conference earlier in the year. "Physical elimination becomes the end stage in the conflict of the revolutionary struggle for a final solution, when removing economic, political and social weapons from counterrevolutionaries fails to put an end to their activities," said their public statement. Colonel Gaddafi was more succinct. "We will follow these people even if they go to the North Pole," he said. After the killings in London, Ambassador Koussa gave an interview to *The Times*. "The revolutionary committees decided last night to kill two more people in the United Kingdom," he said. "I approve of this." The British promptly expelled him, but it didn't put an end to the killings. As many as thirty-five Libyans were murdered in Europe over the next few years.

Undeterred, a group of exiles, led by Gaddafi's former ambassador to India, Mohammed Yusuf Magarief, formed a new opposition party, the National Front for the Salvation of Libya, the NFSL. It provided a secular, nationalist alternative to the Muslim Brotherhood and attracted some of the best educated and wealthiest of the Libyan diaspora, mobilizing opposition to Gaddafi in Europe, America and Egypt, producing pamphlets and holding meetings with students and others who opposed Gaddafi. Cash from the oil boom was washing around the Middle East and London, and Gaddafi had a lot of enemies, so there was no problem getting funds. One former NFSL member recalls going to ask for $100,000 from a Libyan businessman and walking out of the meeting with a check for $1 million.

Ali Abuzeid joined immediately. Huda was never quite sure what her father did. He was no longer an accountant. He traveled a lot, and when he was at home, he was preoccupied. The house was full of men smoking, drinking tea, talking Libyan politics. He was a solid man, someone others trusted, always full of good humor. Family was a safe haven, but he didn't have much time. "I didn't see him very often," recalls Huda. "Revolutionary politics absorbed him. I wanted to get his attention, so I would make little books for him, and write him letters when he was away saying, 'Hey, old man, we miss you.'" Ali warned his children not to talk about Libya, nor to draw attention to their circumstances. Everyone knew what had happened to the Ghesuda kids. Gaddafi decreed that all exiles must return to Libya by June 1980 or face the consequences. A few months after that edict a Libyan named Hosni Farhat, who worked as a ticketing clerk at Libyan Arab Airlines, visited Farag Ghesuda, a former naval officer now living in Portsmouth, on the south coast of England, to try to persuade him to return to Libya. Farag refused and the two men argued. Some months later Hosni Farhat went round to the Ghesuda house ostensibly to apologize, bringing with him a packet of KP peanuts as gift. The following day the Ghesuda children, eight-year-old Karim and seven-year-old Soad, opened the peanuts, and before they had eaten half, fell violently ill. The children were rushed to the hospital; the family dog died after eating the remaining peanuts, which had fallen on the carpet. Farhat had poisoned the nuts with a toxin so deadly that the judge at his trial wouldn't allow it to be named. The children only just survived.

The Crown Court in the English town of Winchester sentenced Hosni Farhat to life imprisonment for attempted murder. Several months before the incident he had met the head of the Libyan People's Bureau in London, but the judge at the trial concluded that his motive was only to punish Ghesuda for refusing to obey Gaddafi, not that he acted on government orders. The Libyan government denied any involvement in the case. It couldn't be proven that Farhat was a member of the *lijan thawriya*, but that was how the system worked. Members had the freedom to act as they saw fit, targeting anyone they regarded as an enemy of the Brother Leader.

When they were imprisoned, as several were after trials in Britain and Italy, others stepped into their place. They were deported on their release and returned to heroes' welcomes in Tripoli, with congratulations for a job well done.

The *lijan thawriya* and the NFSL were battling for the loyalty of Libyan students abroad, just as pro- and anti-Gaddafi factions had clashed on campuses back home in the mid-1970s. In April 1984, a small group associated with the NFSL held a demonstration outside the Libyan People's Bureau in St. James's Square in central London to protest the execution of students in Libya. A counterdemonstration of loyalists turned up, so the police erected barriers to keep the two sides apart, while loud music playing from inside the People's Bureau drowned out the shouting of anti-Gaddafi slogans. Suddenly, gunshots echoed through the square. Eleven people fell to the ground, among them a British policewoman, Yvonne Fletcher. She had been fatally shot in the stomach by a bullet that the inquest concluded had been fired from the first floor of the Libyan People's Bureau. During the eleven-day police siege of the building that followed, her hat remained where she had fallen, an emblem of the lengths Gaddafi would go to to quell his enemies. Gaddafi said the British were attacking the People's Bureau and sent forces to surround the British embassy in Tripoli. Eventually, a deal was done. The British diplomats were allowed to leave Libya, and the Libyans inside the Bureau—many of whom were not diplomats but *lijan thawriya* members—went back to Libya. One of her colleagues removed Fletcher's hat the day the Libyans were expelled, and the next year a memorial was erected on the spot where she had fallen. The Libyan government paid Yvonne Fletcher's mother compensation in 1999, but no one was ever charged with her murder.

The exiles began to plan their next move. The Abuzeid family was uprooted again within a few years, this time to Tunis. Huda, as she approached her teenage years, resented the disruption—she didn't want to have to learn French and go to a new school. She was increasingly aware of the anxiety and danger surrounding her father and his friends. "There was a pro-Gaddafi person living in the next apartment block in Tunis," she remembers. "We had to avoid him. There was always this underlying stress and tension." One day she sneaked into her parents' bedroom, and when she was messing around among her mother's clothes in the wardrobe found something cold and hard. It was a pistol. She dropped it and ran.

What Huda didn't know was that they had moved to Tunisia because her father and his colleagues, including Wanise Elisawi, were plotting to overthrow Gaddafi. Military action, they decided, was the only way. They had the backing of the CIA and the king of Morocco, who had never forgiven Gaddafi for trying to assassinate him, and for supporting the separatist Polisario Front. Sixteen thousand Libyans were studying in America. With a small group traveling on fake Sudanese passports, Wanise went for a month's military training in the Atlas Mountains before he returned to the United States to finish his civil engineering degree. Whether engineers, architects or doctors, they learned the basics of handling weapons but underestimated the skills of subterfuge they would need. As head of the Tunisian branch of the NFSL, Ali was in charge of smuggling fighters into Libya, supervising their accommodation and transport. His links with the people smugglers who had taken Huda and her mother out all those years earlier came in handy. In March 1984, the first fighters entered Libya, rented apartments in Tripoli and Benghazi, smuggled in guns and grenades and contacted supporters within the armed forces. Week by week, more armed men entered the country, waiting for their moment.

On Sunday May 6, 1984, the head of NFSL's military wing, Ahmed Ahwas, crossed the border from Tunisia into Libya with two bodyguards. They tried not to attract attention, got into a taxi, and drove toward Nalut in the Nafousa Mountains. Ali in Tunis and the rest of the leadership in London waited for the signal that he had arrived in Tripoli. It never came. The hours ticked by. Nothing. Then came the Libyan state TV news at

11:00 P.M. A traitor, it said, had been caught trying to enter the country with the aim of assassinating the Brother Leader. Thanks be to God, he had been apprehended and killed. The taxi driver had grown suspicious and taken them to the police in Nalut. A gunfight had broken out in which Ahmed Ahwas had been killed.

The fighters who had already been infiltrated into the country over the previous months were panicked into attempting to storm Bab al Aziziyah earlier than planned, on Tuesday May 8th. It was a disaster. They tried to smash their way in using a garbage truck but were swiftly repelled by the guards and shot dead. Others were killed just outside the apartments they had rented nearby. Worse than that, the authorities had found a list of names and addresses in Ahmed Ahwas's suitcase. They started to hunt down anyone who might have been connected with the NFSL.

Wanise Elisawi was in his home village of Al Marj near Benghazi, waiting for a sign. After the attack on Bab al Aziziyah was under way, he and his men were to assassinate twenty-three key regime leaders, including Gaddafi's brother-in-law, Abdullah Sanussi, and General Al Fattah Younes, then the head of the Garyounis Military Task Force, the biggest brigade in the east. The sign never came. When he saw on state TV that Ahmed Ahwas had been caught, Wanise knew he was a marked man. There was no point in trying to run. Police and soldiers surrounded his house and took him to Tripoli, where a court-martial condemned him to death.

Something inside Wanise was unsurprised. It was almost a family tradition. His grandfather had fought against the Italians, and in 1916 was shipped to Sicily, where he was told he would be executed. He lost his eyesight after years in an underground dungeon, and the sentence was commuted to life in prison. In 1943, during World War II, his father was caught smuggling weapons and was also given a death sentence by the Italians. The hanging was delayed by twenty-four hours, during which time the Italians surrendered and the British declared victory over the Axis powers, so prisoners were released. Now, forty years on, every day state

TV showed the hangings of people involved in the plot he had been part of hatching. "This is the fate of stray dogs who conspire against the Jamahiriya," said the announcer. As he waited on death row, age twenty-nine, Wanise contemplated his short life. He thought of his wife, Farida, pregnant with their third child. They had already decided that if she was a girl, they would call her Isara, meaning the Chosen One. Wanise Elisawi was happy that he might have a third daughter to join the two he already had, but he felt huge guilt that Farida would be bringing up the girls alone.

A gallows was erected in Al Marj. May 27th was the date set for the hanging, but the people of Al Marj had other ideas. The local men, many of whom were relatives of Wanise and Farida, burned down the gallows and the military outpost in the village in the middle of the night. Wanise still doesn't know why the regime backed down. But someone somewhere made a decision, and instead of hanging Wanise, they took him to a newly built prison in Tripoli called Abu Salim. He would spend the next nineteen years of his life there.

At 4:00 A.M., Ali Abuzeid learned that the attempt had failed. His comrades were on the run, arrested or dead. It was the only time Huda ever saw her father cry. But there was little time for tears, because Gaddafi had his spies in Tunis and word came that a hit squad was already en route from Libya. There was a million dollars on his head. Her father vanished that night, leaving the family to follow. Huda packed the books he had given her— she was an adolescent now, and he had just bought her the Judy Blume series. There were the comics he had given her for her birthday some years earlier that she loved, but her mother said she couldn't bring everything, so she had to leave some books behind as they traveled back to London. The family was granted British citizenship, which guaranteed some security, some hope of normalcy, but there were difficult years ahead.

Ali kept up his involvement in the NFSL, which started to fragment under the strain of having lost so many members. In subsequent years they trained fighters in Algeria, Iraq and Chad, with American backing. General Khalifa Heftar, Gaddafi's military commander in Chad, joined the NFSL, and tried to force soldiers to desert with him. The methods he used were as brutal as those of the regime he had turned against. A memo from a U.S. diplomat in the Chadian capital N'Djamena uncovered by Human Rights Watch reports the testimony of three Libyan soldiers, who said that after Heftar deserted, he confined more than five hundred conscripts to "hot, windowless rooms, 40 persons to a room made for twenty." Those who still refused to join the NFSL were placed in another prison, where they lived in sewage, and nine died of gastroenteritis. The three soldiers also testified to seeing Americans at the NFSL training camps N'gora and a place they identify as Ensenina. There is no evidence that they were working for the U.S. government, but when the NFSL fled Chad after a pro-Gaddafi government came to power, Heftar moved to Langley, Virginia, where the CIA has its main office. He was to live there until 2011.

Every plan for Gaddafi's overthrow came to nothing, because the government hosting the conspirators changed, or the Americans pulled out, or the fighters weren't ready. More than five thousand people inside Libya had been arrested in the wake of the NFSL's doomed 1984 adventure. One day Huda went to fetch her father from a friend's house, and as she walked into the living room, she saw the men were watching a video. She watched too, compelled and fascinated. There was a gibbet on the screen, and a man was walking toward the noose. In a flash of horror, she recognized him—he was a family friend whom she always called Uncle Othman. Her father and his friends were watching Othman Zarti, one of their fellow NFSL plotters, being executed. Ali tried to shoo her out of the room, but Huda kept watching. "Uncle Othman read out a bit of the Koran and then stepped up to the gallows," she recalls. "To me it was like the scene in *Lion of the Desert* where Omar Mukhtar is so brave, going to his death in silence, without fear, because he is righteous." She was her father's daughter, steeped in the mythology of a Libyan history in which heroes do not prevail but go to their deaths with dignity, bringing honor upon their family and nation.

Libya was by then a pariah state, and Gaddafi was in the news almost daily, portrayed as a vicious, crazy clown. When asked where she came from, Huda, with her thick, red-brown hair and olive skin, would say Italy. She didn't want to have to explain the strange, peripatetic life her family led, always on the edge of danger—she just wanted to fit into the high school she now attended. Her otherwise normal teenage life— homework, pimples, movies, pop music—was stalked by fear. Sometimes she was aware of a police presence, protection afforded by the British state. Money was a constant worry for Amina and Ali, as they struggled to raise four children. While Ali continued to fund-raise for the NFSL, he never managed to get quite enough for the family to live comfortably. They were always in rented accommodations, always temporary, the dream of Libya receding but never disappearing from the horizon.

The next generation of opposition fighters would be more radical, and more religious. When he first came to power Gaddafi had been keen to present his political philosophy as a more authentic form of Islam than that of the Sanussis. Many young Libyans were convinced—Gaddafi had moved quickly to ban alcohol and build more mosques. But he began to see the *ulema*, the clergy, as an alternative center of power, so he argued that Islam needed no mediation between man and God. He said he could decide how Islam fitted into the modern world; the *ulema* said the Green Book was incompatible with Islam. One day he announced that the Islamic lunar calendar should start from the day of the Prophet's death rather than the date of the *Hejira*, when he fled from Mecca to Medina, the calculation used everywhere else in the Muslim world. This not only offended the religious authorities but confused Libyans—suddenly their country was some ten years ahead of its neighbors. But sometimes he calculated it from the day of the Prophet's birth, which put Libya behind. He refused to go by the religious authorities' sighting of the new moon in Mecca, and would declare the start of Ramadan or Eid himself. At one point he also went against the Western calendar, renaming the months July and August after Nasser and Hannibal and calling January, the coldest month, *ayannar*, which means "Where's the fire?" Libyans no longer knew which day it was.

Sami al Saadi, born a decade after Wanise and Ali, came from a pious, conservative family that had supported the monarchy. He was studying engineering at Tripoli University at the time of the 1984 coup attempt. He remembers tanks on the campus, the arrests and the annual April 7th hangings. His brother, Adel, who was studying medicine in Benghazi, was rounded up with other students and imprisoned for four years in Abu Salim. Sami, like increasing numbers of young Libyan men, was drawn to religion as an alternative to what they saw as the corruption and lawlessness of Gaddafi's Libya. He was not alone. On February 17, 1987—exactly twenty-four years before the start of the uprising that would topple Gaddafi—state TV showed over and over again the public execution of nine men accused of treason, sabotage, plotting, bombing and the attempted assassination of Soviet military advisers. Six of them, all civilians, were hanged in Benghazi in front of a cheering crowd; the three soldiers allegedly involved were shot by a firing squad. They were said to be members of Islamist opposition groups that had never before been heard of in Libya. Nationalists like the members of the NFSL were being replaced by jihadis in the struggle to overthrow Colonel Gaddafi.

There were few job opportunities in Libya—Gaddafi had all but abolished the private sector, and there were no public sector positions for those who opposed the regime so openly, so young men looked outside the country. Some got scholarships or jobs in the West or the Gulf, but others were more restless. In 1988, at age twenty-two, Sami al Saadi went to Peshawar, on the Pakistan/Afghanistan border, to join thousands of other young Arab jihadis, men who had been supporting the Afghan mujahadeen. They also had had the backing of the Americans since 1979, when the Russians invaded Afghanistan. "We believed that the Afghan people were oppressed, because they had been invaded by Russian forces. We thought that they had a legitimate case and we should support them," he explained. "A lot of my friends went." It was the last major confrontation of the Cold War, the Americans and the jihadis making common cause against the godless communists.

The Libyans learned to handle weapons, to fight and to endure hardship, forging strong bonds with fighters from across the Arab world. Sami found that he wasn't much of a military man, but he was interested in the ideology he was hearing all around him. Soon after he arrived, a tall, thin, bearded Saudi with an intense air came to give a short lecture to the Arab volunteers. He was vehement that non-Muslims who occupied Muslim lands were evil. His rhetoric was chauvinistic—he preached against Christians and Jews and for imposing strict limits on women—but in Sami's eyes, this was a pure form of Islam. It was the first of several encounters with Osama bin Laden. Salafism, the rigid form of Islam practiced in Saudi Arabia, was followed by very few in Libya, but bin Laden's explanation made sense to Sami. They were waging holy war. There were two kinds of people, Muslims and non-Muslims, and the only way to bring change, to create a true Islamic state, was through violence. That, thought Sami, was true for Libya as much as for Afghanistan. He found himself increasingly worried about what was happening back home. As the Afghan mujahadeen and their Arab comrades celebrated the 1989 Soviet military withdrawal from Afghanistan, he was hearing news that his two brothers, Adel and Mohammed, and his brother-in-law had been arrested while trying to leave Libya for Tunisia.

Back in Tripoli, football, not religion, brought people out onto the streets. Mukhtar Nagasa, the schoolboy who had loved Gaddafi, was now in high school. Like most young Libyan men, he was thrilled when in 1989—for the first time—the national team was on the brink of qualifying for the World Cup. All they had to do was beat Algeria. He and his friends sat in the main Tripoli stadium waiting for the kickoff. They watched in amazement a while later as a man who looked like a referee walked out onto the pitch and blew a final whistle. The game was over before it had started. Colonel Gaddafi, who thought spectator sports were parasitic, had ordered the cancellation of the match. He was trying to persuade the Algerian government to unite with Libya, so he had told the Libyan Football Federation to announce that "the two teams are, in fact, one team," so there was no need for "conventional competition." The fans started burning the chairs in the stands. The decision meant that Algeria automatically qualified, and Libya had missed its chance. Mukhtar joined the thousands who charged out of the stadium and marched down the street. "I wasn't even political," he said. "I was just furious that he'd given it away to Algeria. We might have been in the World Cup!" For the first time, people chanted anti-Gaddafi slogans in the center of Tripoli. "There is no God but God!" they shouted. "And Gaddafi is the enemy of God!" State media didn't report the disturbances, but Gaddafi noticed the religious tone the protests had taken. The Islamist threat, he said, was "more dangerous . . . than war with the Israelis or the Americans." The secret police rounded up more suspects, and at least twenty-one people were executed.

Sami al Saadi knew he couldn't go home. He married Karima, an Algerian, and they tried to settle in Pakistan. About eight hundred Libyan jihadis had stayed after the Soviet withdrawal, but by 1993, disillusion set in: Instead of building the perfect Islamic state the Afghan mujahadeen were fighting each other, destroying much of Kabul in the process. There was no role for the Libyan jihadis—better to turn their attention to home. The Libyan Islamic Fighting Group, the LIFG, was born in Afghanistan in the early 1990s. Its aim was to wage jihad against Gaddafi. In 1993, its

Shura Council—the governing body—chose Sami, known also as Abu Munthir, as its emir, or leader, a position he held until 1995. His responsibility was to interpret the Koran and find Islamic justification for the group's actions. They declared that Gaddafi's was "an apostate regime that has blasphemed against the faith of God Almighty" and declared its overthrow to be "the foremost duty after faith in God." It would be five years before they came out into the open inside Libya; in the meantime, they scattered. Some quietly returned to Libya as sleeper cells, waiting to strike. Others moved to Sudan, where the Islamist ideologue Hassan al Turabi was ascendant and had invited Osama bin Laden to make his base. Although the LIFG did not join bin Laden's Al Qaeda, they shared its religious ideology and its roots and would be linked to it from then on.

Some, including Sami, claimed asylum in the UK. In the early nineties, London was a center for jihadis, earning the city the sobriquet Londonistan among journalists. Algerians, Palestinians, Egyptians, Saudis, Libyans and others gathered at the Four Feathers Social Club off Baker Street to hear the radical Islamist preacher Abu Qatada and debate the future of jihad. Every group had its own newsletter—the LIFG produced *Al-Fajr*, meaning *Dawn*—that was promoted in the mosques and sent to Arab journalists, many of whom were also based in London. Coming from such a small country that had such tight family and tribal connections, Libyans in London all knew each other, but the jihadis moved in different circles from the secular oppositionists like the members of the NFSL. Arab states, which saw the growing Islamist groups as a threat, complained to the British authorities, but the response Britain gave was that they granted asylum to those whose politics put them at risk of imprisonment back home, and as long as they were not planning violence while living in Britain, they would be allowed to stay.

As the nineties wore on, the British intelligence services began to pay more attention to their radical guests. They infiltrated the groups and listened to what the imams were saying. Libya's neighbors, the Algerians, were the most militant, and the French authorities were pressuring Britain to rein them in. After the Algerian government canceled the 1991 elections that the Islamists seemed set to win, the jihadi Armed Islamic Group, known by its French acronym, the GIA, declared war and embarked on a campaign of murder across Algeria. They used extreme violence, including the indiscriminate slaughter of villagers, politicians, journalists and other jihadis with whom the GIA leadership disagreed. They murdered a group of elderly French monks and carried out bombings on the Paris metro, foreshadowing the kind of violence Al Qaeda would later bring to London and Madrid. The LIFG sent fifteen fighters to help in the jihad in Algeria. They disappeared, murdered, it turned out, on the orders of the GIA leadership. The Algerians, according to one LIFG member who survived, were "devoid of religion or morality." The LIFG denounced their former allies in the *Al-Fajr* newsletter, and the exiles began to think of returning to Libya to join the sleeper cells of activists at home.

In twos and threes, LIFG exiles started to return to Libya from their refuges across the world. Some concentrated on changing Libyan society. The men from the eastern town of Derna became notorious—they tried to make the townspeople conform to the restrictive form of Islam that would later become associated with the Taliban, forcing the closure of theater groups and sports organizations as "unIslamic." Armed skirmishes started around Benghazi and Derna, but the Islamist fighters had neither the discipline nor the numbers to make a big impact. In June 1995, a rogue LIFG unit raided the main hospital in Benghazi to seize one of their number who had been captured during a firefight and was under treatment in handcuffs. Gaddafi's forces tracked them down, arrested and interrogated them, and extracted intelligence about their plans. The LIFG was forced into the open. A few weeks later they announced their existence. "The time has come for the Libyan Islamic Fighting Group to become a recognized movement rather than a secret one," they said.

"Confronting the evil dictators of this era, such as Gaddafi, has become one of the most important duties behind essential belief in blessed Allah." The communiqué was issued from London. Under the close eye of the British intelligence services, MI5 and MI6, the LIFG had started its jihad inside Libya.

In 1998, a former MI5 agent, David Shayler, exposed what he said was a British-backed plot to assassinate Gaddafi. The attempt is undisputed. A group of LIFG fighters threw grenades at Gaddafi's motorcade as it passed through Sirte in February 1996, when he was attending the annual General People's Congress. Although he escaped, several of his bodyguards were killed, as were three LIFG assailants trying to escape the scene. Shayler said he had resigned from the British security services in protest at the involvement of MI6 in paying LIFG operatives to carry out the attempt, an allegation denied by the LIFG and described by then British foreign secretary Robin Cook as "pure fantasy."

A few years later a document emerged dated December 1995 and seemingly written by someone in MI6, saying that they were indeed aware of an assassination plot that they ascribed to "Libyan colonels" who were "not associated with Islamic fundamentalists." The document said the plotters had already distributed weapons among groups of dissident officers in various towns that would take control of the country after the assassination. No doubt the British, like the Americans, would have been happy to see Gaddafi dead, but there is no clear evidence that they were involved in any plot, simply that they knew something was afoot.

The next attempt, in November, was pathetic. After a tip-off about the colonel's itinerary, an LIFG operative threw a grenade at Gaddafi's convoy as it passed through the desert town of Brak. It failed to explode.

The Green Mountain around Derna, where Omar Mukhtar had fought the Italians in the 1920s, became a battleground again. The LIFG numbered less than a thousand, but they had been hardened by their Afghan experience and were far more effective guerrilla fighters than their secular predecessors. They would attack police posts and military units. The response was unremitting. Gaddafi's forces used aerial bombardment and thousands of ground troops to drive the jihadis from their hideouts. This was a secret war—Gaddafi didn't want Libyans or outsiders to know how strong and active the opposition was. In June 1996, the LIFG killed eight paramilitaries in Derna. Martial law was imposed in the area, and the government cut electricity and water to the neighborhoods where the fighters' families lived. Thousands were arrested in the sweep that followed on suspicion of involvement with militant Islamic groups. The Abu Salim prison in Tripoli filled up with Islamists, some fighters, others just sympathizers or family members. Trials were quick and death sentences routine. Many were detained without trial, their families never told the fate of their sons.

Sudan had been a refuge for the LIFG for many years, but the government in Khartoum was coming under increasing pressure from Gaddafi to expel those who remained. Osama bin Laden was also there, building up his jihadi network, Al Qaeda. Although the LIFG was not part of Al Qaeda, bin Laden's actions would change their fate. On August 7, 1998, Al Qaeda operatives drove trucks loaded with explosives into the gates of the U.S. embassies in Nairobi and Dar es Salaam, the capitals of Kenya and Tanzania. More than two hundred people were killed and four thousand injured, some losing their sight or their limbs. The Americans had been watching bin Laden's group for some time, but they were nonetheless taken by surprise by the scale of the attack. The British realized, belatedly, that their policy of infiltrating rather than expelling the jihadis wasn't working. The LIFG were now seen not just as a militant group trying to overthrow Gaddafi but as associates of Osama bin Laden, the most wanted terrorist in the world. Their days as friends of the West, united with the Americans and British in their hatred of Gaddafi, were over.

Sami al Saadi and his wife, Karima, had been moving between London, Qatar and Turkey, but now they wanted to find somewhere to settle. Sudan was no longer an option, because the government had told the jihadis, including Osama bin Laden, to leave after the Americans had bombed a chemical factory outside Khartoum that they said was linked to Al Qaeda. Only one place beckoned. In 1996, after seven years of civil war, a truly Islamic movement had taken over in Afghanistan. Like bin Laden, Sami took his family to Kabul, to live under the protection of the Taliban.

By the nineties, Ali Abuzeid had concluded that there was no hope. Colonel Gaddafi, he thought, could be overthrown only by a revolution from within; the exiles were irrelevant. He was in his fifties now, and his generation had failed. The years in exile had taken their toll. He had lost many friends, abandoned his career, could scarcely provide for his family, and he knew he could never go home. At least the children were all right: Huda had now graduated from a university; the others were doing well at school. But the years stretched ahead, and he had to do something, so he opened a grocery store on Westbourne Grove, near London's Notting Hill. After a while, he began to enjoy it. He was still a sociable man, someone who liked to laugh and talk, and he found that his customers would return more frequently if they enjoyed his company. Some pleaded poverty, and he would give credit when in business terms he really shouldn't, but he didn't mind too much. He made a small profit, and that was good enough. It was the kind of shop you go to for one thing and end up chatting and buying more. He had more time for family too, helping the younger kids with their homework, seeing more of his wife.

Huda felt more settled too. She got a job at the BBC. Her adolescent anxiety about who she was, where she came from, had dissipated. At twenty-two she was still living at home, in the ground floor apartment her parents rented near the shop, but she was free to come and go as she wished and live the life of an ordinary young woman in London, seeing friends, partying, spending time with her parents only when she wasn't too busy.

One Sunday morning in November 1995, her mother knocked on the door to her bedroom. She struggled to get up—it had been a late Saturday night. The guys who worked for her father had rung to say something was wrong—they had arrived at the shop before it opened to find the lights off and the door swinging open. They knew he normally got in early on a Sunday and were worried there might have been a burglary. Huda pulled on her clothes and walked around the corner, worrying that maybe her father had fallen down stairs and hit his head. She walked into the shop and switched on the light. Her father was lying at the far end, blood pooling around his inert body. He had been stabbed in the chest. His face had been mutilated with meat skewers.

Somehow she rang the police. Her fourteen-year-old brother arrived, and she managed to steer him out of the shop and into the police car before he saw their father's body. "My knees collapsed," she recalls. "I remember thinking: My world is over. My life is going to be about this now." The phone rang incessantly as the police secured the crime scene. She knew it was her mother but was not allowed to reenter the shop to pick up the call. Eventually she found a phone nearby and rang home.

"Something's happened to Dad," she said.

"Have they killed him?" asked her mother, and it wasn't really a question.

CHAPTER FOUR

MASSACRE AT ABU SALIM

> Libya is the sole country in the world that has no political
> prisons and no political prisoners, because the political
> problem was solved in a radical, historical and final way
> as all the people attained power.
>
> —MUAMMAR GADDAFI, OCTOBER 1999

> Listen to what they did.
> Don't listen to what they said.
> What was written in blood
> Has been set up in lead.
>
> —JAMES FENTON, "BLOOD AND LEAD"

Muammar Gaddafi climbed into the cab of a bulldozer and drove straight at the prison gates. It was March 1988, and he had decided to make a grand gesture. His acolytes had assembled the diplomatic corps outside to witness the event, but the ambassadors were forced to beat a rapid retreat when the Brother Leader's demolition technique knocked the prison walls outward toward them rather than into the prison grounds. As many as four hundred inmates of Tripoli's Furnash prison climbed over the rubble and into the arms of their waiting families. Some were political prisoners, jailed for their opposition to the regime, but the majority were army deserters or those convicted of common crimes, such as burglary.

"Peoples," said Colonel Gaddafi, "don't triumph through building prisons and raising their walls ever higher." Tripoli radio reported that the Brother Leader's "great historical action of storming the prison, destroying it and freeing the prisoners" had inspired the masses in the desert town of Sabha to do likewise. A few days later Gaddafi arrived unexpectedly at the department of immigration and proceeded to tear up the "black list" of people barred from leaving the country. He handed out confiscated passports and announced that Libyans would no longer need exit visas if they wanted to travel. To reinforce the point, he went to the Tunisian border, got into another bulldozer and demolished the border post.

There was less to this than met the eye. Gaddafi knew that people were fed up with empty shelves in the shops and the arbitrary rule of the *lijan thawriya*, who would persecute or lock up anyone they felt like, so he wanted to give Libyans a little room to breathe. That year about a million Libyans visited Tunisia—the government even gave them money to spend. At the end of March he announced that he was in favor of abolishing the death penalty. There were other ways of punishing people for offenses, he said. You could fine them, imprison them or beat them up, but execution by firing squad or hanging was "abominable." This, however, was just his personal view. The law was in the hands of the people, and according to Gaddafi, they wished to retain the death penalty.

Then came the Great Green Charter of Human Rights of the Jamahiriya Era. It was a new version of his political philosophy, focusing on his bugbears of wage labor and home ownership. "The members of the Jamahiriyan society are free from any rent. A house belongs to the person who lives in it," said the charter, which went on to bar Libyans from employing anyone to work in their homes. Among the verbiage about peace and freedom was one clear paragraph:

The Jamahiriyan society proscribes punishments which attack the dignity and the integrity of the human being, such as forced labor or long-term imprisonment. The Jamahiriyan society proscribes all attacks, physical or mental, on the person of the prisoner.

The message did not get through to the warders at Abu Salim. Gaddafi had tried to ease conditions for Libyans in the hope of regaining favor, but when that didn't work, he unleashed his security forces once more. Within a year the prisons were more crowded than ever before.

The suburb of Abu Salim that surrounded the prison was always a stronghold of Gaddafi supporters. In August 2011, after Gaddafi had fled the capital and the rest of Tripoli had fallen into rebel hands, fighting continued there for more than a week. The day after they seized Gaddafi's compound at Bab al Aziziyah, fighters stormed the prison and released those still inside. They tried to break into the cells while filming on their cell phones as the prisoners crowded around the narrow slots in the iron doors that were used to pass in food, jostling each other to see the chaotic, glorious scene. As the padlocks were smashed, hundreds of prisoners burst out into the courtyards and corridors, shouting, "Allahu Akbhar!" "God is Great!" and hugging the fighters who had freed them.

Three days later I drove to the sprawling grayish-white complex, the gates in its previously impenetrable twenty-three-foot-high concrete walls now swinging open. The low, empty buildings had an eerie stillness. For two decades this had been the most feared place in Libya, the very name Abu Salim synonymous with torture, starvation, sickness and death. Those who entered knew they might never get out, and their families might never know their fate. I wandered around the deserted corridors, looking at the drawings on the cell walls: pictures of the Al-Aksa Mosque in Jerusalem with the legend "God Protect Us" and rows of single digits, a diagonal across each group of five, the universal prisoners' way of counting off the days. Many had written their names and the year of their incarceration, hoping that if they died, at least someone might find out where they had been.

Two small boys cycled down a passageway, one on the seat, one on the crossbar, a bag on the handlebars, searching for loot among the abandoned clothes and dirty mattresses. It was a vast complex covering thirty acres, with dozens of blocks and many wings. The prison had been largely rebuilt in the late 1990s. The new cells had bathrooms, and while the windows were too high to look out of, at least they let in some light. Guard posts, surrounded by barbed wire, stood at every corner of the outer walls, and some of the courtyards were now covered. A few people had found their way into the administration offices the day I was there, and they were searching through the prison's records, trying to find clues that would tell them what had happened to relatives who had been imprisoned. Some people say the victims of the 1996 massacre lie underneath the new buildings, others that they were buried much farther away. Abu Salim is a place of secrets and Libya is a land of hidden graves. There are years of work ahead for forensic scientists and human rights investigators.

That was the day I met Wanise Elisawi for the first time, the opposition activist who had lived through the turbulence at the universities in the 1970s and been sent to Abu Salim after the failed 1984 uprising. In the morning he had woken up with a compulsion to return to the place where he had been incarcerated for nineteen years. After being released in 2002, he had never spoken to anyone outside his family about what he had suffered and witnessed. He struck me as a man with deep feelings, carefully controlled and suppressed, who had endured and survived through stoicism, and even now, as we wandered around the prison yards, could scarcely let his emotions show. His face was creased and his hair gray. He spoke calmly until we walked into cell number seven, which he had shared with thirteen others when first incarcerated. "I stayed here for four years without seeing light," he said. Tears started to well, and he put his head in his hands. "I don't know why I came back here today," he whispered to himself.

Some of his fellow prisoners were driven mad, he said, so he tried to wash and shave them, to keep them clean and give them a vestige of dignity. He talked of being forced to run full-tilt, blindfolded, into a wall, time and time again, of being tortured with dogs and electric prods, of watching cellmates die and their bodies lying in front of him for days on end. "We would wrap them in a blanket and beg the guards to take them away for burial," he said.

The prisoners were mostly young men, in their twenties and thirties, and they were always hungry. "We would have one liter of milk for seven people," said Wanise. "One piece of bread, one spoonful of jam. Dinner was one hundred grams of rice." Wanise was of middle height and build, but after a few years he weighed only 110 pounds. They were given only one prison uniform—no other clothes—and one blanket for two years. It was damp and filthy. Wanise began to suffer from arthritis and hemorrhoids, but prisoners received no medical treatment, so he made trousers from a plastic curtain to contain the blood leaking from his anus. There was not enough room for everyone to lie down at the same time, so they slept in shifts. On one occasion the guards dragged Wanise from his cell to make him confess on camera. He says he told his torturers that they were ruining the country, whereupon they broke his legs in three places with a baseball bat. A cellmate was pulled away to identify new detainees as co-conspirators. He never returned. The torture killed him.

For four years he was allowed no visits, but eventually, in 1988, Wanise's wife, Farida, came with food and clothes. For a while she visited once a month, sometimes bringing their three daughters. "They were very beautiful," said Wanise. "I used to write to them and get letters smuggled out. Sometimes they would write to me. But I was a bad father—my wife gave birth to them, and raised them alone." He felt especially guilty about

Isara, the chosen one, born after his imprisonment. His political adventurism had left her fatherless from birth; he felt he had abandoned her.

Farida had married Wanise at seventeen. This was a traditional marriage within the extended family, as is customary in Libya. She was the daughter of a wealthy relative of the deposed king, Idris. "I thought I would have a happy life, have children. . . ." Her voice trailed off. We were talking in the elegant apartment in Benghazi where they now live. She still finds it painful to look back on those days. Farida had expected to rely on Wanise for everything. She had enjoyed the years they spent in America, while he was studying in Ohio, finding it exciting to learn a little English and venture out alone, but once they were back in Benghazi and he was arrested, her happiness was over. "I thought he would be inside forever," she said. She lived among sisters and brothers, all in the same apartment block. Every week or so she would go to the military police in Benghazi and ask where they had taken Wanise. "They never paid any attention," she said. She wrote letters to the authorities in Benghazi and Tripoli, but it was four years before she got a reply and was told where he was. The first visit was difficult. "He looked weak, and we were only allowed to stay for ten minutes," she recalled. Their daughter Duaa, now a clear-skinned young woman in a brown head scarf and jeans, was in her third year of school when Wanise was imprisoned. She grew used to being ostracized. "Some of the children would say we were dogs, because our father was against the government," she told me. "Others just avoided us when they heard our father was in prison, because they were afraid of what would happen to them." Later on, someone from the *lijan thawriya,* the revolutionary committee, went to the headmaster to tell him that Wanise's daughters should not be allowed to complete their schooling, but luckily that threat was never realized.

Wanise tried to lose himself in study. They were allowed to read the Koran, so he meditated on its meaning, and he taught classical Arabic to the less educated prisoners. The regime would ease for a few months, or even a year, for no apparent reason, and then grow harsh again. So when they were allowed to have books, he improved his English. He devised projects, so one year he taught himself Italian. In the cell they talked endlessly about why successive attempts to overthrow Gaddafi had failed. "I met all of those who had tried coups," he said. "I told them it was good you didn't succeed, because we weren't ready." He told himself that everything was the will of Allah, and he had to submit.

In 1989 the prison started to fill up. Many were first taken to an underground torture center near Tripoli's central hospital, known as the Agency to Combat Atheism and Mental Incapacity, the idea being that anyone who espoused a form of Islam the regime didn't like must be mad or—in Libyan culture, an even worse accusation—a nonbeliever. The new prisoners were then transferred to Abu Salim, where they were divided into three groups: the toughest jihadis, who had been battling Gaddafi, the moderates, and the drunks and smugglers. In 1995, most of the petty criminals were released. Those deemed moderate were brought to the same wing as Wanise, and the others who had been incarcerated earlier. The jihadis were subjected to the worst conditions. "They got no food, no water, no medicine and no visits," recalls Wanise. "About four were dying from tuberculosis every month."

Gaddafi had already made clear his views of such prisoners. "You should forget your imprisoned sons, because they suffer from infectious diseases. They carry HIV AIDS!" he said in a speech in 1989. The people's courts would decide what should happen to Islamists who defied the government. "All such movements are considered atheism, threatening Islam and the Arab Nation. Those who embrace such ideologies must be killed," he said. "Every Libyan family should understand that if it is told that one of its sons has joined this movement, then the family must disown him, as if he has cancer or AIDS. Then, it is over. No one can mediate for him. He is an atheist and must be crushed."

Giuma Atigha was imprisoned in 1990 after being falsely accused of assassinating the head of the Libyan People's Bureau in Rome. The killing had occurred six years earlier and had been claimed by a group called Borkan, meaning Volcano, that said it had attacked several of Gaddafi's envoys. Western intelligence agencies suspected that Borkan might be a front for Palestinian groups that opposed the faction Gaddafi supported. It was active for only a few years, and then disappeared. Giuma, who was a lawyer, had criticized Gaddafi's government but had never been involved with any armed uprising or attempt to overthrow the regime. In his memoir, *Memories of Prison and Exile*, published in 2012, he describes how food at Abu Salim in the mid-1990s was reduced to scraps, a few dates and *zumitta*, a kind of toasted grain. The guards would come, armed with batons and electric cables plaited together to use as whips, lay a tiny amount of food in the corridor and open the cell doors. When the half-starved prisoners tore out to get the food the guards would scream insults and savagely beat them. They were not allowed into the prison yard for exercise, and family visits were stopped. "Every day we heard screaming," he recalled. "In Abu Salim you could be tortured at any time."

One morning, thirteen prisoners who had smuggled in a saw by hiding it within a block of dates managed to escape after they cut through the bars of their cell. The result was collective punishment for those left behind—the assaults grew more violent. Giuma recalls a prisoner from his cell going crazy with anger and attacking a guard. Reinforcements were sent, who clubbed the prisoner over the head until he lost consciousness. They threw his inert body back inside and told his cellmates to bring out their mattresses and clothes until the room was bare. Then the guards poured buckets of water into the cell until it flooded. It was December, when the temperature in Tripoli can drop to 45 degrees Fahrenheit at night. For ten days the prisoners were forced to sit in the cold and wet. "We were in hell," writes Giuma Atigha. "The only escape lay in death through illness or torture."

In the months leading up to the massacre, conditions in Abu Salim deteriorated even further. News seeped in that there was fighting in the east of Libya, as government forces took on the LIFG around the Green Mountain, arresting more jihadis and suspected sympathizers. The prison guards grew more aggressive and cruel. Around 4:00 P.M. on June 28, 1996, other prisoners heard screaming from section four, where the jihadis were kept. "We thought it was a routine punishment given out by a guard against a prisoner, and that now the usual concert of beatings would begin," recalls Giuma Atigha. Then they heard the cry "Allahu Akbhar!" and the sound of shots being fired. Someone was running down the corridors shouting "God is Great!" and "Join the jihad!" The prisoners from section four had risen against the guards, who were shooting to prevent them from freeing the prisoners in other sections.

The prisoners had seized Khalifa al Magtouf, a guard hated for his sadism. "He used to torture people with electricity just for fun," recalls Wanise. The men in section four had been planning their insurrection for weeks, deciding that the only way to get medical attention for ailing prisoners and better treatment for all was to riot and take guards hostage. When al Magtouf opened their cell door to give them food, ten of them went for him with sticks and pipes. Two guards were stationed at the main door to the section, another two where the food was being doled out. Al Magtouf escaped into the yard, prisoners in hot pursuit. Several guards went up onto the roof and shot the prisoners who had run into the yard, killing six and injuring others, before lowering a rope to al Magtouf, who climbed to safety. The remaining prisoners seized a second guard and battered him to death. The prisoners had turned into a lynch mob, killing one of the less cruel guards after the one they hated most had escaped. "In the mayhem, we pleaded with other prisoners out in the corridor not to open our door for fear of harm coming to the sick and elderly men in our cell," writes Giuma Atigha.

Eventually the head warden arrived to talk to the prisoners, who refused to negotiate with him, saying they would only talk to Abdullah al Sanussi, Gaddafi's brother-in-law and the head of internal security. He was among the most feared men in Libya, renowned for his ruthlessness, but they knew they had to deal with someone powerful, because the warden would not have the authority to make a difference. The guards asked the prisoners to nominate representatives, who were brought to Sanussi and the Special Forces commander, Abdullah Mansour, one of Gaddafi's cousins, to discuss the prisoners' demands. Hours went by. Eventually, prison officials announced that an agreement had been reached that sick prisoners would be taken for treatment. "Many of the brothers began clambering over each other to register their names," writes Giuma Atigha. "I tried to warn them that this was a trick, but they wouldn't listen." Four buses arrived at the prison gates and about 120 sick prisoners were escorted out and told they were being taken to the hospital.

The officials said that fair trials couldn't be guaranteed, but Abdullah al Sanussi had agreed that the food would improve, the prisoners would be allowed to exercise in the yard and to receive family visits. "Your demands will be met," said the officials. "A committee will be formed to implement them." By then it was about 2:00 A.M. For a few hours there was peace. The prisoners, who had been taken back to their cells, which now had new locks, tried to sleep. Silence hung over Abu Salim.

Before dawn, soldiers appeared accompanying the hated guard, Khalifa al Magtouf, whose head was wrapped in bandages after the beating he had received at the hands of the prisoners the previous day. Those in Giuma Atigha's cell were ordered to leave carrying only their slippers and blankets. "We were made to jog between two rows of armed guards who were telling us to hurry up and jog faster," he recalls. Some of the prisoners were taken from the civilian to the military prison on the other side of the complex, but there wasn't enough room to accommodate them all, so Giuma and several of his colleagues were made to lie facedown in a yard, guns pointed at their backs. He felt perversely calm, believing this was his last day on earth. At least, he thought, today I am outside seeing the sun rise for the first time in six years.

Wanise was in another block, in a cell with a high window-slit from which he could crane his neck and see two of the yards. Around 11:00 A.M. an explosion echoed through the prison—one of the guards had thrown a grenade into the yard where the prisoners from section four had been assembled just before dawn. As he lay on the ground in the neighboring yard, Giuma Atigha guessed what was happening. He prayed: "To Allah we belong, and to him we return." Wanise hoisted himself up and tried to look through the window. He could see soldiers positioned on the roof around the courtyard where the prisoners were gathered, and Abdullah al Sanussi and other senior officials standing by vehicles at the edge. "When the order came, Sanussi started hitting the car and saying, 'No, not killing, not killing,' " Wanise recalls. "For sure he didn't want to do it. But he got his orders from elsewhere, and then he carried them out."

Did those orders come directly from Gaddafi? Wanise believes they did. Sanussi was among the most powerful men in the country—who else would tell him what to do? Sanussi himself has never given an interview, never spoken about Abu Salim in public, never acknowledged that the massacre happened nor the role he played. How much autonomy he had in the decision to kill the prisoners when the riot had already been quashed is unknown. When the soldiers on the roof opened fire, Giuma could hear it as he lay facedown in the dirt in a neighboring yard. Wanise, whose cell was high up, could see the yard walls as they turned red with blood. Bullets started hitting the window of his cell, and he had to duck down. The prisoners from section four were mowed down by machine-gun fire. There was nowhere for them to run. The few who were still in their cells were shot through the windows. The shooting went on until 2:00 P.M. The dead lay piled up in the yard—other eyewitnesses say that soldiers picked their way through the bodies, finishing off the injured with pistol shots to ensure that none were left alive.

The buses of sick prisoners never went to the hospital but were driven around the corner to the back of the prison. Two men, who for some reason were ordered off their bus, saw their comrades being bound and blindfolded. All but those two who believed they were being taken for medical treatment were shot. By nightfall, 1,270 prisoners were dead. About 500 were left alive in Abu Salim, smelling death and listening to the silence.

The sun rose the next day over Abu Salim, and the guards put on masks and plastic gloves. They moved the bodies and sprayed the prison with disinfectant. "The smell of death was everywhere," recalls Wanise. "It lingered for two days or more." Giuma Atigha was taken to a room, where he believed they trained dogs to torture prisoners, and then to another wing of the jail. As they moved him he tried to look into the section where the massacre had taken place. "There was silence," he recalls. "I could see vultures circling above." Some bodies are thought to have been loaded into containers or refrigerated trucks, but the former prisoners don't know where they were taken. Others may have been buried within the prison walls. Over the next week the guards started to clean and paint section four. "They did a first coat, just to cover up the blood," recalls Wanise. "Then they made us do it. We were made to redo everything."

The residents of the surrounding suburb heard the shooting. It would have been hard not to—it went on for two hours. Did they talk about it? Did they speculate about what had gone on behind those featureless gray-white walls? Or was fear so pervasive that no one dared mention what they heard that long afternoon? Many of the guards lived nearby but none has spoken publicly about what they saw or heard. Inside the jail, Wanise painstakingly made a list of those killed, reaching 550 on his first count, and the number rose steadily as he learned more.

Within a month of the massacre Amnesty International had sketchy information that something had happened, but their public call for an investigation was scarcely reported. Rumors of the massacre didn't break above the tide of other news in the outside world that summer: the war in Bosnia; the bombing of the Khobar Towers in Saudi Arabia; the divorce of the Prince and Princess of Wales. Foreign journalists were rarely granted visas to Libya, and when they were it was usually to interview Gaddafi. The country was almost completely closed, and Libyans were forbidden to talk to foreigners, on pain of arrest. Exiles were the only source, but their opposition to Gaddafi meant that journalists tended to disregard much of what they said, presuming they would be exaggerating the horror of his rule. By the time more information came out it was old news, a massacre referred to in passing, something that had happened in the bad old days before Colonel Gaddafi reformed around 2005 and became an ally of Britain and America.

Gradually, as surviving prisoners were released, the story began to leak out, but the authorities denied everything, and no one seemed to know exactly who had been killed, so the families continued to visit, queueing at the great, green, steel prison gates, hoping that one day they would be allowed to see their brothers and sons. The families learned about the fate of their men piecemeal, like animals foraging for food, finding a scrap here and a scrap there. Fear conspired with hope—not only were they afraid to challenge the authorities, but during all those years of waiting they convinced themselves that their relatives might still be alive. Libya's chaotic system of government bred an almost willful belief in bureaucracy—there was no credible procedure for announcing the death of a prisoner, so the families held onto the notion that until they had a death certificate, they should not lose hope.

Faiza Ahmed Zubi, the woman I met in Benghazi whose brother, Abdul Karim, was among the victims, found out the truth in the year 2000, when a released prisoner came to see her. Her brother, at the time age twenty-six, had been one of the sick prisoners taken away on the buses.

"Can you imagine what they felt?" she asked. "Believing that finally they'd reached a solution, but instead, they tied their hands together, blindfolded them and machine-gunned them down?" She seemed still to be trying to fathom the logic of meting out such punishment to people whose expectations and demands had sunk so low. "They weren't asking to be released, just to be allowed to live like human beings," she said. "They just wanted to eat, to have some fresh air, to see a little sunlight. They weren't asking for anything more."

Sami al Saadi, the emir of the LIFG, was in Qatar when he heard that his two brothers, Adel and Mohammed, had been killed in the massacre. "I was already motivated against Gaddafi, but this made me even more determined," he said.

In 2001, a few Abu Salim families received visits from officials, who gave them death certificates, but the authorities refused to explain the circumstances under which their relatives had died, or to return their bodies. Three years later, in 2004, Colonel Gaddafi himself admitted that something had happened at the prison when he saw representatives from the human rights group Amnesty International, who had been allowed into Libya for the first time. He seemed to know several important details but had a different explanation for the multiple deaths. The prisoners, he said, had attacked and killed a guard as he gave them food, and then stolen his keys, which they used to free other prisoners. According to Gaddafi, some escaped while others took weapons from the guards and started to kill them. When police from outside the prison arrived there was an exchange of fire that left casualties on both sides. It was, he said, "a tragedy" and "families have a right to know."

By then Gaddafi had understood that Abu Salim was an obstacle in his way as he tried to rehabilitate himself and Libya in the eyes of the world, but he couldn't admit the full scale of the massacre. Bit by bit over the years the authorities acknowledged something had happened. In 2005, it was announced that a committee would be formed to investigate. Two years later, after nothing had happened, thirty families from Benghazi, represented by the lawyer Fathi Terbil, filed a civil claim before the North Benghazi Court to compel the Libyan government to reveal the fate of their detained relatives. The court threw out the case, but a year later the families won on appeal and formed the Coordination Committee for the Families of Victims of Abu Salim. They weren't allowed to register their organization but neither were they prevented from meeting, so— knowing full well that demonstrations were illegal—they began to protest every Saturday morning outside the Benghazi courthouse or the People's Social Leadership Building.

The photographs from that time show groups mainly of women holding up black-and-white photographs of those they had lost and banners in Arabic that read: "Where are the graves? Where are the remains?" and "Oh, Gaddafi, where are our children? We want the bodies of the martyred." One picture shows an elderly woman in a turquoise head scarf sitting in a wheelchair, pushed by a slim-faced old man in a gray-striped sweater. She is holding a picture of a fresh-faced young man on her lap. Next to her are two girls in white scarfs who look too young to have been more than toddlers in 1996. Generations of families in eastern Libya were scarred by Abu Salim, defining themselves ever after by their hatred of Gaddafi and their determination to find the truth about their lost relatives. The families grew used to threatening phone calls and intimidation, but by then most were too despairing or angry to care. The security forces would routinely film everyone at the protests and try to pressure the older demonstrators to go home. From time to time they would arrest the organizers, including Fathi Terbil, but even they couldn't bring themselves to lock up dozens of elderly women. The families were no nearer to finding out the truth, but they could no longer be stopped from trying.

They were emboldened partly by Gaddafi's second son, Seif al-Islam, who by 2005 had established himself as the voice of reform, primarily through his Gaddafi International Charity and Development Foundation.

Aware that human rights were a major problem, he turned to someone with firsthand experience—Giuma Atigha, who had been released the year after the massacre. "I didn't trust Seif, but I thought this was a good opportunity to make a first step," said Giuma. "At that time the very words 'human rights' were forbidden." In 2000, with Seif's blessing, he started to work for the release of long-term political prisoners, and to campaign against torture. The two most influential international human rights organizations, Amnesty International and Human Rights Watch, were invited to Libya and given access to some prisons and former detainees. Prisoners were starting to be released, and Giuma was able to discuss human rights issues at the university and on TV. Gradually more of the truth about Abu Salim was emerging.

Seif acknowledged the families' suffering and offered compensation. It was, he said in a speech, "the biggest incident and most tragic problem and incontestably very, very painful." He could not publicly condemn the massacre, but he tried to indicate that he understood the families' need to know the truth. "The reality of this topic should be clarified, especially to the families of the people who died," he said. "You should be told how your children died. What happened on that day and that night exactly? They have to reveal the truth, reveal the lists, and reveal the investigation results, and see if someone is responsible for the operation that led to overcrowding of the prison."

That word "overcrowding" gave the authorities an out, but his statement begged a deeper question. Who was the "they" who should reveal the truth? His father? His uncle, Abdullah al Sanussi? The Libyan system of justice was confused and incoherent. The courts, which came under the Ministry of Justice, would frequently acquit people who nonetheless were kept in prison. When the justice secretary, Mustafa Abdel Jalil, asked the Internal Security Agency, which ran the prisons, to report to him on the Abu Salim massacre, they took no notice. He didn't even have the power to resign—when he tried, after his order to release the remaining political prisoners was ignored, Gaddafi said he had to stay in his post. The revolutionary committees had the authority to detain people, and in the past had been given a license to kill by Gaddafi himself. The people's leadership committees, which were supposed to consist of tribal leaders and eminent persons, were the ones giving out death certificates to the Abu Salim families, but they did not come under the prison authorities or the Ministry of Justice, as they were part of Gaddafi's parallel state. The system was designed to ensure that the families would get lost in the labyrinth and that no one could be held accountable.

In 2009, another inquiry was promised. The judge leading it said the purpose was not justice but "reconciliation," but he never met the families or produced a report. More death certificates were delivered, and more families were offered compensation: 120,000 dinars ($95,000) for a bachelor or 130,000 dinars ($103,000) for a married man. Anyone who took the money had to sign an agreement that they would not sue the authorities, so many families refused. New slogans appeared on the banners at the protests: "We don't want money; we want the butchers" and "No, No, No—we will not sell the blood of our children."

Wanise Elisawi was released in 2002. His daughter Isara had just married. He had missed her birth, her graduation and now her wedding. The family had struggled to cope without a father, and now it was difficult to accommodate the stranger who came home. He was distant, silent, prone to moods. "I couldn't cope," he confessed. "I found the new generation, the new ways of doing things impossible. I felt that people had changed into liars and thieves." He was shocked at how corrupt Libya had become, with Gaddafi's sons at the top of the pyramid and other Libyans more interested in getting out or making money rather than bringing change. Much to

Farida's distress, he took a job with an oil company and went back to the desert. The solitude and the open space suited him. He would work for twenty days and come home for ten. Gradually, they grew to know each other again, but he brooded on the past. He had sacrificed nineteen years of his life, of their lives, and for what? Gaddafi was still ruling Libya, and he could see no chance for change.

CHAPTER FIVE

THAT MAD DOG OF THE MIDDLE EAST

[T]his mad dog of the Middle East has a goal of a world revolution, [a] Muslim fundamentalist revolution, which is targeted on many of his own Arab compatriots. And where we figure in that—I don't know, maybe we're just the enemy because it's a little like climbing Mount Everest, because we're here.

—RONALD REAGAN, PRESS CONFERENCE, 1986

We believe America is practicing all kinds of terrorism against Libya. Even the accusation that we are involved in terrorism is in itself an act of terrorism.

—MUAMMAR GADDAFI, "AN INTERVIEW WITH GADDAFI," *TIME*,

JUNE 8, 1981

Muammar Gaddafi's four-decade-long zigzag trajectory from enemy to friend and back to enemy again has no parallel in modern history. In 1986, U.S. president Ronald Reagan called him a "mad dog" and bombed his compound. Eighteen years later British prime minister Tony Blair praised him as a leader who wanted to make "common cause with us against Al Qaeda, extremists and terrorism" and shook hands in his ceremonial tent. "Old hostilities do not need to go on forever," added U.S. president George W. Bush.

When Gaddafi was killed in 2011, the inconvenient part of the story was carefully omitted, an embarrassingly harmonious interlude that both the British and American leaders could blame on their political predecessors. United States president Barack Obama intoned, "The dark shadow of tyranny has been lifted," and remembered, "all those Americans that we lost at the hands of Gaddafi's terror." The British prime minister, David Cameron, called him a "brutal dictator" and recalled "all of Colonel Gaddafi's victims."

For Colonel Gaddafi the path led from world revolution to survival at any cost. In the 1970s and 1980s he would support any group that challenged what he saw as colonialist or imperialist power. To him there was no difference between the Irish Republican Army (IRA) planting bombs in Britain, the African National Congress (ANC) fighting apartheid in South Africa and the Japanese Red Army that blew up Lod Airport in Tel Aviv and wanted a global communist takeover. He funded Arthur Scargill, the leader of the British National Union of Mineworkers, because he saw him as a major challenge to Margaret Thatcher. (Scargill once said that he kept a goose called Gaddafi.) He lent $8 million to Louis Farrakhan's Nation of Islam in the United States, because he saw it as part of the anti-imperialist struggle. But the same logic of "my enemy's enemy is my friend" eventually drew him close to his old nemeses, the United States and Britain. After 9/11, Gaddafi understood that he could capitalize on the fact that his strongest enemies inside Libya were jihadis allied to Al Qaeda. He needed help in crushing them. As the war on terror got under way, the British and American intelligence services found themselves cooperating with the man who had once armed people trying to assassinate their leaders. They even helped deliver Gaddafi's opponents into Libyan jails.

Then, suddenly, in the spring of 2011, those same intelligence agents were given new instructions: The Libyan contacts they had cultivated so assiduously must now be persuaded to go against Gaddafi. The world had turned on its axis one more time. Gaddafi was the enemy again, an evil tyrant, and Western leaders knew that—however much they might be accused of hypocrisy or flip-flopping—they had to end up on the winning side.

Gaddafi saw himself as the greatest champion of the Palestinian cause and all other Arab leaders as hypocrites. He had a point—heroic statements were declaimed at Arab League meetings but little was done to help Palestinian refugees languishing in camps in Jordan, Lebanon and Syria. Losing wars with Israel in 1967 and 1973 had made Arab leaders cautious, but Gaddafi was forever agitating to attack Israel again. He had a solution for anyone who disagreed: assassination. The Egyptian journalist Mohammed Heikal wrote that President Nasser and King Feisal of Saudi Arabia were somewhat shocked when Gaddafi suggested murdering King Hussein of Jordan as punishment for expelling Palestinian militants in 1971. He never managed to kill an Arab head of state, but it was not for want of trying. "I will take up responsibility and begin terrorism against the Arab rulers, threaten and frighten them, and sever relations," said Gaddafi in 1985. "And if I could, I would behead them one by one."

Nor did he have great regard for Yasser Arafat, the leader of the Palestinian Liberation Organization, which Arab states regarded as the sole legitimate representative of the Palestinian people. Gaddafi found Arafat too emollient, too prone to compromise, so he funded a myriad of Palestinian groups that plotted against the PLO and each other—and probably did more to undermine the Palestinian cause than any of Israel's actions at the time. Arafat angered Gaddafi by refusing to provide hit squads to liquidate the Libyan leader's exiled adversaries, the "stray dogs." In 1982, when Arafat and his Fatah fighters were besieged in Beirut, on the brink of being pushed out of Lebanon by the Israelis, Gaddafi sent him an open telegram suggesting his best option was to kill himself. "Your suicide will immortalize the cause of Palestine for future generations," he said. "There is a decision which, if taken by you, no one can prevent. It is the decision to die. Let this be." Arafat is reported to have replied that if Gaddafi would like to join him, he might consider it.

On May 7, 1984, as the National Front for the Salvation of Libya prepared for its doomed assault on Bab al Aziziyah the next day, Colonel Gaddafi was in his tent inside the compound meeting a new friend. Abu Nidal was not only an Arafat enemy, he was also a ruthless operator and a gun for hire. It was, according to the writer Patrick Seale, "a meeting of like minds." Abu Nidal wanted to move his base from Damascus, because his always uneasy relationship with the Syrian government was on the point of breaking down. Gaddafi, for his part, needed someone he could task with getting rid of enemies overseas. The next day's NFSL attack served to reinforce his resolve.

It would be three years before Abu Nidal and his men moved to a camp in the desert a hundred miles south of Tripoli, but the cooperation started earlier. On December 27, 1985, four Palestinian gunmen attacked the check-in counter of the Israeli airline El Al and the U.S. company Trans World Airlines (TWA) at Rome's airport, killing sixteen and injuring eighty passengers. Within a few minutes, three gunmen carried out a similar attack at Vienna's airport, killing four and injuring thirty-nine. The Abu Nidal Organization claimed responsibility, saying the attacks were in response to Israel's bombing of the PLO's headquarters in Tunis. The attacks were described on Libyan TV as "heroic operations," and—although Gaddafi denied involvement—defectors from Abu Nidal's group later said Libya had provided the weapons and the stolen Tunisian passports on which the gunmen were traveling.

In his memoir, President Reagan wrote that his intelligence chiefs told him that Gaddafi began plotting to assassinate him soon after he moved into the White House in 1981. The two men grew fixated on each other over the next five years. Gaddafi extended the customary national maritime exclusion zone by twelve miles, claiming the bay extending from

Misrata to Benghazi, known as the Gulf of Sirte, as Libyan rather than international waters. Reagan sent naval patrols to test the new limit. In 1981, U.S. planes, operating from warships in what Gaddafi said were Libyan waters, shot down two Libyan aircraft. Five years later, Gaddafi declared that foreign vessels that sailed into the Gulf were crossing "the line of death." President Reagan promptly sent three aircraft carriers and more than twenty warships for maneuvers, a move that looked dangerously likely to lead to conflict. In late March there were skirmishes at sea and dogfights in the air, as each side provoked the other. The Libyans fired at U.S. ships and aircraft with newly installed Soviet missile batteries along the coast, while the Americans sank Libyan patrol boats at the cost of several Libyan sailors' lives.

In 1982, Gaddafi had announced the formation of his World Center for Resistance against Imperialism, Zionism, Racism, Reaction and Fascism, known as the *mathaba*, meaning the center. In mid-March 1986, following the buildup of tension through the early months of the year, Gaddafi hosted an international conference during which seven hundred organizations, movements and political parties from around the world gathered to condemn the United States, and announce the establishment of a "fighting international revolutionary force," with Gaddafi as its commander and sponsor. Revolutionary movements from Nicaragua, Cuba and Colombia, which Reagan saw as the enemies in America's backyard, all were in attendance and would soon be among those sending men for military training at the *mathaba*.

Reagan was looking for a trigger, and it came with the bomb targeting U.S. servicemembers at La Belle discothèque in Berlin on April 5th. The subsequent U.S. attack on ports, military training facilities and the Libyan air force in Tripoli and Benghazi, as well as on Colonel Gaddafi's compound, was the biggest U.S. air raid since the Vietnam War. U.S. fighters took off from bases in the UK and from aircraft carriers in the Mediterranean, because European countries other than Britain opposed the U.S.

raids. They had commercial interests in Libya and thought this would simply twist the serpent's tail. France and Italy refused to allow over-flights, so the U.S. warplanes had to go by a circuitous route and refuel in the air. Even the CIA had counseled against the raids, saying that other states, especially Syria and Iran, were greater sponsors of terror. American intelligence analysts believed attacking Gaddafi would elevate his status in the Arab world and might provoke him into sponsoring more terror attacks. They were right. Arab leaders who privately loathed Gaddafi now lined up to express support, and his status as an emblem of resistance even convinced some of the Left in Europe. This was the era of wars in Central America, when the Reagan administration funded death squads in El Salvador and the right-wing contra guerrillas in Nicaragua. Gaddafi was now David to Reagan's Goliath, the little guy who refused to bow down in the face of American aggression.

Among the dead was a baby girl whose body was shown to reporters. This was the baby who Gaddafi said was his fifteen-month-old adopted daughter, Hana. In the years that followed he frequently referred to her death as a cause of enduring sadness for him and his wife, Safia. On the twentieth anniversary of the raids the regime organized the Hana Festival of Freedom and Peace in her memory. In the outside world it became an accepted truth that—whatever the rights and wrongs of the raid—it had killed Gaddafi's child, which had had a profound effect on him.

Inside Libya, not everyone was convinced. Rumors of Hana's continued existence spread, and as she grew up, people began to meet her. In 2011, I came across medical students who told me they were a couple of years behind her in medical school. "We would never dare speak to her, and she always had two bodyguards," said Amira al Tarhuni, a young doctor who had worked in a secret hospital during the revolution. "They gave her an office, even when she was just an intern." In the ruins of Bab al Aziziyah, I met Dr. Yunus Mohammed Ali, who said that four years earlier he had been Hana's examiner in her final exams to qualify as a doctor.

"Are you Hana? We thought you were dead!" he told me he had asked her, but she refused to reply. In 2011, after Gaddafi's overthrow, journalists combing the complex found a room that appeared to belong to a young woman. The documents inside included a British council certificate for an English-language course completed in 2007 in the name of Hana Muammar Gaddafi. It was later revealed that the British embassy had given her a visa on more than one occasion, and she had come to London for dental treatment. The documents suggest that she was six months old, not fifteen, at the time of the bombing, which leaves some room for doubt. (Seif al-Islam once wrote that Hana was four years old when she died, leading to more confusion.) One of the people closest to Hana told me that an infant named Hana did indeed die in the raid, and afterward Gaddafi's wife went to the Tripoli orphanage and adopted a second baby girl, who they named in honor of the dead child. Few Libyans I met believe that. The death of Hana Gaddafi, they say, was simply propaganda, a way for Muammar Gaddafi to present himself to the world as a grieving father.

Gaddafi turned the ruins of his house into a place of pilgrimage. His multicolored ceremonial tent for receiving visitors was placed outside, so everyone who came to see him was confronted with the evidence of his victimhood. As I wandered around it after his fall I read grafitti on the walls written by his international followers. Most were African: "ZANU PF with you forever!" read a line written by one of Robert Mugabe's envoys from Zimbabwe. Gaddafi had been one of the biggest backers of Mugabe's ZANU PF party. There were names from Zambia, Niger and Mali. In front of the house, fighters, holding up two-finger V for victory signs, were posing for photographs around the statue of a giant golden fist grasping a tiny silver jet fighter that Gaddafi erected after the U.S. raid, an emblem of his survival. It was about twelve feet tall, and dressed in a *jird*, Gaddafi often made his theatrical speeches standing next to it, against the backdrop of the bombed-out house. It had been the symbol of what

Gaddafi claimed as his victory over Reagan; now it was the symbol of the fighters' victory over him.

The Provisional IRA began its armed struggle just a few months after Colonel Gaddafi seized power in 1969. "We support the revolutionaries of Ireland who oppose Britain and are motivated by nationalism and religion," said the Libyan leader. To him, IRA men like Gerry Adams or Martin McGuinness were the Irish equivalent of Omar Mukhtar, the Libyan hero who had fought the Italians. Within a few years they had established an office in Tripoli to facilitate the transfer of weapons and money and to organize trainings. It was in one of Gaddafi's desert camps that Thomas McMahon, who was later convicted of the 1979 murder of Prince Charles's uncle Lord Mountbatten, learned to make the type of remote-controlled bombs believed to have been used in the killing. When Margaret Thatcher took office that same year, relations between Libya and Britain began to worsen. The street on which the British embassy stood in Tripoli was renamed Bobby Sands Street after the IRA hunger striker who died in the Maze prison in 1981. A few months after the British expelled Libyan diplomats because of the shooting of Police Constable Yvonne Fletcher in April 1984, a senior Libyan intelligence official, Nasser Ashour, traveled to Ireland on a false passport. According to Ed Moloney in his book *A Secret History of the IRA*, he offered the IRA Army Council $10 million and three hundred tons of weapons. For the Libyans it was a form of contracting out—far easier to get the IRA to attack Thatcher's government than to do it themselves. For the IRA, it was a move into the big time.

The weapons, which were transferred from Tripoli to the remote Irish beach of Clogga Strand, in County Wicklow, and hidden in arms dumps across Ireland over the next two years, would transform the IRA's arsenal. Previously, they had pistols and rifles, mostly smuggled in from the United States, but now, as well as hundreds of AK-47 assault rifles, revolvers and ammunition, Gaddafi was giving them rocket-propelled grenades, heavy machine guns and shoulder-launched SAM 7s, surface-to-air missiles, to bring down aircraft. Most significantly, he gave them five tons of Semtex, a plastic explosive made in Czechoslovakia. Gaddafi had bought seven hundred tons of it at the height of his arms shopping spree, so he had enough extra for his friends.

"Every IRA bomb since 1986 has Libyan Semtex in it," says Jason McCue, a lawyer who acts for the families of IRA victims. He lists the most famous incidents—Enniskillen, Warrington, Manchester, the Baltic Exchange, Canary Wharf—all the bombing incidents in Britain and Northern Ireland that killed and injured hundreds. After the Good Friday Agreement that brought the Troubles to an end, a splinter group called the Real IRA that refused to accept the peace deal is believed to have removed some of the stock of plastic explosive. The bomb that killed 29 and injured 220 in Omagh three months after the peace agreement is believed to have been made with Libyan Semtex. There may be Libyan Semtex out there still.

The Libyan point man was a familiar figure. Musa Koussa, the former head of the Libyan People's Bureau in London, had expressed support for the IRA before being expelled by the British for threatening to murder Libyan dissidents in the UK. An elegant and urbane diplomat, fluent in English and fond of Italian shoes, he was given a senior position in external intelligence. He built on the IRA contacts he had made in London and ensured that the provisionals got the weaponry that was promised. An estimated 120 tons of weapons were delivered in four shipments during 1985 and 1986. Vessels hired by the IRA would draw alongside Libyan ships off the coast of Malta to transfer the cargo; from there they sailed to Clogga Strand. The IRA men were grateful and impressed.

They began to plan for a big offensive in which they would attack British targets in the air as well as on land. This time, the ship they chartered, the *Eksund*, sailed direct to Tripoli—the 150-ton consignment of weapons was too big to transfer at sea. Onboard were Captain Adrian Hopkins, four crew members, including a senior IRA man, and an Alsatian dog, a gift from the IRA to Nasser Ashour, the intelligence official who had organized the deal. It took two nights to load the *Eksund*, but she never reached her destination. The crew realized soon after setting sail from Tripoli that a spotter plane was tracking them. As they neared Roscoff, on the Brittany coast, they tried to scuttle the ship, but French and British intelligence were already onboard. According to Moloney, in the hold they found

> 1,000 Romanian-made AK-47 automatic rifles, a million rounds of ammunition, 430 grenades, 12 rocket-propelled grenade launchers with ample supplies of grenades and rockets, 12 heavy Russian DHSK machine guns, over 50 SAM-7 ground-to-air missiles capable of downing British army helicopters, 2,000 electric detonators and 4,700 fuses, 106 millimeter cannons, general-purpose machine guns, anti-tank missile launchers, flame throwers, and two tons of the powerful Czech-made explosive Semtex.

On arrest, the captain, Adrian Hopkins, told police about the arms that had been imported earlier. Many of the heavier weapons were designed for conventional combat, not the hit-and-run attacks that the IRA mounted, and the British army neutralized the surface-to-air missiles with countermeasures on their helicopters. That left the Semtex. One of the first foreigners to arrive in Benghazi after the 2011 revolution was Jason McCue, the lawyer for the IRA victims' families. "The IRA victims feel a kindred spirit with recent victims in Libya," he said. "They never got even an apology from Gaddafi." Their campaign for compensation from Colonel Gaddafi had failed, so he was now lobbying the new National Transitional Council. It was one of the many legacies of Gaddafi's rule that they would have to face in the coming months.

. . .

More than anything else, it was the downing of Pan Am Flight 103 over the Scottish town of Lockerbie that brought international opprobrium on Colonel Gaddafi's head. The aircraft took off from London's Heathrow Airport on Wednesday, December 21, 1988, bound for John F. Kennedy International Airport in New York. Many of the passengers were American students flying home for Christmas. It blew up in midair above the town of Lockerbie; the crash killed all the passengers and crew, and eleven people on the ground. The victims included 189 Americans and 43 Britons. Bodies and debris lay scattered across the Scottish countryside for days, as police did a fingertip search for evidence. In the end they concluded that the bomb had been in a Samsonite suitcase that had been transferred off a flight from Frankfurt. The suitcase contained a cassette recorder with traces of Semtex, a timer of the kind the manufacturers said had previously been supplied to Libya, and baby clothes that were traced to a shop in Malta. Presented with a police lineup, the Maltese shopkeeper identified a Libyan intelligence agent called Abdel Basset al-Megrahi as the man who had purchased the clothes a couple of weeks before the bombing. A secret CIA investigation concluded that the Libyan government was responsible and named Musa Koussa as the official in charge of the operation.

The families of the victims on both sides of the Atlantic became a powerful lobby group that shaped relations with Libya and ensured that the bombing was never forgotten. There were plenty of other suspects, including the Iranian government, which had an obvious motive, as the Americans had shot down one of their passenger planes over the Persian Gulf just five months earlier, and several Palestinian groups, which had carried out similar attacks in the recent past. Abu Nidal said he did it, but then, he often claimed to have carried out attacks that were later shown to be the work of others. Colonel Gaddafi denied responsibility, but the investigation centered on Libya, and arguments over responsibility and compensation dogged him to the end.

It took three years to issue warrants for Megrahi and another Libyan, Lamin Khalifa Fhimah, and a further eight to bring them to trial. Gaddafi refused to hand over the Libyan agents, arguing that they wouldn't get a fair hearing in Scotland. In 1992, the UN Security Council imposed sanctions in response. The happy days of the 1970s oil boom were long gone, and Libya was already suffering from a decline in oil prices, mismanagement of the economy and the impact of unilateral U.S. sanctions, which had first been imposed in 1981 and were made tougher every year. Eventually, Gaddafi agreed to an unprecedented formula: The Libyans would be tried by Scottish judges but in the neutral venue of a military camp in the Netherlands. The trial began in May 2000; Megrahi was convicted and Fhimah acquitted in January of the following year. The judges said they didn't believe Megrahi had been acting alone, but they couldn't say who had given him orders, merely that "the Libyan origin of this crime" had been proven.

Gaddafi never admitted to Lockerbie. After long negotiations, Libya's representative to the UN submitted a letter accepting "responsibility for the actions of its officials," and the Libyan government offered compensation of $10 million per family. The money was to be paid in stages, and there were delays while the Americans prevaricated on removing Libya's name from its list of "state sponsors of terror." Libyan officials, including Seif al-Islam Gaddafi, quite openly said that they were "buying peace" rather than accepting blame. Similarly, the Libyans paid compensation but never admitted responsibility in the 1989 bombing of a plane operated by the French company Union de Transports Aériens, UTA, which exploded and crashed in Niger, killing 170 passengers and crew, including 54 French citizens. Six Libyan agents were found guilty in absentia in Paris and given life sentences. More money—Seif al-Islam Gaddafi called it "a humanitarian gesture"—was paid to Germans injured in the La Belle discothèque. Libya was trying, if not to atone for the past, at least to settle accounts.

In the Great Green Charter of Human Rights, Gaddafi called for "the suppression of nuclear, bacteriological and chemical weapons," but that didn't stop him from trying to acquire them. He understood that as long as Israel had the bomb and no Arab country did, the balance of power would never shift. Within a year of taking over, he sent his deputy, Major Abdul Salam Jalloud, on a shopping trip to Beijing, but Premier Zhou Enlai told him that Chinese nuclear technology was not for sale. For a while Gaddafi bought bits and pieces here and there: uranium concentrate, or "yellow cake," from Niger; uranium prospecting and processing equipment from Argentina; a research reactor from the Soviet Union; medical isotopes from India. None of it could be used for a bomb, but Libya was also developing missiles and getting its soldiers trained. In the 1970s, ninety-six soldiers went to Sweden to learn how to operate guided missiles. A West German company, OTRAG, started to test midrange rockets in the desert near Sabha that might have been capable of carrying a nuclear warhead, until the U.S. authorities got wind of the project and pressured the German government to get it closed down.

By the mid-1990s, when Libya was under sanctions, Colonel Gaddafi's dream of a nuclear weapon came closer to being realized. The scientist A. Q. Khan, the father of Pakistan's nuclear bomb, had established a clandestine global network for the supply of nuclear components and materials. Having achieved his goal of building a bomb in his home country, he started to sell the technology to others, including North Korea and Iran, using middlemen in Malaysia and Dubai. The Libyans bought centrifuges to manufacture enough highly enriched uranium for roughly ten nuclear weapons annually. The nuclear expert David Albright says the network intended to provide Libya with a "turnkey gas-centrifuge facility . . . and ongoing technical assistance to help overcome any obstacles in assembling and operating the plant." The A. Q. Khan network supplied blueprints for nuclear warheads, of the same 1960s Chinese design that Zhou Enlai had refused to sell Major Jalloud twenty-five years earlier. Libya never got the bomb—as with the conventional weapons, some components never left the box—but by the late nineties they were making progress.

Possibly inspired by Saddam Hussein, who had used chemical weapons in his war with Iran in 1988, the Libyans began to build a facility at Rabta, southwest of Tripoli. They had no trouble getting the materials and expertise they needed. The West German company Imhausen-Chemie did much of the construction, avoiding regulations by sending the equipment via Hong Kong and failing to tell thirty German subcontractors, including Siemens, that Libya was the ultimate destination. Japan's Toshiba was subcontracted by another Japanese company to provide equipment for a machine shop, but both companies said in their defense that they had only supplied general purpose industrial materials. Several West German businessmen were later prosecuted for selling Libya equipment that could be used to manufacture chemical weapons, and—after a plea bargain with the West German authorities—the director of Imhausen-Chemie ended up serving a brief jail sentence. To the great frustration of the Americans, who had intelligence reports from the site, Belgian, French, Thai and Chinese companies were also involved, and Libya started to produce nerve and blister agents. Some reports suggest that the Libyans used chemical weapons during the war in Chad: The three defectors from the Libyan army whose testimony to the U.S. embassy in N'Djamena was uncovered by Human Rights Watch said that General Khalifa Heftar "used poison gas against the Chadians." Libya built a second chemical weapons factory at a military facility in the desert near Sabha, and a third in Tarhuna, south of Tripoli. By 2003, when they declared their arsenal, they had a stockpile of forty-four thousand pounds of mustard gas.

Gaddafi's decision to surrender his weapons of mass destruction, announced by President Bush on December 19, 2003, marked his public rehabilitation, but the process of rapprochement with his old enemies had started five years earlier. By the 1990s, Gaddafi's status as a pariah was no longer bringing him the controversy and international attention he craved. No one seemed to listen to him. Libya was getting poorer, and he recognized that his economic policies hadn't worked. "We cannot stand in the way of progress," he said. "The fashion now is free markets and investments." The World Bank said the UN embargo had cost Libya $18 billion; the Libyans put it at $33 billion. Gaddafi could no longer manipulate the oil price, but he knew he had to get the sanctions lifted. His son Seif was keen for Libya to escape its political isolation, so he spearheaded the plan that led to the Lockerbie suspects being handed over for trial. Libya expelled the Abu Nidal Organization and stopped supporting the anti-Israel groups, Hamas in the Palestinian territories and Hizbollah in Lebanon.

In 1999, the UN suspended the sanctions, and Libyan diplomats approached the Clinton administration about the possibility of lifting the more draconian U.S. embargo. Secret talks got under way—the interlocutor on the Libyan side being their smoothest and most plausible spy-cum-diplomat: Musa Koussa. "At the first meeting, in Geneva in May 1999, we used the promise of official dialogue to persuade Libya to co-operate in the campaign against Osama bin Laden and provide compensation for the Lockerbie families," wrote Martin Indyk, a senior State Department official at the time, in an article in the *Financial Times*. "Libya's representatives were ready to put everything on the table, saying that Mr. Gaddafi had realized that was not the path to pursue and that Libya and the US faced a common threat from Islamic fundamentalism." According to Indyk, the Libyans offered to declare their chemical weapons stocks, but the Americans didn't feel that Libya's WMD were an "imminent threat" and wanted a settlement on Lockerbie first.

The Bush administration had not yet formulated its policy toward

Libya when Al Qaeda flew its planes into the Twin Towers on September 11, 2001. Colonel Gaddafi was among the first leaders to condemn the attacks. "In spite of the political conflict with the United States, it is our humanitarian duty to present condolences to the American people and to share with them this heavy, sad and horrible day," he said. He realized very quickly that this was his chance—he had been saying for years that the jihadi Libyan Islamic Fighting Group, which worked alongside Osama bin Laden in Afghanistan, was a threat not just to him but to the world. Now he was in a far better position to persuade the Americans. Musa Koussa was barred from visiting the United States because of his alleged involvement with Lockerbie, but the British were always more accommodating. One month after 9/11, he met William Burns, the U.S. assistant secretary of state for near eastern affairs, and a senior CIA agent at a mansion belonging to Prince Bandar, the Saudi ambassador to the United States, just off London's Regent's Park. Koussa had information the Americans wanted about Libyans, including members of the LIFG, who were close to bin Laden. The Americans held their noses, and started to deal.

One by one the pieces fell into place. In May 2002, the Libyans agreed to compensation for the victims of Lockerbie. The following March, as U.S. and British forces massed in Kuwait to invade Iraq, the Libyans approached MI6 with a new offer: Colonel Gaddafi wanted to negotiate the surrender of his chemical and nuclear weapons. This time the interlocutor was Seif al-Islam, who met MI6 officers to assure them that his father was serious. It wasn't the first time the Libyans had discussed giving up their WMD, but the timing was significant—the Americans and British were fighting Saddam ostensibly because he had refused to surrender his. If this worked, President Bush and Prime Minister Blair could use it to prove that their policy of killing the chicken to scare the monkey had worked.

An MI6 team, led by Mark Allen, and another from the CIA, led by Steve Kappes, made several visits to Libya, and even met the Guide.

Slowly they started to get the measure of the WMD program, even as Saddam Hussein was swept from power eighteen hundred miles away in Iraq. But there was no trust. Then, following a tip-off, a ship called the *BBC China,* en route to Tripoli, was diverted to Italy. When the security forces opened the containers they found nuclear parts. The British and Americans confronted the Libyans, who agreed to more site inspections. Eventually, the Libyans produced a pile of documents with the information the spies wanted: the design of the nuclear weapon the A. Q. Khan network had sold them. The final agreement was made in the shabby chic surroundings—mahogany furniture and brass light fittings—of the Travellers' Club on Pall Mall, guaranteeing the discretion required. Musa Koussa was the senior Libyan envoy. Two weeks later George Bush and Tony Blair made their announcement that Libya was no longer an enemy. Colonel Gaddafi's rehabilitation had begun.

While the Brother Leader was figuring out how to get into America's good books, Sami al Saadi, the emir of the Libyan Islamic Fighting Group, was on his way back to Afghanistan. He welcomed the protection afforded to him by the Taliban. The cruel, doctrinaire nature of their rule seems to have left him unbothered, although he did tell them he disagreed with the dynamiting of the statues of Buddha in Bamian, which the Taliban had destroyed as idolatrous. I met Sami in 2011—a mild-mannered, bearded man in a *jird,* speaking good if slightly hesitant English—in his family home, the large villa in Tripoli where he had spent his childhood. He showed me a faded picture of himself about age seven, in a smart, Western-style gray suit with a little red hanky in his jacket pocket, a typical upper-class Libyan boy of the time. As we spoke, Sami's teenage daughter, wearing jeans and a T-shirt, was relaxing in her room, while his sixteen-year-old son, who said he had fought in the revolution, was in military fatigues. Karima, his wife, was praying before getting ready to go out, wearing a long dress and head scarf with her face showing, no more covered than any normal Libyan woman. Yet Sami was full of praise for the Taliban leader, Mullah Omar, whom he had met on several occasions. "He was strict but in the right way, in a positive way. He was charismatic, and even elderly people respected him. He didn't speak much." I asked about harsh Islamic punishments, like the stoning to death of adulterers.

"I never saw that," he said.

But it happened, I pointed out. You can't deny it.

"Anyway, this is a matter for the Taliban regime, not me."

"What about cutting off people's hands?"

"The Western media exaggerates. They said the Taliban did that to those who wore henna on their hands. It wasn't true."

But they did cut off people's hands, I thought.

"What about the role of women?"

"Many scholars say the burqa is not compulsory, and I agree. My daughter is at university."

But the Taliban forced women to wear the burqa.

"The Taliban made mistakes," he replied, and changed the subject.

In 1998, Osama bin Laden asked the LIFG to amalgamate with Al Qaeda, but they refused, saying they were only interested in fighting Gaddafi not in joining a worldwide jihad. Bin Laden tried to get Sami, who as the LIFG's ideological guide had profound influence on the group, to change his mind. "He tried to persuade me that we should fight America from Afghanistan, but I knew that Mullah Omar didn't agree with it either," he told me. Two months before 9/11, Sami saw bin Laden in Kandahar. "We had a long discussion. I said he should obey Mullah Omar, but he believed what he was about to do was legitimate from an Islamic point of view," he said. "Everyone in Kabul and Kandahar knew bin Laden would carry out activities against America, but we had no details."

According to Noman Benotman, a former senior member of the LIFG who was also in Afghanistan in 2001, and who now advises the British government on countering jihadism, the LIFG as an organization did not support bin Laden's international campaign against "the Crusaders and the Jews," because for them Gaddafi, not the Americans, was the enemy. Nonetheless, individual Libyan jihadis who were not members of the LIFG rose to high positions within Al Qaeda, and the LIFG didn't distance itself from Al Qaeda in the late 1990s or early 2000s, refusing to criticize their brother jihadis publicly. Like all jihadis, they didn't distinguish between civilians and soldiers, only between Muslims and non-Muslims, so while they didn't see the terror campaign as useful for their purposes, nor did they condemn it. The LIFG's opposition to attacks on America was practical as much as ideological—they knew America would hit back, and that would make their lives difficult. So it proved. As U.S. forces gathered to attack Afghanistan in the wake of the 9/11 attacks, Sami and many of the Arab jihadis remaining in Afghanistan were forced to move again. "We knew the safe period was over," he said. For three years he went from country to country, with his wife, Karima, and four children, traveling on a variety of fake passports, trying to stay ahead of U.S. intelligence, which Sami guessed would be onto him.

First they went to Iran, but after a year they were deported to Pakistan, then to Malaysia. Karima was teaching the children at home, but Sami knew they needed to go to school, and he had to find a way to stay in one place. He tried to register at the university in Kuala Lumpur, but the authorities realized he was traveling on a fake Moroccan passport and deported the family to China. The throbbing, roaring streets of Guangzhou in southern China are a magnet for traders from around the world, especially Africans and Arabs who buy cheap Chinese jeans, shoes, DVDs and computer parts for export. Sami met up with the Abdel Hakim Belhaj, who had succeeded him as LIFG emir, and who had come by an equally circuitous route, using any number of fake passports. "We decided to settle there as merchants," he said.

It was not to be. On a trip to Hong Kong, the immigration authorities became suspicious of Sami's fake passport and arrested him. "The Hong Kong people interrogated me in English for twelve days," he says. "I slept on the chairs. They asked about my origin, and I told them I'd been in England, so they asked about the streets and things. They asked me what I thought about jihad in Iraq against U.S. forces. I told them that people who want to should help the Iraqi people build the country." His answers didn't satisfy the Hong Kong authorities, who consulted the British intelligence service MI6. Documents found in the wreckage of Libya's Intelligence Ministry in September 2011 reveal the rest of the story.

Sami al Saadi also went by the name of Abu Munthir. On March 24, 2004, the CIA sent a cable to Libyan Intelligence entitled: SECRET // US ONLY// EXCEPT LIBYA. RENDITION OF LIFG DEPUTY ABU MUNTHIR. They were offering to help the Libyans get Sami back. "We are aware that your service had been cooperating with the British to effect Abu Munthir's removal to Tripoli," reads the cable. The Hong Kong authorities had denied the Libyans permission to land their plane, for fear of breaching sanctions, so the CIA offered to pay for a non-Libyan plane. "If we pursue that option," they said, "we must have assurances that Abu Munthir and his family will be treated humanely and his human rights will be respected."

The policy of "extraordinary rendition" was one of the most controversial aspects of George Bush and Tony Blair's war on terror. The practice dated back to the 1990s, but after 9/11 it was stepped up, and hundreds of people from a variety of nationalities were arrested—sometimes kidnapped—and either deported back to their home countries, from which they had fled persecution, or to third countries that didn't have British or American strictures against torture and coercive interrogation. It was a way of farming out the dirty work to dirty regimes so the U.S. and British governments could say their hands were clean. The program was highly secret, and illegal under international law. Given the Libyan government's human rights record, it is hard to know what kind of human rights assurances they might have convincingly provided. Colonel Gaddafi had after all said in 1999, just three years after the slaughter at Abu Salim, "Libya is the only country in the world that has no political prisoners." By 2004, there were fewer hangings, but Amnesty International, which was allowed to send a delegation to Libya for the first time that year, reported the continued use of torture to extract confessions, as well as unfair trials and prolonged detentions, with no access to the outside world.

Sami was taken to a plane and told he would be sent back to mainland China. The plane never took off, and he was returned to the terminal for a few more days. "The night before I was finally taken, I could hear the guards talking Chinese as I lay on the chairs," he recalled. "I couldn't understand what they were saying, but I heard them mention 'CIA' four or five times." Karima and the children were brought to the airport. The Hong Kong police again told the family that they were being flown back to mainland China, but when they reached the tarmac they found an Egyptian plane and four Libyan security officers, easily recognized by their accents. Sami began to shout, and the police handcuffed him and Karima together and bundled them onto the aircraft. "My wife was crying, my children were crying," he recalls. "The officers seemed worried about my health, because I'm a diabetic, but that wasn't for humanitarian reasons; it was because they wanted me alive."

As they landed in Tripoli, they were hooded. Karima thought they were going to be executed, but they were taken to the External Security headquarters in the Tripoli suburb of Tajoura. Karima and the children were put in one cell, Sami in another. It wasn't long before Musa Koussa arrived. Sami said he introduced himself and said, "Sami, the world has become very small since 9/11. Before we couldn't arrest you in many countries, but now I can call the CIA or MI6 directly and get all the most recent information on you and your group." At first Sami's treatment was good, but after a month it deteriorated. "They used electric shocks with a baton, and beat me on my hands, legs and the soles of my feet with a wooden stick. They insulted me and threatened to hang me." Karima was also detained, but in a separate room. "They insinuated that my wife was not safe."

They asked him about LIFG members in Libya, and when he didn't cooperate, beat him more.

After about a week, two Americans, a man and a woman, came to see Sami. They asked him a lot of questions about the LIFG and about bin Laden. "I think the CIA knew that we were not involved with Al Qaeda, because most people in Kabul knew that we were a separate organization," he said. Six months later a team of five Americans came and asked similar questions. After a few months, British officials turned up. "Again, it was a lady and a man," recalled Sami. "I don't think it was a real inquiry—they just wanted to know my situation, but I couldn't tell them, because there was a Libyan there and his eyes were on my face all the time. If they were very clever, they knew, but I couldn't give a clear indication." The British, he says, discussed "how to help face terrorism in the world." They never returned. Sami seems to have become a regular for intelligence agencies. "The Italians were very polite," he says. "They asked if I knew anything about Al Qaeda in Italy and Iraq. Then there were the French— although maybe they were Canadian, I don't know. I just know they spoke French."

Karima and the children, to Sami's relief, were released after two months. He spent more than two years in prison in Tajoura before they came to move him, but any hopes of release were quickly dashed. They took him to Abu Salim, where his brothers Adel and Mohammed had been killed in the 1986 massacre. He despaired that he would ever get out.

The documents found in the rubble of the intelligence ministry reveal a chummy relationship between MI6 and their Libyan counterparts. Mark

Allen, the MI6 head of counterterrorism, signed his letters to Musa Koussa "Your friend, Mark." Someone called Khaled is thanked for a gift of "oranges and dates." The same month that Sami al Saadi was "rendered" from Hong Kong, the LIFG leader Abdel Hakim Belhaj—also known as Abu 'Abd Allah Sadiq—was rendered from Thailand under similar circumstances. "Congratulations on the safe arrival of Abu 'Abd Allah Sadiq," writes Mark to his friend Musa. "This was the least we could do for you and for Libya to demonstrate the remarkable relationship we have built over recent years." The British intelligence service's perennial rivalry with their allies the Americans, so elegantly conjured in the novels of John le Carré, is revealed to have a basis in fact. "Amusingly, we got a request from the Americans to channel information from Abu 'Abd Allah Sadiq through the Americans," writes Mark to Musa. "I have no intention of doing any such thing. The intelligence about Abu 'Abd Allah Sadiq was British. I know I did not pay for the air cargo. But I feel I have the right to deal with you direct on this and am very grateful to you for the help you are giving us."

That same cable deals with preparations for Colonel Gaddafi's reentry onto the world stage, an event the staff at 10 Downing Street planned with precision, like a coming-out ball for an aging debutante. Tony Blair was to go to Tripoli, accompanied by sixty journalists, to shake hands with the Brother Leader. "No 10 [sic] are keen that the Prime Minister meet the leader in his tent," explains Mark. "I don't know why the English are fascinated by tents. The plain fact is the journalists would love it. My own view is that it would give a good impression of the Leader's preference for simplicity which I know is important to him." Happy to oblige, the Libyans put up the Leader's tent in an appropriate bit of desert, carefully positioned not too far from the hotels from where the journalists needed to write and file their stories. The footage shows Blair, in a dark suit and a plain tie, shaking hands with Gaddafi, who is wearing his brown *jird*, a black fez and glasses. They stride around the tent for the benefit of the cameras, so the world can witness the moment the Guide is rehabilitated, a rebirthing-through-television ritual like total-immersion baptism. The press pack watches off camera, and a herd of camels sways up, nuzzling at the sparse green desert grass and belching loudly.

The jihadis in Libya's restive east were unimpressed by all this peace and harmony. As far as they were concerned, Gaddafi was still the enemy, and the British and Americans were becoming the enemy by association. Moreover, the Americans were—in their eyes—behaving just like the Soviets occupying Afghanistan back in the 1980s. Documents seized by U.S. forces after a raid on a militants' base in Iraq in 2007 revealed that of 600 foreign fighters who had entered from Syria, 112 were Libyan. Libyans, it turned out, were second in number only to Saudis among those blowing up American military convoys and Iraqi civilians. The majority came from the eastern towns of Derna and Benghazi, and the scant details in the documents suggested that they were unexceptional young men— one record describes a student, a traffic policeman and a teacher, all from Derna, who traveled through Egypt and Syria to blow themselves up as suicide bombers in Iraq. Why? Derna—the hometown of fifty-two of the jihadis mentioned—had been anti-Gaddafi from the beginning, and many of the LIFG were from there, but never before had they targeted Americans or civilians.

In early 2008, Chris Stevens, a U.S. diplomat, set out from Tripoli for Derna. He managed to throw off his government tail and get talking to Libyans freely, who explained how anger against Gaddafi had morphed into hatred of the United States. In a cable published by WikiLeaks, he writes: "Fighting against U.S. and coalition forces in Iraq represented a way for frustrated young radicals to strike a blow against both Qadhafi and against his perceived American backers." Derna, he noted, was deliberately neglected by Gaddafi's regime and had missed out on the building boom now under way in Tripoli as the oil companies returned. Young men were unemployed, so they often couldn't marry until their late thirties. There was a lot of pent-up sexual frustration as well as political anger in Derna. "One Libyan interlocutor likened young men in Derna to Bruce Willis's character in the action picture *Die Hard*, who stubbornly refused to die quietly," he writes. "For them, resistance against coalition forces in Iraq is an important act of jihad and a last act of defiance against the Qadhafi regime."

The history of eastern Libya, where the Sanussis, another religious group, had fought colonial occupation, may have contributed to their sense of mission. For them, jihad, the violent creature born of religion and politics, was thoroughly modern: It was global, and absolute. On Al Jazeera and other satellite channels they saw the occupation of Muslim lands from Palestine to Iraq and Afghanistan. Western TV channels sanitize war, censoring out the blood and the broken bodies, but Arabic TV shows the unflinching visceral horror of it—dead babies, flesh flying after bombing raids, heads separated from bodies, everything. Sometimes the most disturbing images are set to music and played on a loop in between programs. On the Internet they found Western movies with action heroes like Bruce Willis, and pornography. The young men of eastern Libya inhabited a world in which nothing, in their view, was changing for the better, and in which they had no role unless they went to fight the *kafir*, the infidel. Gaddafi's government ensured that they saw no benefit in the rapprochement with the West. Quite the opposite—they saw the hated Brother Leader being feted by Western prime ministers and presidents while they remained jobless and liable to arrest if they spoke against the regime. U.S. support for Gaddafi was matched by U.S. support for Israel. In small, scattered mosques, which Gaddafi's spies frequently failed to monitor, they listened to imams influenced by the Salafi current spreading across the region, preaching hatred of the Zionists and Americans. These, then, were the young Libyans who went to Iraq to fight America, and who—in yet another rapid and unforeseen twist of history—only a few years later would find themselves united with America against the old enemy, Gaddafi.

CHAPTER SIX

KING OF KINGS OF AFRICA

There are inevitable cycles of social history: the yellow
race's domination of the world, when it came from Asia,
and the white race's attempts at colonizing extensive
areas of all continents of the world. Now it is the turn of
the black race to prevail in the world.

—MUAMMAR GADDAFI, THE GREEN BOOK

Kiss the hand you cannot sever.

—TUAREG PROVERB

The Aberdeen-based company KCA Deutag produced oil-drilling equipment at their compound on the outskirts of Tripoli until the day in May 2011 when soldiers turned up and ordered the workers to leave. From that moment it became a top-secret military facility where Gaddafi's engineers would take rockets and missiles and mount them on trucks. A week after Gaddafi's forces were driven out of Tripoli, I found myself tripping over missile launchers and welding equipment, as I accompanied a group of former employees surveying the place, as they contemplated how to describe the mess in their compound to their German and Scottish bosses, who had fled back to Europe at the beginning of the conflict.

We wandered around a giant workshop, which had a corrugated iron roof like an aircraft hangar, poking at Russian-made mortar tubes still inside their wooden crates, 30mm cannons and boxes of ammunition scattered carelessly on the concrete floor. The prefabricated trailers where the expats once lived had been taken over by soldiers, and then abandoned in a hurry. Camouflage jackets and berets lay among German-language paperback novels. One of the men I was with handed me a 2007 desk diary with a dark red cover that he had found lying around. Inside, random pages were filled with scribbling in blue ballpoint—most in Arabic script, some French, the odd phrase in English. Much had been crossed out. On one page someone had drawn the emblem of the Thirty-second Brigade, the feared unit led by Gaddafi's son Khamis. I asked my companion to translate some words. "It's in Tuareg, not Arabic," he said. "Hard to understand." We had happened across a notebook used by nomadic fighters from the southern desert near the border with Niger, the people the new revolutionaries most resented for their support of Gaddafi.

For Gaddafi, the pastoralist Tuareg, who herded their camels and goats across the vast sea of sand in defiance of national borders, were natural allies, because like him they spurned the state. Tuareg culture is distinct and enduring. A tall people with fine features, the men swathe their heads in yards of cloth, so their faces are covered and only their eyes show, protection against *el ghibli,* the harsh desert wind. Their traditional robes are indigo blue, and they make an impressive sight driving camel caravans across the featureless pale sand. Their ancestors are thought to be the Garamantes, described in the fifth century BC by the Greek traveler Herodotus, as "an exceedingly numerous people . . . who raise crops by spreading earth over the salt, and hunt . . . with four-horse chariots." For two millennia they drove caravans across five routes through the Sahara, bringing salt, cloth and slaves to the Mediterranean ports of Cyrenaica and Tripolitana, the only link between the interior of Africa and Europe's southern shore. They were spread across six countries—Libya, Algeria, Niger, Mali, Morocco and Burkina Faso—and resisted the French

Mervat Mhani of the Free Generation Movement, which carried out acts
of civil disobedience in Tripoli during the 2011 revolution.
Lucy Young / lucyyoungphotos.co.uk

Mohammed Mustafa Saudi, who makes copper moons for minarets
in the metal-workers section of the Tripoli souk.
Lucy Young / lucyyoungphotos.co.uk

Wanise Elisawi, with his ID card from the 1980s. After participating in a failed coup attempt, he spent nineteen years in Abu Salim prison.

Lucy Young / lucyyoungphotos.co.uk

Huda Abuzeid with a photograph of her father, Ali. She returned to Libya from London during the revolution.

Lucy Young / lucyyoungphotos.co.uk

Mukhtar Nagasa in the ruins of Saadi Gaddafi's house, which was
bulldozed a few weeks after he and other fighters broke in.

Lucy Young / lucyyoungphotos.co.uk

Sami al Saadi with his daughter Khadija. A leading member of the Libyan Islamic
Fighting Group, he was "rendered" from Hong Kong to Libya in 2004.

Courtesy of Cori Crider / Reprieve

Me doing a piece for the camera in the ruins of a building
destroyed by a NATO airstrike in June 2011.

Martin Fletcher

Me with rebels driving into Tripoli just after it fell on August 22, 2011.

Sarah Corp

Pictures of the missing, including those killed in the 1996 Abu Salim prison massacre, posted on the wall of the North Courthouse in Benghazi, February 2011.

Ivor Prickett / Panos Pictures

Rebels fighting Gaddafi's troops as a multiple-rocket launcher is fired, between Ras Lanuf and Bin Jawad in March 2011.

Goran Tomasevic / Reuters

In August 2011, rebel fighters celebrated on the statue Gaddafi erected in the
Bab al Aziziyah compound after the U.S. bombing of 1986.

William Daniels / Panos Pictures

Rebel fighters congratulate each other inside the ruins of
Gaddafi's house, bombed by the United States in 1986.

William Daniels / Panos Pictures

Tripoli Street in Misrata, destroyed by months of fighting and siege.
David Rose

Celebrating the revolution in Martyrs' Square, previously
known as Green Square, in Tripoli.
Ricardo Garcia Vilanova

Colonel Muammar Gaddafi at the Prado in Madrid, December 17, 2007.

Pedro Armestre / AFP / Getty

In August 2011, researchers from Human Rights Watch found an archive of photographs in the ruins of Gaddafi's ministries and other buildings.

Soviet president Leonid I. Brezhnev welcomed Colonel Gaddafi to Moscow in April 1981 as a "comrade in the struggle for the rights and freedoms of peoples, against imperialist oppression and aggression."

Courtesy of Michael Christopher Brown / Human Rights Watch © 2012

In May 1954, Queen Elizabeth II visited King Idris in Tobruk,
where the British maintained a military base.
Courtesy of Peter Bouckaert / Human Rights Watch

Colonel Gaddafi in the early 1970s.
Courtesy of Michael Christopher Brown / Human Rights Watch © 2012

Enthusiastic crowds greeted Gaddafi, Egyptian president Gamal Abdel Nasser and President Jaafar Nimieri of Sudan in Tripoli, December 1969.

Courtesy of Peter Bouckaert / Human Rights Watch

Gaddafi said he felt most relaxed in the desert, where he was born.

Courtesy of Michael Christopher Brown / Human Rights Watch © 2012

Gaddafi with Nasser, greeting a fan at the stadium in Benghazi in June 1970. They
were celebrating the handover of the U.S. and UK military bases to Libya.

Courtesy of Peter Bouckaert / Human Rights Watch

Gaddafi, Nasser and Nimieri greet the crowd in June 1970. Nasser, who died
a few months later, said, "As I bid farewell, I leave amongst you my brother
Muammar Gaddafi as the trustee of Arab nationalism."

Courtesy of Michael Christopher Brown / Human Rights Watch © 2012

Gaddafi visiting East Germany in the late 1970s. The child on the right is Seif al-Islam. The East German government cooperated closely with Gaddafi and facilitated the bombing of La Belle discothèque in 1986.

Courtesy of Michael Christopher Brown / Human Rights Watch © 2012

Gaddafi and Yasser Arafat. Despite the display of affection, the two men mistrusted each other.

Courtesy of Michael Christopher Brown / Human Rights Watch © 2012

On April 7, 1977, two students and two others were hanged in Benghazi, heralding a period of repression.

Courtesy of the estate of Tim Hetherington / Human Rights Watch

Gaddafi's wife Safia and his second son, Seif al-Islam, in one of the giant water pipes used for the Great Man Made River.

Courtesy of Michael Christopher Brown / Human Rights Watch © 2012

Gaddafi and family in a tent, probably in the Bab al Aziziyah compound.

Courtesy of Michael Christopher Brown / Human Rights Watch © 2012

Gaddafi and an unidentified child. The photograph on the wall shows him with the Polish leader, General Wojciech Jaruzelski, whom he visited in 1982.

Courtesy of Michael Christopher Brown / Human Rights Watch © 2012

Gaddafi shakes the hand of an unidentified child. The young man on the left is his son Hannibal.

Courtesy of Michael Christopher Brown / Human Rights Watch © 2012

Gaddafi in his latter years with three unidentified children.

Courtesy of Michael Christopher Brown / Human Rights Watch © 2012

colonial authorities in the nineteenth century; more recently, they had fought postindependence governments that had tried to control their migrations or make them settle. Colonel Gaddafi determined to exploit their restlessness both at home and abroad.

In the 1970s, Gaddafi recruited thousands of Tuareg for his Islamic Legion, sending them to fight in countries where he was trying to extend his influence or unseat his enemies. He didn't distinguish between those born in Libya and those from across the borders, recruiting Tuareg from all the Sahelian states and promising Libyan documents to anyone who fought. As a result, even Tuareg who really were born in Libya find it hard to persuade Libyan officials to give them birth certificates for their children—like bureaucrats everywhere, Libyan officials hate anyone who refuses to settle in one place. Despite Gaddafi's purported backing, the Tuareg remained stateless, the Kurds of Africa, an undocumented people without a homeland. In 2005, Gaddafi came up with the idea of a border-less Islamic Republic of the Sahara, through which he would become the Guide of a far larger stretch of territory than just Libya. He announced the formation of the Popular and Social League of the Great Sahara Tribes in Timbuktu in 2006, a forum which was supposed to be a peaceful plat-form for the rights of the Tuareg and other nomadic peoples, but instead he armed the Tuareg, precipitating uprisings in Mali and Niger.

Unsurprisingly, he earned the ire of other governments in the region. The Tuareg had any number of legitimate complaints—they were poor and marginalized in all the countries where they lived, and successive droughts had driven them into shantytowns, so their traditional way of life was becoming more difficult every year—but the backing of Gaddafi didn't help. Adding to the confusion, Al Qaeda in the Maghreb was by then operating across the Sahel, smuggling weapons and kidnapping Western tourists. The Bush administration started to train regional armies, who quickly ran up against Gaddafi's Tuareg warriors. So Gad-dafi, who by then had given up overtly antagonizing the Americans, set himself up as a peace broker, negotiating between Tuareg leaders and various governments, still presenting himself as a champion of the nomads.

I showed the notebook to a Tuareg living in Britain. Akli Sheita had little time for the idea of Gaddafi as his people's defender. In 2009 he had fled Libya after a friend was arrested and taken to Abu Salim prison as punishment for a film they had made about the walled ghetto of Al Kambo in which Tuareg live in Sabha. The film, which they had posted on YouTube, showed Tuareg women in cardboard houses complaining about how Libyan police had bulldozed their mud dwellings and arrested their sons. "A person without a country is like a dog. No one shows him respect," they said. With the police on his tail, Akli disguised himself as an old woman, wrapping his head in a black cloth with just one eye showing, and took a taxi to Tripoli, where he delivered himself to a people smuggler. He paid 1,200 dinars ($953) to stow away on a cargo ship for the twenty-day voyage to Europe. In the daytime he hid among boxes and crates in the ship's hold dressed in overalls, as if he were a crew member; at night he was allowed into the cabin of the people smuggler, who worked onboard. After docking at several European ports, he was unloaded in Britain—he has no idea where—and stuffed into a fish van, ending up at a London railway station, where he was arrested and transferred to the northern town of Halifax to await the result of his asylum application.

Akli told his story with no rancor but considerable apprehension at the possibility of returning to Libya. While other Libyan exiles who had been persecuted by Gaddafi's regime felt it was safe to return after the 2011 revolution, he did not. Like most Tuareg, he had no papers, so he had been allowed to attend only primary school in Sabha. Without papers, you cannot get a job in Libya. More worrying, the Tuareg were regarded by the new authorities in Libya as the Brother Leader's personal militia, enemies of the new order. Although he opposed Gaddafi, Akli knew that any Tuareg risked imprisonment or worse in the new Libya.

We turned to the notebook, where Tuareg fighters had recorded their thoughts.

"Memories of the Tuareg youth in the middle of the battlefield; we are the mujahadeen, the victory will be very soon," read one. "We are Muammar Gaddafi's soldiers and lions, and we'll do whatever it takes to protect him." Another had written, "Khamis Muammar Gaddafi—we will stay with you" and—in a reference to the rebels they were fighting—"those rats are annoying me, but we will keep our pledge." But from time to time Akli found opaque but dissenting views in the book. Someone had written, "Whoever tells the truth will be killed," and another, "Evil is the action you take against wanted individuals." In the middle, in clear handwriting, one of the soldiers had written a screed: "The Tuareg in Libya are merely tools for playing games, and none has a position in politics, business or the environment. They don't have identity documents to prove they are Libyans. Whatever problem you find in Libya, they will be right at the front as human shields."

I wondered about the men who had written with such bitterness. Gaddafi did deals with Tuareg leaders, paying them huge sums of money to deliver fighters for the cause. These men had been recruited to the Thirty-second Brigade, commanded by Gaddafi's son Khamis. Largely uneducated, with no job prospects and no papers, drought having destroyed their traditional way of life, young Tuareg men had little alternative but to fight for the Brother Leader, but the freedom other Libyans had fought for was unlikely to bring them anything good.

If the Tuareg were mistrusted by those trying to overthrow Gaddafi, Africans from farther afield were actively loathed. Libyans come in all shades, but I learned that to call someone black was an insult. I once pointed out to a rebel fighter who had been complaining about blacks fighting for Gaddafi that many on his side were black too—at least, they looked black to me. He looked around as if seeing his colleagues for the first time. "We can tell the difference," he said. Gaddafi's decision to identify increasingly with Africa rather than the Arab world was unpopular with the majority of Libyans, partly because they saw him lavishing money on other countries and neglecting their own, and partly because their aspirations made them look north over the Mediterranean to Europe or east to the Gulf rather than south to the Sahara and beyond.

Libya was full of Africans who were looking in the same direction. Refugees from conflicts and brutal regimes trekked across the Sahara to Tripoli, Benghazi and Misrata where—like the Tuareg Akli Sheita—they paid people smugglers to ship them to Europe. While in Libya, they hid in the shadows, sleeping dozens to a room. They were frequently arrested and sent to squalid detention centers and camps, where they risked beating and rape by Libyan police and prison guards. Libya had not signed the UN's convention on refugees, so they had no rights and no recourse to law, only the charity of a handful of Filipina and Indian nuns who tried to ensure they didn't starve or die on the street. Once they managed to get on a boat—sometimes after years on the run—the risks were not over. By 2011, around thirty thousand African refugees were arriving in Italy every year, so before they landed, Italian government vessels frequently forced them back to Libya, where they faced arrest again. Some boats sank, and dozens onboard drowned. Colonel Gaddafi championed Africa as his sphere of influence, but there was no mercy for African refugees in his country.

To be a black African in Libya as the revolution started was dangerous indeed. African migrant workers were immediately suspected of being mercenaries. In Tobruk, I came across a hapless young man from Sierra Leone who dared not make the journey to the Egyptian border for fear of being hauled out of a vehicle and accused of being a fighter for Gaddafi. He had been working for an oil company but now slept at the hospital, where the staff had agreed to protect him. Libya's eastern and western borders were packed with undocumented Africans who had tried to flee but had been blocked—the Tunisian and Egyptian authorities were worried that the Africans would start looking for work in their countries rather than go back home. So they lived for months in a squalid no-man's-land between border posts, waiting for someone to sort out their papers and let them through.

Throughout those months, I kept coming across small groups of Africans who had been detained by the rebels. Some had allegedly been caught on the battlefield, but most had been turned in by suspicious neighbors. In Benghazi, a busload of journalists was taken to a courtyard surrounded by barbed wire inside a large military complex to see thirty African men, all accused of being mercenaries. They were from Mali, Niger, Chad, Ghana and Sudan. All denied being fighters. A Gambian showed me an ID card from one of Gaddafi's revolutionary committees, the *lijan thawriya*, saying he was head of the Gambian community. The rebels said that that proved he had been a fighter, but actually it just proved that he had cooperated with the regime. That group was released eventually, but human rights groups reported dozens of instances in which groups of freelance rebels detained Africans at their own pleasure, sometimes beating or torturing them, determined to prove that they were mercenaries.

Only once did I find a prisoner who confessed to being a mercenary. A group of 130 men were being held in a school in Zintan, in the Nafousa Mountains. Their jailers, who wanted to show me that they were not mistreating prisoners, and also to ask if I could get the Red Cross to visit, had assembled them in a classroom. I asked if any spoke English, and a thin man with buckteeth, a blue towel slung around his neck, put his hand up. He said his name was Gaddafi Ismad Harun, and he was from Darfur in Sudan. His parents—who had presumably given him the name Gaddafi— lived in Zem Zem, a huge refugee camp created when the Sudanese government and its militia started attacking the people in the area. When I told him that I had once visited Zem Zem, while covering the conflict in

Darfur, he smiled, amazed to meet anyone who might have a clue about his origins. He said he had first come to Libya in 1992, working on building sites and sending his wages home. He had gone back and forth several times, returning to Libya most recently in 2009. When the uprising started he had volunteered to fight, after recruiters told him that Gaddafi's enemies were an unholy (and unlikely) alliance of colonialists and jihadis. "When we came to this area from Tripoli, we were looking for the French army and for Al Qaeda, but when we arrived we never saw them," he said. Surrounded by the rebels who had imprisoned him, I didn't feel I could ask a crucial question: Had he also fought in Sudan with the Justice and Equality Movement, the rebel group Gaddafi had been arming and funding in Darfur? Gaddafi's mercenaries were not all simple guns-for-hire; many had been fighting in their own countries in wars Gaddafi had fomented. He had been calling in favors.

The threads of Gaddafi's involvement in conflicts across the continent were tangled, his motives and interests changing through the decades. Africa had been his backyard, the place where he could most easily buy influence, but what had started as ideological commitment had ended up as vanity. In the 1970s, it had been about countering imperialism and colonialism, so he backed liberation movements, offering arms and training to those fighting in Portuguese Guinea, South Africa and Rhodesia.

The late Joshua Nkomo, the leader of the Zimbabwe African People's Union (ZAPU) who fought alongside Robert Mugabe's forces to overthrow white rule in Rhodesia, recalled in his memoir a meeting with Gaddafi in the desert. "He was sitting on a mat, with camels nearby beside an ancient castle, as his troops paraded past in their modern armored vehicles," he wrote. Nkomo hadn't realized how easy this was going to be. "I explained our problems to him and his reply was to ask me how many men we wanted to train. When I said two thousand, he agreed at once; as soon as our troops were ready he sent an aircraft down to Zambia and flew them up to Libya. . . . [O]ur men were given uniforms, weapons and a

full training in how to use them. That was the promptest and most generous help we ever received with our military efforts."

Gaddafi became an icon for those fighting apartheid in South Africa.
He supported the African National Congress with money, weapons and
training, earning the undying gratitude of Nelson Mandela, which caused
immense diplomatic inconvenience in later years, when Gaddafi was still a
pariah and Mandela the toast of the world. When Mandela was released
from jail in 1997, he broke UN sanctions and traveled to Libya to see Gaddafi, despite admonitions from then U.S. president Bill Clinton. "Those
that yesterday were friends of our enemies have the gall today to tell me
not to visit my brother Gaddafi," said Mandela. "They are advising us to be
ungrateful and forget our friends of the past." He used his position to
lobby for Abdel Basset al-Megrahi, the Libyan intelligence officer convicted in the Lockerbie bombing, to be moved from Scotland to a Muslim
country. To Mandela, Gaddafi was a fellow freedom fighter.

Libyan soldiers were less impressed with Gaddafi's African adventures. For a
decade and a half, they were deployed to the former French colony of
Chad, on Libya's southern border. "It was for the glory of Gaddafi, not for
Libya. He wanted his own personal empire," said Mustafa Abozeid, a
retired air force commander. "If he had conquered Chad, he would have
gone on to Sudan. He was always picking on poor countries, because they
were an easy target." It was hard to imagine Mustafa as the young pilot he
had been in those days. He was now an elderly man with a gray beard,
dressed in a beige *jird* fringed with gold brocade, living in Misrata. He was
the uncle of a young medic I met, who, with his friend, had been translating for journalists who covered the 2011 revolution. As we sat around on
cushions in the family home, and I asked questions about Chad, I realized
he wasn't really talking to me but to his nephew and his friends. They listened avidly, young men who before the 2011 revolution had thought of

little but downloading the latest computer game or Metallica album, fascinated to learn about their country's hidden history. The war in Chad had been a source of shame, said Mustafa. It had brought ruin to the Libyan armed forces that he had joined with patriotic pride in 1977. And for what? For a bit of desert that in the end was surrendered.

In 1973 Gaddafi's forces invaded the narrow belt of sand called the Aouzo Strip, claiming it—as Mussolini had done—as Libyan territory. Some said it had uranium reserves, so he wanted it for his nuclear program, others that it was to provoke the Chadian government, which was backed by the French. Certainly there was no obvious advantage to Libya in moving the border south by sixty miles. In the 1980s he sent in more troops, backing different Chadian rebel groups with improbable acronyms, which proliferated and fragmented as the conflict wore on. "We were young and had no idea about politics," said Mustafa. "We just saw it as an opportunity to improve our fighting capability." He realized the orders he was given were wrong, but he obeyed nonetheless. "We were ordered to shoot anything, even a camel caravan carrying goods across the desert. I didn't want to do that, because it wasn't a military target, but we were told to consider everything moving as an enemy." The pilots had no ground navigation equipment, and it was hard to know where they were as they circled above the featureless, burning desert. One day, two of Mustafa's comrades failed to return. For a month, other pilots kept looking for them whenever they went on a mission, and eventually a team spotted an aircraft half submerged in sand, from the *ghibli* that blew across the desert. Flying around trying to find their bearings, the pilots had run out of fuel and made an emergency landing. There, in the 104-degree heat, they had waited and waited. The rescue team scraped the sand away and found the two bodies and, in the cockpit, a letter dated sixteen days earlier. "We are about to die of thirst," it said. "Please bury our bodies in Tripoli, and pour a glass of water over our grave."

Such stories were never told. In official propaganda, the war in

Chad—which sputtered on for nearly a decade—was a series of victories in which the glorious Libyan forces had prevailed over cowardly Chadian renegades backed by the colonialist French. Soldiers and airmen like Mustafa knew that to tell the truth about the conditions in which they fought, or about defeat and death, would invite court-martial. There were no official figures for how many Libyans died in Chad, nor how many Chadians. Mustafa believes at least twelve thousand Libyan soldiers perished, but he has no way of knowing. Most were buried in the Chadian desert, because Gaddafi didn't want Libyans to see bodies being repatriated. There would be no heroes' acre for those killed in a war of utmost futility, which he pursued against the advice of his military high command. Much of the air force resigned after the war, while senior officers were forcibly retired. The commander of the forces in Chad, who had defected to the opposition National Front for the Salvation of Libya, forcibly accompanied by some of his soldiers, was resented because while he ended up in exile in America, many of them were killed. Many former military men believe that Gaddafi used the war in Chad to weaken the army, so it could never mount another coup against him. As for the Aouzo Strip, in 1987 Chadian forces pushed the Libyans out, and seven years later an international boundary commission awarded the strip to Chad.

Men like Mustafa Abozeid also remember the debacle in Uganda, where Gaddafi sent forces to the aid of Idi Amin, one of Africa's most notoriously cruel and arbitrary dictators. In the early seventies, Gaddafi persuaded Amin, who was a Muslim, to sever his ties with Israel, and after that, the two became allies. When—after years of bloodshed and civil strife—a guerrilla force backed by neighboring Tanzania tried to oust Amin, Gaddafi sent troops to help his friend. "Some of those recruited were civilians," recalled Mustafa. "They were told they were going to Tobruk for a celebration, but they were taken to Uganda. When they saw how green it was, with all the trees, they thought it must be an agricultural project!" The conscripts were joined by Gaddafi's Islamic Legion and a few professional soldiers. With Russian-made tanks and fighter-bombers, they were relatively well equipped, but Amin's forces looted the towns they entered and fled, so the Libyans were left fighting the Tanzanians alone. At least four hundred Libyans were killed, and the rest gave up. The new Ugandan government had them repatriated; Idi Amin followed them into temporary exile in Tripoli before he settled in Saudi Arabia.

Just outside Benghazi, in a heavily guarded complex unseen by the outside world, Gaddafi built the World Revolutionary Headquarters, a training facility for anyone who might like to have a go at overthrowing a regime he didn't like. It was part of the *mathaba*, the World Center for Resistance against Imperialism, Zionism, Racism, Reaction and Fascism. In the early nineties Musa Koussa became its director. Students came from all over the world, but the list of African alumni is striking for the chaos they brought to their home countries: Charles Taylor, who turned Liberia into a killing ground and ended up on trial for war crimes; Foday Sankoh, whose forces in Sierra Leone were notorious for chopping off people's arms and legs, raping little girls and forcing little boys to kill members of their family; Laurent Kabila, who ousted Mobutu Sese Seko in Zaire and presided over an equally brutal replacement regime; Blaise Compaore, who overthrew his best friend, the popular left-wing leader Thomas Sankara, in Burkina Faso; Kukoi Sanyang, who mounted a coup against the democratically elected government of Gambia.

The recruitment methods Gaddafi employed were not dissimilar in some ways to those used by Western countries trying to attract young Africans to the ideas of democracy and the free market or Christian missionaries to win converts. Gaddafi would give grants of money to build mosques and sponsor African Muslims to go on the hajj, the annual pilgrimage to Mecca. Like any foreign government, the Libyans used their embassy to win friends and influence people. The Libyan People's Bureau would be well stocked with copies of the Green Book, which were widely distributed, something that was very welcome in countries where there were few books or libraries. In Sierra Leone, the students' union started a Green Book study group, so some were invited to Tripoli as guests of Gaddafi's revolutionary committees for the annual Green Book celebration. They would get lectures about the Libyan system and suggestions about how to bring a Libyan-style revolution to their home countries. It wasn't hard to exploit discontent. Sierra Leone was among the poorest countries in the world, and the pocket money the Libyans provided enabled students to continue at the university or start a small business. Libyans might think their capital was dilapidated, but to a West African student in his midtwenties who was accommodated in a hotel for the first time, it looked pretty good. This pattern was followed in several African countries. After a while, those who were most enthusiastic about Libya would become contact people through whom the Libyans channeled funds. They might be tasked with "revolutionary assignments," such as attacking a government facility or a foreign diplomat. Their Libyan friends, who would be in the *lijan thawriya*, would ask them to recruit more like-minded youth for the cause of pan-African and world revolution and—if they had the right revolutionary fervor—invite them to Benghazi for further training.

The war in Chad was in part a struggle against the remnants of French colonialism, but by the late eighties, after the Reagan bombing raids, Gaddafi was focusing on the United States. Liberia was the base for American intelligence activities in West Africa, so an obvious target. Charles Taylor, a Liberian American who had escaped from prison in Massachusetts in 1985, and was wandering around West Africa looking for young men to fight in Liberia, became Gaddafi's point man, fomenting war not just in his own country but across West Africa. Each impoverished, weak state was another piece in Gaddafi's jigsaw of world revolution, but it's hard to believe that what happened was the picture he had planned to create.

Charles Taylor and his forces overthrew President Samuel Doe, the pro-American Liberian president Gaddafi had in his sights, sparking off more than a decade of conflict. Foday Sankoh, a Sierra Leonean who had also been trained in Libya, provided forces to assist Taylor, and then the two men started an equally brutal war over the border in Sierra Leone. Both wars were characterized by plunder and the extreme cruelty meted out to civilians. Fighters, often dressed in wigs and women's clothing and wearing juju amulets around their necks, manned roadblocks where anyone regarded as an enemy might be killed with a machete, and disemboweled. Cannibalism was not uncommon. Children were forced to murder and mutilate, and became the most feared fighters of all. There is no suggestion that such tactics were taught in the World Revolutionary Center— the fighters trained in Libya tended to wear uniforms and show a certain degree of discipline—but the impact of the wars Gaddafi stirred up was devastating. Liberia and Sierra Leone were brought to ruin, their peoples killed, maimed and left destitute. Gaddafi saw Africa as a crucible for his world revolution, but the fire his ambition sparked consumed millions of lives.

On September 9, 1999, Muammar Gaddafi turned his back on the Arab world. It was, he pointed out, the ninth day of the ninth month of the ninety-ninth year, an auspicious day, an echo of the eleventh hour of the eleventh day of the eleventh month in 1918, when the armistice was signed, bringing an end to World War I. He had been growing increasingly impatient with Arab leaders who had dismissed his idea of creating Isratine, the single state combining Israel and Palestine, just as they had dismissed his ideas for Arab unity back in the 1970s. At a summit of the Organization of African Unity, which he hosted in his hometown of Sirte, he announced: "I have a vision—a United States of Africa, similar to the United States of

America." He gave the attending African leaders medals, which he called the African Regalia, and they responded by issuing the Sirte Declaration, which called for the rapid establishment of a pan-African parliament, an African Monetary Union and an African Court of Justice. "[W]e have been inspired by the important proposals submitted by Colonel Muammar Gaddafi, Leader of the Great Al Fatah Libyan Revolution," they said in the declaration.

A month later, Gaddafi explained to Libyans:

The world, and particularly Africa, from now on is looking to you, Libyans. They consider us as the driving engine of Africa, the decisive factor, the dynamic force, the source of support, supply, aid, political solutions, military assistance, economic aid, loans, donations, trusts, arms, opinion and advice. America and Europe now are envious of Libya's prestige.

Gaddafi's vision turned into the African Union, a bureaucratic structure that replaced the regional talking shop, the Organization of African Unity, but which stopped far short of being the governing body of a United States of Africa. AU summits saw regular clashes between Gaddafi and the South African leader, Thabo Mbeki, who regarded the Libyan leader's vision as at best utopian and at worst a vehicle for his malign ambition. "Gaddafi influenced events because he was a very insistent man," recalls Patrick Mazimhaka, a Rwandan who worked as a senior official in the AU secretariat in Addis Ababa. "Those who didn't like his program for a United States of Africa just had to use delaying tactics." Gaddafi designed the AU flag in—of course—his favorite color, green. He paid 15 percent of the costs to run the AU and the dues of those countries too poor or too uninterested to pay. "If you don't pay, you don't vote!" points out Patrick Mazimhaka. "So it was a strategic payment to get his ideas through the

AU." But Gaddafi failed to get the AU headquarters relocated to Sirte—there was a limit to how far African leaders would become beholden to the Leader.

As African leaders like Mbeki tried to present a modern face of the continent, and Western countries made aid increasingly dependent on what they called "good governance" and progress toward democracy, Gaddafi tried to pull the continent in a different direction. "We don't want your democracy," he said at a summit in Sirte in 2005. Gaddafi grew frustrated with the intransigence of leaders like Mbeki, who blocked a debate on his plan to scrap all borders in Africa, so he took matters into his own hands, put together a long caravan of vehicles and drove across the continent along back roads and through the desert. "He took his soldiers, his vehicles and some camels and just passed through," recalls Patrick Mazimhaka. "Most of the borders in Africa are unguarded. He did it in West Africa, and then he drove from South Africa to Swaziland, Mozambique and Malawi. It was just to prove his point that those borders couldn't be defended by anyone."

Alhaj Habib Kagimu, one of Uganda's most successful businessmen, was Gaddafi's host whenever he visited Kampala. Their connection went back a long way. In 1971, at age fourteen, Habib had won a scholarship to Benghazi, part of a scheme started by King Idris and continued by Gaddafi to provide educations for Muslim boys from around the world. Most Ugandans are Christians, but Muslims make up a significant minority. Two years later, when Idi Amin visited for the first time, Habib was taken to Tripoli to represent Ugandan students. "Gaddafi was very impressed when I spoke classical Arabic," recalled Habib. "He said to Amin, 'This young man speaks Arabic better than I do!'" From then on, whenever Amin was in Libya, Gaddafi insisted that he bring the young Ugandan to visit. Habib married a Libyan and stayed in his adopted homeland during the years when Milton Obote governed Uganda. Gaddafi hated Obote, because he had ousted Amin. He armed a new guerrilla group, the

National Resistance Army, led by a dynamic young leader, Yoweri Muse-veni. For once, Gaddafi and the West were on the same side. Obote had brought even more killing and mayhem to Uganda than Amin. Museveni won a bush war, and promised better. He restored a degree of stability and prosperity to Uganda, after the long years of violence and misrule. Habib went home.

I met Habib Kagimu over lattes in a five-star London hotel. He had brought his lawyer along as a witness. "I don't normally give interviews," he said. He drummed his fingers on the table and shifted in his chair, full of pent-up energy and enthusiasm. He was funny and flirtatious, keen, despite his stated reluctance, to give me a different picture of a man he regarded as a friend. In 2001, Gaddafi attended Museveni's swearing-in after he was elected president. It was a time when the Guide was thinking about the tribal nature of Libyan society and whether it could be har-nessed more effectively than through the almost moribund revolutionary committees. "At the function he was introduced to our traditional lead-ers," recalled Habib. "He was amazed." Habib explained to Gaddafi how, although Uganda was a republic, it had restored the traditional kingdoms as a form of customary authority, because many Ugandans still respected their tribal leaders. The kingdoms of Uganda had existed before the Brit-ish colonized the country but had been suppressed under Amin and Obote. Now they had to accept the central government but could mediate in disputes and local matters that had always been the responsibility of the tribe. "This is a wonderful idea—if only we had something like that in Libya!" responded Gaddafi, and he promptly invited the kings and queens of Uganda to Tripoli.

So began Gaddafi's liaison with the kingdom of Toro in southwestern Uganda. King Rukiraba Saija Oyo Nyimba Kabamba Iguru Rukidi IV was only three when he ascended the throne in 1995. During their visit to Tripoli, his guardians invited Gaddafi to attend the *empango*, the anniver-sary of his coronation. Habib Kagimu accompanied the Brother Leader as they drove from Kampala. "The convoy must have been three hundred vehicles," he recalled. "There was a massive bus with his bedroom onboard. I couldn't believe the numbers of people who came out to see him—there were crowds at the side of the road in every town and village. He stopped at every point to embrace people." Here, in the heart of Africa, Gaddafi got the adulation he craved. It must be said that any three-hundred-vehicle convoy would draw curiosity and excitement in the placid villages of western Uganda, but Gaddafi was generous. He saw a lame man sitting on a mound and instructed his aides to buy him a wheelchair. He stopped to talk to women in their traditional *basuti* dresses. He let children grab hold of his robe. "The bodyguards were not impressed—they said he'd catch a disease. I said, 'I can't tell him, you tell him!'" recalled Habib. The two-hundred-mile journey to Fort Portal took two days. Gaddafi loved the people and the subtropical vegetation. His favorite color was everywhere—few places on earth are quite as green as Uganda. When he saw the king of Toro's ruined palace, he immediately offered to rebuild it. He bought the young king homes in Kampala and London, and helped fund his education.

Habib is reluctant to talk about Gaddafi's relationship with the Toro queen mother, Omujwera Best Olumi Kemigisa Akiiki. "It would be unfair to personalize," he said. The Ugandan newspapers carried stories of lavish gifts Gaddafi reportedly gave her, until the Libyan embassy sued, and Uganda's Media Council found that speculation about their relationship was damaging relations between the two countries. She described him as her "best friend," and made him an honorary guardian of her son. In 2008 he appointed her secretary general of the Conference of African Traditional Leaders, founded when he invited two hundred tribal chiefs, kings, queens, princes, sultans and sheikhs from all over the continent to a gathering in Benghazi. There they proclaimed him King of Kings of Africa. It was a title he was only too happy to adopt, but Africa's political leaders were getting suspicious that he was undermining their authority.

When he tried to hold a follow-up meeting in Uganda, inviting traditional leaders from around the continent whose positions were unrecognized or even proscribed by their governments, President Museveni swiftly banned the event.

Gaddafi transformed the Kampala skyline by building a huge mosque on the ruins of what had been the house of Sir Frederick Lugard, the British military administrator of Uganda at the end of the nineteenth century. It appealed to his anticolonial ideas. As he was driving Gaddafi around the city on his 2001 visit, Habib explained that the British had divided the city's land among all religions except the Muslims. Idi Amin had given a hill to the Muslims as compensation, but the mosque had never been completed. "Gaddafi said his people should build the best mosque in Africa, whatever it costs," Habib recalled. "He attended the opening."

African leaders liked such grandiose gestures, but they grew impatient with Libya's haphazard investment in Africa. President Museveni told Gaddafi that his dream of a United States of Africa with a million-strong army was meaningless without economic progress. "Museveni told a delegation from the Leader that Africa needed a union of stomachs before a union of politics," said Habib. "Instead of pushing for political union, he should push for investment in Africa." In response, Gaddafi created the $5 billion Libya African Investment Portfolio. In Uganda, they invested in hotels, coffee processing and textiles and bought a 69 percent share in Uganda Telecom. Habib, who was by then chair of the East African subsidiary of Tamoil, a Libya-owned company running gas stations in Europe, grew frustrated. He ran his own successful investment company and felt he knew what needed to be done. "I told Gaddafi personally that if you don't have serious management it will lead to very little change. He was nationalistic. He wanted Libyans in charge. I said you should buy in European and American management expertise. If they had done that they would have had a more profound effect."

But Gaddafi was not a man for practical detail, and he started looking for increasingly novel ways to prevail in Africa at the expense of the West. Even tropical diseases and AIDS could be a weapon against Europe and America, he suggested to a baffled assembly of African leaders in Mozambique one year. "AIDS is a peaceful virus. Don't be scared; it is not an aggressive virus," he said. "If they come to our continent to establish bases and occupy it for a second time, the tsetse fly, malaria, AIDS and all other diseases will kill them. God will unleash them. These are armies sent by God to defend Africa." It was a new vision of Africa as the white man's grave.

"Begging," said Gaddafi, "does not make the future of any country and cannot make the future of Africa." But while he railed against Western aid programs, his own actions turned Africans into beggars. Razia Sholeh, a protocol official in the Foreign Ministry, accompanied the Guide—as she always called him—to Mali.

"I had to go to the market in Bamako to buy clothes for men, women and children," she said. I asked her how much money Gaddafi gave her to spend on the Malian poor.

"A million dollars."

"A million dollars!" I couldn't believe I had heard right. "In cash?"

"Yes, a million in cash. I had to change it into Malian money."

I remembered a visit I once paid to the market in Bamako, wandering around stalls of secondhand clothes, vegetables, baskets, carved wooden masks and the intriguing corner where they sell fetishes—bones, dried toads, snakes in bottles.

"Is it possible to spend a million dollars in the market in Bamako?"

"Well, I bought clothes, and others bought things like food. And what we couldn't spend we just gave out in envelopes of money. It made me happy to do it. People in Libya often resent how much money the Guide gave to Africa, but the people there are poor, and I think it was a good thing to do."

As foreign companies returned to Libya, and the economy started to grow, high-rise hotels and office blocks were built along the shorefront in Tripoli. Every month at least one African leader would turn up at the Guide's invitation to be accommodated in the five-star Corinthia Hotel, the haunt of oilmen and others cashing in on Libya's newfound prosperity. It was Razia's job to entertain African first ladies. A young, cosmopolitan woman who spoke French and English, and happened to be very close to Gaddafi's wife and daughters, she was the ideal hostess. She took wives, daughters (and probably the occasional mistress) around the ruins at Lepcis Magna, the Tripoli Museum and sometimes the Green Mountain near Beyda or the cave paintings in the desert near Sabha. She soon figured out what her guests liked best. "I learned always to wear flat shoes," she recalled. "We had to spend four or five hours every day shopping. They loved shopping more than anything." Pocket money was provided.

"What did they buy?" I asked, trying to imagine what Gargaresh, a somewhat broken-down street of small shops, had to offer that the first ladies couldn't find on the Champs Élysées or Bond Street. "Anything," she replied. "Clothes, shoes. Whatever they could find."

After the uprising started in February 2011, African leaders issued a statement condemning the violence meted out to protesters in Tripoli and Benghazi, but—in contrast to Western countries—they urged compromise to bring the conflict to a close. When the International Criminal Court issued arrest warrants for Gaddafi, Seif and Sanussi, they pointed out that since the court was created in 1998, it had prosecuted only Africans—Libya was just the latest. They put forward a plan for a ceasefire and a transition to democracy. South African president Jacob Zuma went to see Gaddafi in Tripoli. Having brought an end to apartheid through a long process of negotiation, the South Africans tend to believe that any conflict, however bitter, can be solved by compromise. Gaddafi said he accepted, but the National Transitional Council in

Benghazi—which by then had NATO on its side—wasn't interested in the plan, because it didn't require the Brother Leader to step down. He said that he had no position to step down from—he was just the Guide, not the president. NATO countries, having committed themselves to bombing, purportedly "to protect civilians," were not about to stop for what they believed would be a long, drawn-out process during which Gaddafi's forces would consolidate. The AU plan was never taken seriously, because the AU was seen as Gaddafi's creature.

"I am really feeling sorry for the suffering the people are going through. It is really bad and a trying time for my best friend, President Muammar Gaddafi," said Best Kemigisa, the queen mother of Toro. Habib Kagimu was more outspoken. "There were two opposing forces in Libya," he said. "If they had followed the plan of the AU, which the Europeans arrogantly ignored, there could have been a reasonable compromise." To Habib's mind it only went to prove that Gaddafi was right about one thing: You can't trust colonialists. "He made a deal to give up his WMD. The only reason they attacked him was because he was weak. They wanted to take revenge for his so-called terrorist attacks from before." Habib grew more animated. "The way we Africans look at it, the West thinks they own the world. They have the attitude that you must do as you're told, or else you'll be bombed."

Habib refused to tell me if he had spoken to Gaddafi after the uprising started, but he seemed to know what the Brother Leader had been thinking as his erstwhile NATO allies attacked him and his African friends found themselves unable to help. "He knew nothing would change his destiny," said Habib. "He was taken by overwhelming force. He decided he was going to die in Libya. He knew that NATO was targeting him, and whatever measures he took were just delaying the inevitable."

CHAPTER SEVEN

SONS AND DAUGHTERS

Love and fear. Everything the father of a family says
must inspire one or the other.

—JOSEPH JOUBERT, *THE NOTEBOOKS OF JOSEPH JOUBERT*

I think it is inevitable that, by virtue of who my father is,
the way I live my life is not identical to the way that an
ordinary Libyan citizen would. It is, of course, true that I
am afforded certain privileges which other Libyan people
might not be.

—SEIF AL-ISLAM GADDAFI, CLAIMANT WITNESS STATEMENT, 2000

Seif al-Islam, Gaddafi's second son, set himself up as the only person who
could move Libya beyond dictatorship. With his fluent English and cosmopolitan ease, he made a convincing case. I met Seif in late 2003, when a
Lebanese friend called to say he wanted to introduce me to someone
important. The following evening, I was ushered into a luxurious apartment near Harrods. Seif was sitting at the far end of a huge room, with
cushions on the floor around the walls, in the Arabic style. He was wearing casual, Western clothes, his hair was short, and his face smooth. We
drank tea, and he tried to convince me that Libya was changing, journalists could now work freely, reporting and filming as they wished. The
following morning I got a call from an aide, inviting me to accompany Seif

to Tripoli on his private plane that very day—an offer I reluctantly refused, as I couldn't drop everything else to go. I had the feeling that he was keen to prove something that wasn't quite true; other reporters had gone to Libya with Seif and found that once they emerged from his protective shield the same old rules applied—everyone was afraid to talk, and you could be arrested for filming on the street.

But on many occasions his contacts and charm worked. An early success came in 1999, when he helped negotiate the release of Western hostages captured by the Abu Sayyaf group in the Philippines, channeling ransom money through his Gaddafi International Charity and Development Foundation. In the first decade of the twenty-first century, he became the face of a North African glasnost, an opening up that his supporters in the West thought might—as had happened in the Soviet Union three decades earlier—lead to a perestroika, a restructuring of the system. He was instrumental in persuading his father to compensate the victims of Lockerbie, the Berlin discothèque bombing and the downing of the UTA flight over Niger. He managed the release of five Bulgarian nurses and a Palestinian doctor who had been imprisoned and tortured in Benghazi on an unproven allegation that they had willfully infected children with the AIDS virus. Determined that Libya should cast off its pariah status, get sanctions lifted and be accepted back into the world, he led negotiations on abandoning weapons of mass destruction. Gradually, it became clear that he was his father's heir apparent, and anyone who wanted to do business in Libya had to do business with him.

A court case from 2000, when Seif was twenty-eight and just emerging into the limelight, gives an intriguing insight into his view of himself. He was suing the *Daily Telegraph* newspaper for libel—a case he won, as they had accused him of several crimes for which they had no proof. In a personal statement, which he wrote to explain his background for the benefit of the court, he explains that his feelings were hurt by allegations that he was corrupt or dishonest. What fascinates is the breathtaking sense of entitlement and the inability to distinguish between himself and the country his father ruled that the document displays. Despite his famous name, writes Seif, he is a normal student with normal hobbies, such as reading, painting, working out, falconry and keeping pet tigers. He had breached no international convention by bringing his beloved white tigers to Austria, where he was studying for an MBA—at least not knowingly, because someone else dealt with the paperwork. "When I arrived in Vienna, I discussed the tigers with the Mayor of the City, and with the head of the Schonnbrun Zoo," he writes. "They both said they would be delighted to have my tigers, which are very rare, in Vienna, and we therefore arranged for them to be transported. . . . I was certainly delighted to have my tigers nearby, because it meant that I was able to go and see them and play with them."

Keen to prove that he was not a representative of the government, he writes that he is just an ordinary Libyan student, albeit one with certain privileges, such as being chauffeured around Vienna in a car with diplomatic plates and living in a house with a swimming pool and sauna. His enthusiasm about the accommodating nature of the Austrian authorities is tempered some time later, when they fail to extend his residency permit. "Fortunately the Libyan government treated this insult to me very seriously and threatened to deny Austrians visas to enter Libya if the decision was not revoked. The Austrians changed their mind very quickly, and I was allowed to stay," he wrote. He thinks back to previous insults. "A similar incident occurred in Switzerland in 1997 when the Swiss government refused to extend my visa and the Libyan government threatened sanctions."

The document provides a glimpse of home life chez Gaddafi at Bab al Aziziyah. "I am close to my father, and talk a lot to him when I see him, often about our family, but sometimes also about public affairs, on which we sometimes disagree (although we do not often fall out!)." I love the parentheses and the exclamation mark, like a child who is rather proud of himself for daring to defy his dad. "I know that I have taken many qualities from my father," he quickly adds. "Especially my religious faith and my love of reading."

He had an unusual circle of friends. At a party in Vienna he bonded with the Austrian fascist Jörg Haider over their mutual dislike of the then Austrian government that had tried to revoke his visa. He introduced his new friend to his father, and the acquaintance resulted in several successful business deals. He denies that he was a friend of Saddam Hussein's son Uday, saying it was just that "on the occasion of his severe injury, my brothers and I sent a letter wishing him a speedy recovery." (Uday's injuries were sustained in an assassination attempt in 1996—he survived, unlike his father's valet, whom Uday had murdered with an electric carving knife at a party eight years earlier.)

As he developed his reputation as a reformer, Seif al-Islam found himself invited to gatherings of the wealthy and influential. He spoke at the World Economic Forum at Davos in Switzerland, met Prince Andrew and was invited to parties at Nat Rothschild's house in Corfu, where he mixed with the Russian aluminum tycoon Oleg Deripaska and Tony Blair's close associate Peter Mandelson. He celebrated his thirty-seventh birthday at the Hotel Splendid in Montenegro—a local society columnist noted the seventy-nine-yard and sixty-nine-yard luxury yachts moored nearby and the dozen Lear jets that arrived the day before, bringing guests reportedly including Prince Albert of Monaco, the Canadian gold magnate Peter Munk and the steel tycoon Lakshmi Mittal. It was, said the columnist, not dissimilar to parties Seif had thrown in Monaco and Saint-Tropez, and definitely was "the most glamorous party ever seen before in the entire Adriatic."

While Libya was emerging from isolation, the regime was becoming less of a dictatorship and more of a mafia. The Brother Leader, who had once argued that the tribe was a backward concept, now trusted only those within his own clan. Three tribes—his own Gaddafa, the Mergaha from Sabha and the country's biggest tribe, the Warfalla, supported the regime. There were dissidents within each tribe, but the leaders were with Gaddafi, and most families followed the crowd. Almost every other tribe was regarded as suspect. Gaddafi's cousins and in-laws had always been appointed to senior positions, but now it was the children's turn. Libya was growing prosperous, the old socialist policies long forgotten. They picked whichever businesses and franchises they wanted: telcoms, football clubs, shipping, soft drinks—all were controlled by the sons. They were seemingly unaware of how bizarre or terrifying they might appear to the outside world. Rivalry between the brothers was a substitute for politics, and sometimes turned to violence. When Mohammed—Gaddafi's son by his first wife—quarreled with Mutassim—the fifth son—over ownership of the Tripoli Coca-Cola bottling plant, Mutassim's men abducted and beat up a relative of Mohammed's on his mother's side. Mohammed and Saadi supported rival football teams—on one occasion, fans of Al Ittihad, Mohammed's team, invaded the pitch, and Saadi sat and watched from his special place in the stand as uniformed men restored order by shooting into the crowd, killing at least twenty. The fans marched through the streets of Tripoli burning green flags and shouting slogans against father and sons. Any family that wanted the body of their son or husband back had to sign a form saying he was a football hooligan and the state was not culpable in his death.

Mutassim, who held the rank of lieutenant colonel, felt that he would be a far better successor than Seif. He found it hard to wait; in 2001, at age twenty-three, he tried to mount a coup against his father and was banished to Egypt. "I found myself involved," said Abdelsalam Abu Zitaya, a distant relative of Gaddafi's who worked as a guard at Bab al Aziziyah, who I met in October 2011. He was reluctant to explain the role he had played, saying only that he had been imprisoned after the failure of the coup and sentenced to death. He was freed after six months but doesn't think it was Mutassim who argued on his behalf. "Mutassim threatened to kill me," he said. "He is heartless and bloody. I lived in hell, because I was caught up in the conflict within the family." Every Friday, he said, the family would gather at Bab al Aziziyah, but if Seif came, then Mutassim would not. They were not on speaking terms.

Gaddafi saw himself as some kind of supranational leader, King of Kings of Africa, and an elder statesman, presiding over a kingdom he had bequeathed to his sons. Sometimes he tasked his daughter Aisha with mediating between them, while at other times he tried to manage their rivalry himself. When President Mubarak of Egypt persuaded Gaddafi to let the errant Mutassim return to Libya—possibly because he didn't want him in Egypt any longer—Gaddafi made him national security adviser. The position had no place in the government hierarchy or bureaucracy—it was simply a gift from father to son. Mutassim was sent on diplomatic missions, notably to Washington in 2009, where he met U.S. secretary of state Hillary Clinton. A tall, slim young man, with long, dark hair and fashionable stubble, he shook her hand and smiled for the photo op. "We are delighted to welcome you to the State Department, Mr. Minister," she said, a formulation of words that was presumably worked out with the Libyans in advance, as Mutassim was not a minister at all.

Mutassim wanted to have his own militia, maybe because his younger brother, Khamis, was in charge of the Thirty-second Brigade and had just ordered $165 million in communications and other equipment from General Dynamics UK, a contract facilitated by Tony Blair. He sent his envoys to demand $1.2 billion in cash or oil shipments from the National Oil Corporation to fund his new project. The head of the NOC, former prime minister Shukri Ghanem, a reformer who was close to Seif, went to see Colonel Gaddafi, who reportedly laughed, and told him to ignore the request. Ghanem survived in his post, but others were not so lucky. Giuma Atigha, the lawyer who had witnessed the Abu Salim massacre and gone on to be a human rights adviser to Seif, found himself caught in the rivalry between the brothers. He had resigned his position but carried on giving lectures and writing about reform. Mutassim and his allies within the security establishment didn't like his liberal views, so in 2009, he was rearrested on the same trumped-up murder charge that had been dismissed by the court nearly twenty years before. He spent two weeks in jail before Seif managed to have him released. Giuma had got the message. "It was a warning," he said. "I became very cautious."

For those who want to live a playboy lifestyle, Tripoli is not the place. For a start, there are no nightclubs. Alcohol is banned, so if you want to drink you must do it at home. For real fun, the Gaddafi brothers had to travel. The suspension and then lifting of sanctions enabled them to live the glamorous lifestyle they craved. Talitha van Zon, a Dutch model who had once been a *Playboy* centerfold, began an affair with Mutassim after meeting him at a nightclub in Rome in 2004. He bought her an entire collection of Louis Vuitton bags, took her to the Grand Prix in Monaco and flew her in his private jet to the exclusive Caribbean island of St. Barts where stars such as Beyoncé and Mariah Carey would perform at Gaddafi family private parties. He told her he spent about $2 million a month on travel, gifts and parties. "He worshipped his father," she told a British journalist. "He talked a lot about Hitler, Fidel Castro, Hugo Chavez. He liked leaders who had a lot of power."

Mutassim seems to have been close to his brother Hannibal, who was two years older, and not interested in vying for power. Politics seems to have interested him only inasmuch as the family name enabled him to avoid prosecution in European capitals where he vented his violent temper. Between 2001 and 2009 he variously assaulted three police officers in Rome; attacked French traffic police after being stopped for speeding the wrong way down the Champs Élysées; received a four-year suspended sentence in France for beating up his pregnant girlfriend; was arrested with his wife, Aline, in Geneva after they assaulted two of their staff in the President Wilson Hotel; and narrowly escaped arrest in London in 2009 after he broke Aline's nose on Christmas Day in their $6,400-a-night suite in Claridge's.

In the last instance, the Libyan embassy intervened, claiming Hannibal had diplomatic immunity. As trade with Libya was booming by then, with BP and a dozen other companies having signed lucrative contracts, the British Foreign Office was in no mood to argue. After all, everyone knew what had happened to the Swiss. Following the incident in Geneva, Libya imposed trade sanctions, stopped oil supplies, withdrew $5 billion from Swiss banks, canceled all flights, recalled its ambassador, refused to issue visas to Swiss citizens and ordered the arrest of two Swiss businessmen, who ended up sheltering in the Swiss embassy in Tripoli for more than a year. (Colonel Gaddafi's ire was increased by a referendum in November 2009 in which the Swiss voted to ban the construction of minarets.) He submitted a proposal to the UN suggesting that Switzerland be abolished and the land divided up among Germany, France and Italy. The Swiss president, Hans-Rudolf Merz, eventually flew to Tripoli to deliver an "official and public apology for the unjustified and unnecessary arrests," while $1.2 million was paid into a German account as compensation, after a September 2009 edition of the newspaper *La Tribune de Genève* published police mug shots of Hannibal.

It was not easy to say no to Hannibal. When UN sanctions were suspended in 1999, Morajea Karim—the naval officer who had struggled to keep Libya's merchant navy going through the difficult days of the seventies and eighties—was appointed CEO of the General National Maritime Transport Company. Frustrated after failing to get the government bureaucracy to sign off on guarantees the company needed for a loan from a British bank, he resigned. Hannibal, who had trained at the Marine Academy and saw shipping as his preserve, was displeased. "He rang me from Spain to say I couldn't leave," recalls Morajea. "I said the prime minister had signed me off." Hannibal replied: "The prime minister means nothing. I want you to stay." Eventually a deal was done. Morajea could leave, but he now had to create a private shipping company for Hannibal.

The company made $1 million in its first year, through brokerage work and contracting ships to the National Oil Company. "He was the owner and I was the general manager," said Morajea. "His whole way of working was odd. He would call me at midnight and say, for example, 'Tomorrow before noon, you must send $100,000 to X in Lebanon.'" Morajea, fearing that he might be accused of corruption or theft, asked for written instructions. "He would say that for security reasons names could not be written down. Sometimes the amounts could reach millions." Morajea did as he was instructed. Hannibal was moody, and there was no question of countermanding his orders or challenging his opinion. The fear Hannibal inspired was such that no one would use his name on the phone. "If I needed to refer to him I'd say 'the top guy,'" said Morajea, who gradually eased himself out, until he was just a consultant to the company.

The week Tripoli fell I persuaded a group of fighters to take me into a compound that Mutassim and Hannibal had shared in the Ben Ashur district of the capital. Curious neighbors came too—never before had they been able to see beyond the sixty-feet-high concrete walls that surrounded the manicured gardens and single-story concrete mansions within. It didn't seem to be a residence; there was little furniture, and some of it was half built. Inside one building we found a group of local men trying to force open a massive, pale green metal security door with a combination lock, the kind you might find at the entrance to a bank vault. They couldn't do it, but another beckoned us to a door that had already been forced, and we walked downstairs into a labyrinth of subterranean passages. The corridors forked and divided, some routes blocked by more vault doors. We found a hospital, complete with several wards and an operating theater, medical instruments carefully stowed in cabinets. The rooms were not luxurious; they had more the feel of a nuclear bunker, but one which seemed to extend for miles. The passages were painted white and had no decoration. After a while I began to feel disoriented and confused—each passage was identical, but some seemed to be leading downhill and others were level. It was impossible to know if we were going deeper into the earth or where we might end up. The neighbors were fascinated but afraid—could someone still be hiding down here? The fighters readied their weapons as we walked around the corners. None of us knew where Hannibal or Mutassim were; it suddenly seemed possible that they might be lurking in the silence of their bunker, waiting to make their last stand.

I stopped to look through a pile of books heaped on the floor in one of the side rooms. I found a manual for an electronic target system made in Saudi Arabia and a report by a British company, Janes, on the reorganization of the Libyan Armed Forces. In among the catalogs for weapons I came across a paperback with careful underlinings and bookmarks. It was entitled: *The Only Book of Astrology You'll Ever Need*. "Libra," it said on a marked-up page. "You are known for being charming." I laughed. "Charming" was not a word I had heard to describe Hannibal or Mutassim. I flicked through the pages about destiny and the stars. Mutassim and Hannibal had tried to look into the future, but I doubt they foresaw their fate.

A few days later I went to Saadi's beach house, which was in the center of Tripoli near the Corintha Hotel. A few fighters were camped on the sand in front, playing with the Jet Skis that Gaddafi's third son used to use to get to a little island, half a mile out to sea, where he also moored his speedboats. I climbed into the villa through a broken window and picked my way through the debris—anything that hadn't been looted had been trashed, and graffiti had been sprayed on the walls inside and out. Libyans frequently hated the sons more than the father. It wasn't that anyone necessarily wanted to use the rocky outcrop in the bay, but it was a daily affront to see it and know that only Saadi and his guests could go there. Gaddafi's speeches about how the Libyan people were the real rulers of the country, and he was just an adviser and guide, a simple Bedouin living in his tent longing for the desert, seemed more insulting when Libyans thought about the behavior of the Gaddafi children.

Like all the brothers, Saadi seemed to have unlimited wealth, the source of which was never clear. His interference in football made him particularly unpopular. He had made himself president of the Libyan Football Federation, captain of the national team and captain of Tripoli Al Ahly, even though he had failed drugs tests and was an indifferent player at best. No one forgot how he had destroyed Benghazi Al Ahly, and watched as the supporters of Al Ittihad, his brother Mohammed's favorite team, were killed. Libya never qualified for the World Cup, which didn't help either. Rumors abounded that he was bisexual, which went down badly in conservative Libya, as well as the reports that all the brothers drank, took drugs and went to prostitutes. At one point Saadi invested in a film company in Hollywood called Natural Selection. His name appears in the credits as associate producer of a film the company made: *The Experiment*, starring Forest Whitaker, which was never shown in cinemas but went straight to DVD. "Twenty-six men are chosen to participate in the roles of guards and prisoners in a psychological study that ultimately spirals out of control," says the blurb on the Web site. To Saadi it might have been fiction but to many of his compatriots such experiences were only too real.

Razia Sholeh—the young protocol officer who escorted visiting first ladies and accompanied Colonel Gaddafi around Africa—had another view of the family. At thirty-five, she was a high-flyer in the Foreign Ministry, and her marriage to a relative of the Gaddafis ensured that she could penetrate if not the inner, at least the outer circle. She had studied political science in Paris and, unlike most Libyan women, didn't wear the head scarf, instead pulling her dark wavy hair back in a scrunchy decorated with a black cloth flower; instead of a tunic covering her thighs, she wore neatly cut waist-length jackets with jeans or black trousers and high heels. She became part of the entourage attached to the female members of the

Gaddafi family. "Safia wasn't like other first ladies," recalled Razia. "She was always with the family, the children and grandchildren. She didn't want to be known, to make speeches or anything like that." Razia became almost part of the family.

She was especially fond of Hana, the adopted daughter who she said had been named after the toddler killed in the 1986 bombing (and others said was the same child). The "new" Hana, Razia said, was Gaddafi's favorite, his little darling, his pet. As she grew up, the other Gaddafi children learned to go through her if they wanted to tell their father something unwelcome—they knew she had his ear. "She adored her father," Razia recalled. "I was with her and the daughter of the president of Burkina Faso, walking around Tripoli, when we saw a big picture of her father. I will never forget it. She said: 'I love that person. If he dies, I want to die with him.'" It worried Razia. Hana was thirteen at the time, and Razia knew that in five years she would be told the truth, that she was not Gaddafi's natural but rather his adopted daughter. This was the Libyan way, she explained; an adopted child would be told of his or her true origins only when he or she was eighteen and deemed old enough to cope. "I was with Hana after he told her," she recollected. "She was in shock. She cried. I think it was very tough for her for a couple of years, until she learned to accept it."

Razia was also close to Aisha, Gaddafi and Safia's only biological daughter. Like the wives of the younger generation of Arab leaders—Asma al Assad of Syria and Queen Rania, the wife of King Abdullah of Jordan—Aisha presented herself as the modern face of Arab womanhood: glamorous, socially concerned, at ease in New York or London but unquestioningly supportive of the big man who ruled back home. Trained as a lawyer, Aisha was ferocious in defense of her father. "She's very strong, just like him," Razia said. "She hates to cry. Sometimes, the look on her face is just like him." Aisha's face could be seen on a gift from her father placed in the entrance hall to her luxury villa in eastern Tripoli: a sofa with a golden frame in the shape of a mermaid. Aisha's head rose at one end, long hair sculpted to sweep along the sofa back, while her bare-breasted torso morphed into a scaly tail extending beneath the cushions. By the time I got to see it fighters had knocked the face out, so you could see into Aisha's hollow golden head, evidence not just of gross bad taste but of the fury the Gaddafi family inspired.

Aisha was rich—Razia said she couldn't be sure where, exactly, the money had come from—and generous, sponsoring projects for the poor and deprived. The problem was, the poor and deprived didn't benefit. Others creamed off the money, it seemed, and Aisha never had the time to follow up or find out what was going on. "She had these associations for orphans and the destitute, but on the ground there was nothing," said Razia. Aisha was part of Saddam Hussein's defense team after he was charged with war crimes, genocide and crimes against humanity—the Iraqi leader was, after all, a family friend. After a while she moved onto the international stage, becoming a UN goodwill ambassador for something or other. Razia couldn't remember for what exactly, but she thought it might have been peace.

As I listened to Razia, a line from Joan Didion came into my head: "We tell ourselves stories in order to live." Those who support the insupportable have a lot of stories to tell. Razia sounded like a mother whose son has fallen into a life of crime—he didn't mean it, he fell in with a bad lot, you have to give him another chance. It's never the leader but those around the leader. Never the intention, just the unforeseen outcome. Razia didn't blame Gaddafi or his children for what had gone wrong, but those closest to them, who hadn't told them the truth. She listed some officials. They said everyone loved the Gaddafis, and that wasn't true. The neglect of eastern Libya? That was the fault of the Benghazi authorities who had failed to spend well the money that Gaddafi had given them. The murder of 1,270 men at Abu Salim? That was the fault of his brother-in-law, Abdullah al Sanussi. I suggested in that case, maybe Sanussi should have been fired. Or put on trial. She thought about it and shook her head. Not possible. Sanussi was married to Safia's sister, Fatima, so obviously he couldn't be fired. What was more, he was from Sabha, in the desert south, so if he had lost his job, his tribesmen would have risen against Gaddafi. Not just Sabha, but Bani Walid and Sirte would have joined in too. It was a shame—she didn't like Abdullah al Sanussi one little bit—but there was no way to get rid of him. "We're a family country," she said. "That's how it works in Libya."

Tarek Ben Halim came from an important family too. He grew up in Tripoli in the 1960s, during the reign of King Idris. When he went to the movies with his brothers and sisters, they never had to pay for tickets but were respectfully ushered straight in. One day a magnificent elderly woman with dyed black hair in a beehive style came to visit—it was the Egyptian singer Umm Kulthum, the "star of the east," the most famous woman in the Arab world. Tarek's father, Mustafa, had been prime minister of Libya in the 1950s and remained close to King Idris and Queen Fatima, entertaining sheikhs and princes at the family home and numbering King Feisal of Saudi Arabia and Lord Mountbatten among his friends. Every summer the family would decamp to Europe for six weeks, returning at the end of August before the school term started.

In the summer of 1969 Tarek's mother, Yusra, suffered a minor ailment, so they delayed their return to Tripoli from Geneva, where they had been staying, rebooking their tickets for September 2nd. On September 1st, the coup that brought Gaddafi to power changed their world. Overnight the Ben Halim family went from being part of a secure elite to refugees on the run, moving between Lebanon, London and Saudi Arabia. Tarek was thirteen; it would be thirty-six years before he returned to his homeland. By then he had long since lost the sense of entitlement he had enjoyed in his youth. "I firmly believe that the Middle East needs relief from the self-serving, unrepresentative governments that have, with few exceptions, ruled the Arab world since the 19th century," he wrote in an opinion piece for an American newspaper. "Wealthy people are prepared to see poor people as beneath them. As Arabs, we should do something about it."

In 2003, Tarek gave up a lucrative career as an investment banker and started looking for a way to use his skills and money in the interests of democracy. I met him when he worked briefly for the ill-fated Coalition Provisional Authority, advising on the privatization of Iraq's inefficient and corrupt state-owned companies. Disillusion set in quickly, and he told me that he felt his bosses were more interested in promoting the ideology of the Bush White House than in doing what was best to help Iraqis. He started a "venture philanthropy fund," investing his own resources and those of a few wealthy Arab friends to finance projects in Egypt that were intended to promote social change. Then, in 2004, another prominent Libyan son came to him with a proposition: Come back and do something for your own country. Seif al-Islam Gaddafi wanted Tarek as part of his project to reform Libya.

In September 2004 Tarek and his older brother Amr climbed the steps onto the private jet Seif had been lent to take them from Malta to Tripoli. It was not a comfortable moment. Tarek found himself thinking back to the day in 1970 when, while brushing his teeth in the morning at boarding school, another boy said to him: "Oh, did you hear? Your father's been kidnapped." He dropped his toothbrush, ran down the hill to the pay phone and called home. It was true. His father, who campaigned against Gaddafi from exile, had been hijacked by armed men while driving home from his office in Beirut. He was beaten up, stuffed into the trunk of a car and driven toward the Syrian border. But just as some kindly fate had intervened to keep the family out of Libya on the day of the coup, his father miraculously survived this ordeal too. It was the beginning of the era of hostage taking in Beirut. The kidnappers, it later emerged, were from a Palestinian extremist group allied to the Syrians and paid by Gaddafi. Driving along roads made slippery by early rains, the driver lost control of the vehicle, which careered off the verge opposite the last restaurant before the border. The kidnappers fled, leaving Mustafa to shout from the car trunk until people came out of the restaurant and rescued him. Thirty-five years later, Tarek leaned back in the seat of the luxury jet and—for just a moment—wondered if this invitation was an elaborate hoax, another kidnap attempt on the Ben Halims. Only this time they had willingly put themselves at the mercy of the Gaddafis.

Tarek had told Seif he would only go to Libya if he could visit the family home. Gaddafi had given the magnificent villa of his childhood to the Islamic Republic of Iran to use as an embassy. He knocked on the door and, as it opened, said: "I am Tarek Ben Halim and this is my house." The Iranians had been warned. He was politely ushered in and allowed to stand downstairs for a while. (A few years later, on a trip with his American wife, Cynthia, and their three children, the Iranian ambassador invited the family upstairs for tea and pistachios.) Tripoli was not as he had remembered it. The façades of the old Italianate buildings had crumbled, and sewage ran in the backstreets, in contrast with the new glass-and-concrete towers under construction along the seafront. Gaddafi's face was like a malevolent Mona Lisa, eyes following Tarek everywhere from billboards and murals, a constant reminder that change would not come easily.

Seif told him that Libya had to modernize, to move into a transition period, to become more representative. All over the Arab world sons were following the fathers, talking of reform—Bashar al Assad in Syria, King Mohammed VI in Morocco, King Abdullah in Jordan. It was a beguiling model, holding out the possibility of a gradual evolution toward a more democratic order without too much social disruption. Tarek didn't like Seif's arrogance—maybe because he saw in him something of his own younger self—but he saw the offer as an opportunity. He told himself it would be self-indulgent to wait until the regime changed, that Libya would need functioning and transparent institutions if it was ever to be democratic. He agreed to help modernize the banking sector.

His brother Ahmed, who accompanied him on a later trip, recalled how differently the three brothers reacted. "Amr was always practical, wanting to know if we could get our assets back," he said. "I just thought these people were ugly and I wanted nothing to do with them. But Tarek—always the idealist—said, yes, they're ugly, but he wanted to change them, to try and do something."

By 2006, Seif al-Islam's reform program had attracted not just Tarek but many lost sons and daughters of Libya. Mukhtar Nagasa, who as a teenager had sat with his father's hunting rifle across his knees during the 1986 Reagan bombing, had lost his hero worship of Colonel Gaddafi in the genteel English town of Bath, where he went to study dentistry in the late 1990s. After a few months he had Googled "Muammar Gaddafi" and been stunned to read about Lockerbie, the IRA and what had happened to the "stray dogs" in exile. He bought a book about Arab dictators and read it avidly. A Libyan he met told him about Abu Salim. Soon he was the one criticizing Colonel Gaddafi while Arabs he met from other countries defended the Brother Leader, saying he was still the only honest leader in the Arab world. Mukhtar married Amel, a fellow dentist, and they felt free and relaxed in Britain. Then, on July 7, 2005, commuters were blown up by jihadis on the tube in London. Mukhtar—tall, slim and dark— began to get suspicious looks on public transport. "I think they thought I looked like Osama bin Laden," he said. "I was respected in the hospital but outside I got racial abuse." They read about Seif al-Islam and the reform program. "We heard that Libya was coming in from the cold, that foreign companies were coming back. We were looking to Seif to be our hero."

He and Amel went back home and started a family. He had a private dental clinic, which wasn't doing badly, but he felt frustrated. "Seif said a lot of good things about multiparties, a new constitution, freedom of expression. But then I started to hear about billions of dollars in corruption. It was Seif and his people—I knew them, because we had been at university in Tripoli together. It was my generation, and they were more corrupt than the old guard." It gnawed at him—he didn't want to go back to the UK, but he felt angry about the Libya to which he had returned.

Seif al-Islam turned the Green Book Studies Center, which his father had established in the 1980s so people could study his philosophy, into a space where people could debate the future of the country, attracting some of the most prominent political scientists and economists in the world. Money was the key to getting the caliber of speaker he wanted. According to documents uncovered by the Libyan opposition in exile, the Libyan government paid the U.S.-based management consultants Monitor Group $750,000 a quarter plus expenses to bring prominent speakers to lecture on democracy and globalization. Francis Fukuyama, Joseph Nye and Bernard Lewis were among the intellectuals who gave talks, and who also got to see the Guide. The academics might have believed they were contributing to reform, but Monitor's contract was with Abdullah al Sanussi, the intelligence chief responsible for the 1996 Abu Salim massacre. In a memo to Sanussi, Monitor's CEO, Mark Fuller, said their aim was to "enhance international understanding and appreciation of Libya." It later elided into a new project "to enhance the profile of Libya and Muammar Qadhafi" and "to introduce Muammar Qadhafi as a thinker and intellectual, independent of his more widely-known and very public persona as the Leader of the Revolution in Libya." Monitor knew how things worked in Libya—their senior adviser was Sir Mark Allen, now retired from MI6, who had been so friendly to Musa Koussa when rapprochement between Britain and Libya started.

Intellectual legitimacy was important to Seif, who seems to have regarded himself as a polymath, a Libyan version of a renaissance man. Ned McClennen, a U.S. academic temporarily at the London School of Economics, lobbied hard for Seif's admission as a PhD student, and became something of a mentor. Professor McClennen wasn't blind to Seif's shortcomings—his English wasn't good and his background in architecture scarcely qualified him for his preferred field of study, which was government. Still, he saw other reasons to accept him. "I think we are dealing here with someone who is likely to emerge as the new leader in Libya, and that we are in the position to contribute constructively to his education," he wrote in his letter of recommendation in 2003. Rejected nonetheless by the Government Department, Seif ended up in the Philosophy Department. He asked Professor McClennen to join the panel he had drafting a new Libyan constitution. "He seemed very much a committed and idealistic individual," wrote McClennen in an article after the 2011 revolution. It was hard to accept that his protégé may have been less promising politically and morally, as well as academically, than he had thought. "Seif seems to have changed," he concluded.

What Professor McClennen may not have realized at the time was that Monitor Group helped Seif write his thesis, which was put together by a process of "dictation." According to an investigation headed by Lord Justice Woolf into the LSE's relations with Libya, Seif would chat to Omar Bukhres, a Libyan working as a professor at Purdue University in Indianapolis, who would write up the conversation and consult the Monitor Group Research Department. Seif's involvement in writing his own thesis seems to have been fleeting—after all, he was busy negotiating the freedom of the Bulgarian nurses; lobbying the British government to release Abdel Basset al-Megrahi, the man convicted of the Lockerbie bombing; and arranging a traveling exhibition of his paintings, *The Desert Is Not Silent*.

His connection with the LSE blew up into a major controversy after the revolution started in 2011. While Seif was studying at the LSE its director, the economist Sir Howard Davies, was appointed by then prime minister Tony Blair as an "economic envoy" to Libya (a post from which he later resigned); he also went onto the international advisory board of the Libyan Investment Authority, the country's sovereign wealth fund, which had been founded by Seif in 2006. Six weeks after Seif finished his PhD in 2008, Professor David Held, the head of the LSE's Department of Governance, approached Seif for a donation; the grant of $2.4 million from the Gaddafi Foundation was announced the day Seif graduated. The Woolf Inquiry established that the Gaddafi Foundation had a budget of around 27 million dinars ($21 million), 25 million dinars ($20 million) of which came from the Islamic Call Society, an organization founded by Seif al-Islam's father in the 1970s to promote Islam in Africa and around the world, and to fund Palestinian causes. Much of the rest of the money came from international companies that made donations to grease the wheels of their reentry into the Libyan market. As with everything in Libya, nothing was transparent: There was no public audit nor register of donors. No one in authority at the LSE had investigated the origin of the money nor thought through the implications of receiving a donation from a country that, while it might be reforming, could not be described as reformed.

Professor Fred Halliday, an expert on the region who had been a senior academic at the LSE for decades and had recently left, warned against accepting the donation. He saw the merits of engaging with the regime, and had lectured at the Green Book Studies Center, but he believed that taking money from such a tainted government was a step too far. When he heard about the donation he sent a memo saying that the idea that the Gaddafi Foundation was in any way separate from the state was incredible, describing it as an entity that solicited from companies "a form of down payment, indeed of taxation, paid to the Libyan state, in anticipation of the award of contracts." As for Seif, he was a central member of a regime based on patronage and kinship. Professor Halliday's warnings were dismissed and derided. According to the investigation, his allegations that senior academics had acted improperly during Seif's time as a student could be libelous, so his memo should be deleted from the record. It was, wrote Professor Held in an e-mail, "so potentially damaging to Fred that it is in his interests that we all do this." Fred Halliday died of cancer in 2010; he did not live to see himself vindicated.

If Libya hadn't been so rich, foreign governments and organizations like the LSE might have treated Seif al-Islam Gaddafi's flirtation with glasnost with more circumspection. But Libya was growing at 9 percent a year. The antics of the other brothers and Seif's own playboy side were regarded as an embarrassing sideshow. The real issue was that oil and gas prices were shooting up, and by 2007 Libya had a budget surplus of 39 percent. Companies jostled for the $65 billion capital of the Libyan Investment Authority, the country's sovereign wealth fund, which employed HSBC and Goldman Sachs as its bankers and invested in European companies, including the publisher of the *Financial Times* and the Italian football club Juventus. Tarek Ben Halim, even as he was trying to reform the banking sector, refused to go near the LIA: It was too corrupt and too dangerously close to the Gaddafi family and the inner circle for reform. He was proved right. The LIA's deputy chairman, who made most of the decisions, was one of Seif's best friends, and Musa Koussa's son worked as a broker on its cash equity desk. An audit by KPMG in 2010 found that the LIA had no audited accounts and no risk management; it was impossible to work out where the money went and why.

As soon as UN sanctions were suspended in 1999, European, Russian, Turkish and Chinese companies rushed into Libya. There were opportunities in banking, accounting, construction, hotels and shipping, but the biggest draw was energy. In 2005, oil and gas companies, including the U.S. majors ExxonMobil, Chevron and Occidental and the Italian company ENI, bid for exploration rights. Libya had the largest proven oil reserves in Africa, bigger than Algeria or Nigeria. At current production levels there was enough oil for seventy-seven years and enough gas for ninety-eight years. Tony Blair was determined that British companies should profit from the diplomatic lead his government had taken in rehabilitating Gaddafi. British diplomats, accompanied by executives from Shell, met Libyan officials at least eleven times between 2004 and 2007 to press the Anglo-Dutch company's interest in Libya's liquefied natural gas. BP—which had employed the ubiquitous Sir Mark Allen as an adviser—secured a $900 million deal, which the company described as its largest single exploration commitment. It was signed in 2007, during Tony Blair's second visit to Libya.

Seif was determined to secure the release of Abdel Basset al-Megrahi, who was still jailed in Scotland for the Lockerbie bombing. The British government was in a bind. Technically, the decision to release Megrahi was in the hands of the Scottish justice secretary. Politically, the outcome was critical for relations between Libya and the UK, not to mention for British businesses. Every time Seif met advisers to Tony Blair and his successor, Gordon Brown, he raised the issue of Megrahi. Every time they say they told him it was not their decision to make. Despite having left office, Blair visited Libya five times in the run-up to Megrahi's release. He says his private meetings with Gaddafi were to discuss Libyan investment in Africa, and he toed the line whenever Gaddafi raised the issue of Megrahi, explaining there was nothing he could do. But the pressure was mounting. Sir Mark Allen—worried about BP's investments—lobbied Jack Straw, the British justice secretary, twice about a general prisoner transfer arrangement that had been held up by the controversy over Megrahi. "We were aware that this could have a negative impact on UK commercial interests, including the ratification by the Libyan Government of BP's exploration agreement," said BP in a press statement issued when the matter became public.

In the end, the Scottish authorities released Megrahi on compassionate grounds, because he was suffering from terminal prostate cancer and expected to die within three months. The deciding factor may have been Megrahi's announcement that he would drop his appeal—if he had proceeded, it would have reopened the Lockerbie case, with all its controversies, just as everyone was getting back to business. A week later, Colonel Gaddafi sent a plane to collect Megrahi, accompanied by Seif, who saw the release as a triumph for his personal diplomacy. Celebrations were held in Green Square, and Colonel Gaddafi was shown on TV kissing Megrahi. The British government maintained that the decision had nothing to do with BP or any business interest, but that's not how it looked from Tripoli. The Brother Leader thanked "my friend Brown, the prime minister of Britain, his government, the queen of Britain, Elizabeth, and Prince Andrew, who all contributed to encouraging the Scottish government to take this historic and courageous decision, despite the obstacles."

Two years later, after the 2011 revolution, Megrahi was still alive, hooked up to an oxygen supply and lying on a hospital bed installed in the family home in the upscale Tripoli suburb of Hey Damas. I stood outside with a dozen other journalists, hoping for an interview, or at least for a glimpse of the man who must know the last great secret of Gaddafi's regime: Did the Brother Leader order the downing of Pan Am 103? Every now and then his brother would appear and apologize for not letting us see Megrahi. When a camera crew was eventually allowed in, Megrahi's comments were delphic. "The facts will become clear one day, and hopefully in the near future," he croaked. "In a few months from now, you will see new facts that will be announced."

Ministers who had defected from Gaddafi's government hinted that there was more to come out. Abdel Rahman Shalgam, a former foreign minister who had run the Libyan People's Bureau in Rome in the 1980s, said the UTA bombing was entirely the work of the Libyan government, which thought—wrongly—that the leader of the National Front for the Salvation of Libya was onboard. "The Lockerbie operation was more complex," he said. "While the Libyan services were implicated, I do not think it was a purely Libyan operation." Mustafa Abdel Jalil, who had been Gaddafi's justice secretary, told a Swedish journalist after he joined the revolution in February 2011: "I have information that is one hundred percent sure that Gaddafi is behind the tragedy at Lockerbie. It is not something that I think—it is something that I know and am one hundred percent sure about." But he provided no proof for his statement even after he became interim president under the National Transitional Council. "The answer to the riddle is that Gaddafi gave the orders," he said. Megrahi, he added, knew everything. But Megrahi wasn't talking.

Once the European Union arms embargo was lifted in 2004, the countries that had armed Libya in the 1970s dived back in. France signed a $140 million agreement to refurbish the aging fleet of Mirage jet fighters and a $400 million contract for antitank missiles and military communications equipment. In 2007, when Gaddafi made a state visit to Paris, the two countries discussed a $6 billion deal for Rafale fighter jets, military helicopters and a radar defense system, plus twenty-one Airbuses for civilian use.

When Libya staged the Libya Defense and Security Exhibition in 2008 and again in 2010, more than half of the one hundred companies represented were British, touting their wares at the UK pavilion under the slogan "Securing an Insecure World." The British Ministry of Defense identified Libya as a "priority area" for arms exports, granting export licenses for $83 million worth of components for tanks and armored vehicles, as well as for the General Dyamics communications system for the Khamis Brigade. During Tony Blair's second visit in 2007, Prime Minister al Baghdadi al Mahmoudi announced that Libya would buy British air defense systems and missiles. Only the Americans seemed to be missing out on the new bonanza, because even after sanctions were lifted they maintained a ban on the export of lethal weapons. But for the Europeans, nothing, it seems, was off-limits. The French company Amesys even sold the Libyan intelligence service "deep packet inspection technology," a system for monitoring its citizens' e-mails, which came in very handy during the uprising.

Sami al Saadi, the former emir of the Libyan Islamic Fighting Group, was in solitary confinement for more than two years in Tajoura prison, frequently handcuffed and blindfolded, and he had no idea what was going on outside the prison walls. For him, Libya had not changed. The CIA and MI6 had delivered him into the hands of the regime, and for all he knew he would spend the rest of his life in prison. Then, in 2006, he and other imprisoned members of the Libyan Islamic Fighting Group were invited to a meeting with intelligence officials, who said they wanted dialogue. The LIFG leadership were allowed to discuss their response among themselves. Was it a trick? Could they trust their enemies? What other choice did they have? "At the beginning we were suspicious, but by the end we believed they were genuine," said Sami.

It was Seif al-Islam's idea. In 2005, he approached Noman Benotman, the former senior member of the LIFG who had established himself as a person who could explain to Western governments the thinking of men like Sami al Saadi and the LIFG emir Abdel Hakim Belhaj. Noman had spent years in Afghanistan and knew Osama bin Laden and other Al Qaeda officials, but he was now part of the Quilliam Foundation, a "counter-extremism think tank" in London that aimed to persuade jihadis that violence was not the only way. "After dozens of meetings we built some trust," recalls Noman. "It took time—Seif was the enemy. He had been one of our targets. We talked a lot about the prisoners, and he was amazed to hear the stories, how widely they'd traveled and how Sami had ended up in China. After all these conversations, he decided to do something."

Seif came to believe that the only way to curb the opposition in Libya was to make a deal with the leadership; when the intelligence officials approached Sami and his companions in Tajoura, they were acting on his behalf. "They thought the LIFG was weaker but not finished," said Sami. "So it was for their own benefit, but they also wanted to make Libya secure." It was the beginning of what became known as the "deradicalization process," modeled on similar programs with jihadi prisoners in Egypt, Algeria and Yemen but tailored specifically for Libya. Over a period of three years Noman would travel to Libya once or twice a month to hold meetings with the prisoners and discuss their ideas. An influential Qatar-based Libyan cleric, Ali al Salabi, who was close to the Muslim Brotherhood and spent eight years in Abu Salim in the 1980s, led the discussions.

The LIFG were focused on Gaddafi's regime and had never attacked civilians or foreigners. But violence was at the heart of their ideology. Negotiating or reconciling with an enemy was forbidden; their beliefs were absolute and incontrovertible. They drew no distinction between civilians and soldiers, only Muslims and non-Muslims. "In my first meeting with them in prison, I said, 'you have to renounce violence, that's the point of departure,'" recalled Noman. "I asked them if they thought I was there to negotiate Islam or to discuss a political issue. It was man who produced this ideology, not God. It was us. They understood that it wasn't about religion, and that was a radical, major change."

For three years the LIFG leadership and Seif al-Islam's interlocutors debated the ideology of jihad and the conditions under which the prisoners—now transferred to Abu Salim—might be released and reintegrated into Libyan society. It wasn't easy. "One of the main obstacles was Mutassim," recalls Noman. "He was my worst enemy." The younger Gaddafi brother managed to stop the deradicalization process several times by getting his people within the security service to undermine the LIFG leadership in the eyes of other prisoners. He insisted that court proceedings should continue at the same time—Sami al Saadi was condemned to death by the court in 2009 despite being central to the deradicalization program. As no political organizations were permitted in Libya, the security services refused to deal with the LIFG as a body, only as individuals. "Are you crazy?" they asked Noman. "Do you want to help the LIFG reorganize?" After a while, Abdullah al Sanussi came down on the side of Seif and supported the program, but the attempts to derail it never stopped. "Mutassim was behind all that," said Noman. "He said it was a security issue."

There was also the problem of Libyan jihadis who had remained in Afghanistan after 9/11. Two prominent members of the LIFG, Abu Laith al Libi and Abu Yahyia al Libi, had joined Al Qaeda and risen to high positions in its ranks. Abu Yahyia's brother, Idris, was among those in prison in Tripoli, rethinking the group's philosophy; now the two would turn in very different directions. In an attempt to delegitimize the deradicalization process, in 2007, Ayman al Zawahiri, Osama bin Laden's deputy, announced from Aghanistan that the LIFG had joined Al Qaeda. In fact, the organization had split, with those in Afghanistan fully embracing the campaign against "the Crusaders and the Jews" while the imprisoned LIFG leadership in Libya was moving away from everything Al Qaeda represented. In 2008, 136 activists renounced violence and were released from prison with ten thousand dinars ($8,000) each to start a new life. The next year the LIFG in Libya published a book that outlined its new thinking. Entitled *Corrective Studies in Understanding Jihad, Accountability and the Judgment of People*, it started with the renunciation of violence and opened up the possibility of reconciliation. Sami and Belhaj were the main authors, but the text was reviewed by several leading Islamic scholars, including the influential theologian Yusuf al Qaradawi in Qatar.

It wasn't enough for Muammar Gaddafi. Maybe Mutassim had talked to him, but four months after the publication of the book, he came out against the release of the LIFG leadership. "When they are released they will continue to blow things up and assassinate," he said. "They will disperse across Libya and walk toward Egypt, Tunisia, Algeria and Afghanistan and to other countries around us. They will return and recruit others. The entire world is now fighting this terrorist network. . . . How can we release them without thinking of society's interests?" It took Seif another three months to convince his father that this had been a bargain and that the LIFG leadership had kept their part.

On March 21, 2010, Abdullah al Sanussi called Sami and Belhaj to tell them they would be released. Two days later they found themselves at the Rixos Hotel, holding a press conference with Noman and Seif al Gaddafi. Sami felt bounced into making that public appearance, but he was happy to be free. The remaining 409 jihadi prisoners were slated for release within a few months. "Today's event is historic," said Seif. "The journey will continue until the last person is released from prison. . . . The prison will be open for all: the press and diplomatic experts will be able to visit it, and it will become a center for the rehabilitation of our brothers."

How to judge Seif al-Islam Gaddafi? Western governments and academics who study Islamism regard the deradicalization program as a model, a textbook example of how to rehabilitate Islamist extremists. Without Seif it would never have happened. Sami al Saadi might have been executed, or remained in prison until he died, the violent ideology of jihad still unquestioned by Islamists who opposed Gaddafi. Seif battled his brother Mutassim and at times his father to liberalize the country and to lift the heavy presence of the security services. By 2010, despite the success of the deradicalization program, he felt he was losing. His international reputation was in decline. The Americans in particular were critical of his role in negotiating with the British government for the release of Abdel Basset al-Megrahi. The Americans were also unimpressed when the Gaddafi Foundation sent an aid ship to Gaza, an attempt to break the Israeli blockade, which the United States saw as a political, not a humanitarian, gesture.

Back home, he was also losing ground. His father had given him the position of general coordinator of the People's Social Leadership Committee, which, under Libya's idiosyncratic system, was the formal head of state. But Mutassim and his allies were moving against him. They scuttled his attempt to introduce the new constitution that his friend Professor McClennen and other eminent figures had drafted, which would have allowed for more freedom of speech and the right to organize. After he championed the formation of NGOs—the subject of his LSE PhD thesis—his father said publicly that there was no place in Libya for civil society. The two newspapers he had founded, which were sometimes mildly critical of the regime, were closed down. The board of the Gaddafi Foundation announced that his position as chairman would now be "honorary," suggesting that he would have less autonomy there too. "He wasn't really capable," said a former director of the foundation. "He lacked depth and consistency, and he had the same superiority complex as his father. He just wasn't solid enough."

As time went on, Tarek Ben Halim found himself ever more anxious. He had organized consultants for the central bank and arranged for twelve star employees—including a couple of women, which took some persuading—to attend an English course at his alma mater, Warwick University. He would go to Libya every month and tell himself that the intervention of technocrats like him was not only improving Libya's economy but nudging it gradually into becoming more democratic. But he was beginning to lose confidence. There was so much unnecessary poverty, not the kind of abject misery you would see farther south or west in Africa, but deprivation that you shouldn't find in the country with the world's ninth-largest oil reserves. He tried to see his work as a kind of subterfuge, a way of supporting a few Libyans who shared, or might share, his ideals, but the fear of Gaddafi he saw everywhere was making him angry. It humiliated everyone, even him, and he was still half on the outside.

Tarek tried to keep his distance from Seif al-Islam, but his wife, Cynthia, felt he needed the protection the link would bring, so he went to visit him at his country house overlooking Tripoli. The villa, with its deep pink walls, crenellations and courtyard, had been a gift to Seif's father from King Hassan II of Morocco. Tarek was taken to see Seif's pet Bengali white tiger, Freddo, and his hawks, the customary accoutrements of an Arab prince. His conduit was one of Seif's aides, who on this occasion had irritated his master in some way. It was a burning hot summer day. Seif and Tarek sat under a tree, sweating despite the shade. Seif ordered his aide to go and stand in the sun. And there he left him for two unbearable, sweltering, long hours.

"I said to Tarek when he got home, why didn't you do something?" recalled Cynthia. "He looked at me with this sad expression and said there was nothing he could do. The reason Seif had done that was to demonstrate to Tarek that he could do anything he wanted."

Tarek resolved never to see Seif again. He made one more trip to Libya but grew increasingly uneasy. It was becoming ever more difficult to get anything done. The state seemed immovable. Then Gaddafi made a speech in which he referred to Tarek's father, Mustafa, the former prime minister, as a traitor who had left the country. Mustafa responded with an open letter criticizing the Brother Leader for reopening the old wounds. Tarek was at Tripoli Airport when he learned that the letter had been made public. He climbed up the stairs onto the British Airways flight back to London with his heart beating as loudly as that first time, when he and his brothers had flown into Tripoli from Malta on the private jet Seif had hired. The plane taxied down the runway and stopped for a long, long time. Tarek closed his eyes. If they came for him, there was nothing he could do. No explanation was given. No one came. As the plane took off, he breathed deeply and decided he would not go back. Not while Gaddafi was still in power.

On February 20, 2011, as he prepared to address a rebellious nation, Seif al-Islam Gaddafi faced a choice: He could either proclaim himself the reformer, the one who could answer the cries for change, or he could vow to defend his father to the death. He did the latter. Someone who spoke to him afterward, who wants to remain anonymous, told me that the speech went through several drafts. "Seif thought he could calm people down, but in the end he had to appear as the most radical so his brothers couldn't blame him," he said. "It was because of the conflict within the family. That's why he was so angry." Seif's hope was that the regime could restore order and give him the opportunity to prevail over his brothers. The ideological disputes over reform were long gone—this was now simply a fight within the clan. The person who spoke to him said Seif made one catastrophic error. "He thought the international community was on his side."

CHAPTER EIGHT

SPIES, DIPLOMATS AND DRONES

Prepare yourselves for colonialism, on top of everything
else. Colonialism is coming back. It will return. The
Europeans and Americans will return and will enter Libya
by force.

—SEIF AL-ISLAM GADDAFI, FEBRUARY 2011

Decent people cannot sit back and watch systematic,
state-directed massacres of other people. Decent people
cannot fail to come to the rescue if the rescue action is
within their power.

—VACLAV HAVEL, 1999

Britain, France and the United States were in a dilemma. On the one hand, Muammar Gaddafi had become an ally. On the other, as uprisings erupted across the Arab world Western governments were looking at best ineffectual and, at worst, on the side of dictators. President Sarkozy of France had just fired his foreign minister, Michèle Alliot-Marie, after it emerged that she had enjoyed Christmas as a guest of a businessman friend of President Zine al-Abedine Ben Ali as the uprising in Tunisia got under way. When it became clear that the Tunisian leader might be unseated she had offered him the expertise of the French police, who had, after all, a lot of experience dealing with pesky North Africans in the *banlieues* of Paris.

Then it emerged that the Egyptian leader, Hosni Mubarak, had paid for the French prime minister, François Fillon, and his family to spend New Year's on the Nile, but Mr. Fillon kept his job on the grounds that at least his holiday was over before the revolt got under way.

President Obama was also under pressure. Tunisia had largely passed the U.S. government by—it was a francophone country anyway—but Egypt was America's closest Arab ally in the Middle East, the second-largest recipient of U.S. aid in the world, after Israel. As tens of thousands gathered on the streets of Cairo calling for Mubarak's overthrow, President Obama's envoy to Cairo, Frank Wisner, told a diplomatic gathering in Munich, "President Mubarak's continued leadership is critical: It's his opportunity to write his own legacy." The White House quickly distanced itself from Wisner, but the damage was done. President Obama had gained popularity across the Arab world when he gave a speech in Cairo in 2009, showing respect for Islam and trying to suggest that he had a more subtle understanding of democracy in the Arab world than his predecessor, George Bush. "America does not presume to know what is best for everyone, just as we would not presume to pick the outcome of a peaceful election," he said. "I do have an unyielding belief that all people yearn for certain things: the ability to speak your mind and have a say in how you are governed; confidence in the rule of law and the equal administration of justice; government that is transparent and doesn't steal from the people; the freedom to live as you choose." If there was a time when those sounded like empty words, it was now.

David Cameron, the British prime minister, was under pressure over British arms exports to the region. Unfortunately for him, a scheduled trip to the Gulf, accompanied by executives from eight British arms manufacturers, coincided not only with Gaddafi's *zenga zenga* speech but also with demonstrations in Bahrain, which were suppressed with tear gas and live fire. British arms manufacturers—more than ninety of which were at the time exhibiting their wares at the Idex 2011 arms fair in Abu Dhabi, in the presence of Defense Minister Gerard Howarth—had supplied weaponry to both Libya and Bahrain. Licenses were rapidly revoked, and Cameron made a hastily arranged six-hour stopover in Cairo to show his support for democracy. Libya had been part of the new Conservative government's export-led foreign policy, but Cameron was keen to distance himself from the former prime minister, Tony Blair, whose praise for Colonel Gaddafi as an ally in the "war on terror" was coming in for criticism in the media.

Moving against the Brother Leader was beginning to look like the best option politically, but there was a gamble to be taken: If Gaddafi won, he might expel Western companies like BP and ExxonMobil, which had gained their lucrative contracts so recently. Then again, if he lost, the next leadership would be better disposed to those who had provided support. China and Russia, which also had big energy and construction interests in Libya, were backing Gaddafi—if he prevailed, they would be favored. It was not a situation where you could easily hedge your bets.

The turning point was February 21st. The tricolor rebel flag was hoisted over the North Courthouse in Benghazi. Six Libyan ambassadors resigned, while the Libyan deputy ambassador to the UN, Ibrahim Dabbashi, gave a series of interviews saying that Gaddafi had started "genocide against the Libyan people" and asking for the UN Security Council to impose a no-fly zone to stop him from bringing in mercenaries. Two air force pilots flew into exile in Malta, saying that they had refused orders to bomb demonstrators. Helicopter gunships and fighter-bombers circled low over Tripoli, while Gaddafi's forces on the ground fired at demonstrators in the streets. Al Jazeera carried an interview with an eyewitness who said that protesters had been shot from aircraft. The story is unproven, and was probably the result of the fog of war—the sound of antiaircraft weapons, which are known to have been used against demonstrators, plus the presence of helicopter gunships may have led the eyewitness to believe the shots came from the air—but it was picked up across the world and became emblematic of Gaddafi's ruthlessness. The British foreign secretary, William Hague, said he had heard that Gaddafi had fled to Venezuela, while news agencies reported that the Warfalla, Libya's largest tribe, had turned against Gaddafi. Again, neither report was true, but both added to the sense of a regime crumbling. The justice secretary, Mustafa Abdel Jalil, who later became the head of the National Transitional Council, resigned his position and joined the rebellion. Fact and fiction combined into an irresistible narrative—Colonel Gaddafi's regime was making a final, brutal stand before collapsing. The next day Gaddafi made his *zenga zenga* speech, and his fate was sealed.

Moving against Gaddafi was made easier by the fact that he was loathed by Arab leaders, especially the Saudis, whom he had made a point of insulting whenever the opportunity arose. None were impressed when in 2009 he had stomped out of an Arab League meeting after declaring himself "leader of the Arab leaders and the imam of the Muslims." Worse, five years earlier, even as the West had been reengaging with Libya, the FBI had uncovered an alleged Libyan plot to assassinate Crown Prince Abdullah. President Obama was concerned not to look like President Bush, intervening in a resentful region and stoking up more anti-American sentiment, but stopping Gaddafi might be popular not only with Arabs calling for freedom and democracy but also with their leaders.

Gaddafi said on February 22nd that his model for dealing with the protests was Tiananmen Square, and like the Chinese government in 1989, he would mow people down with tanks if he felt it necessary. If he succeeded in quashing the revolt by force, it would prove what the cynics said—never mind Rwanda, where eight hundred thousand had been killed as UN troops fled the country; never mind Srebrenica, where seven thousand Bosnian men were slaughtered while Dutch peacekeepers looked the other way; never mind the UN doctrine of "responsibility to protect," which had been formulated in response to those two catastrophic failures. It would send a message that at the beginning of the twenty-first century any leader, however ruthless, could kill as many of his own people as he liked and no one would do anything about it. "More than anything it was the *zenga zenga* speech and the folk memory of Rwanda and Srebrenica which made us act," said Alistair Burt, the British minister for North Africa and the Middle East.

Western leaders called on Gaddafi to step down. The United States and then the UN imposed economic sanctions. The Security Council referred Gaddafi and his closest aides to the International Criminal Court. British diplomats, who knew many of Gaddafi's officials well, tried to persuade them to defect. Meetings were held, contacts made, threats uttered. Still Gaddafi's forces advanced, and it became clear that the rebels were too weak militarily to extend their reach beyond the east and the isolated pockets of Misrata and Zintan. As the military situation deteriorated an earnest group of young men thrust a banner into my hands in Benghazi, saying, "Give this to David Cameron!" It read: INTERNATIONAL COMMUNITY: LIBYAN PEPOLE SAY'S WITCH THE CHEAPEST—LIBYAN OIL OR LIBYAN BLOOD?

On February 27th, the rebels had formed the National Transitional Council, the NTC, under the former justice minister Mustafa Abdel Jalil, which reassured Western governments that this revolution had leadership and some chance of forming a replacement regime if Gaddafi fell. President Sarkozy announced that France would recognize it as the legitimate representative of the Libyan people. "I think Mr. Sarkozy has a problem of mental disorder. He has said things that can only come from a madman," responded Colonel Gaddafi, in an interview with an Italian newspaper.

One early British foray into rebel-held Libya bordered on the farcical. A report surfaced the first weekend in March that British diplomats had been detained in Benghazi. I called a contact close to the NTC who said that they had nothing against the British—in fact, they were grateful for their support—but they didn't understand why a British delegation had landed by helicopter in the middle of a field in the early hours, arousing the suspicion of a passing goatherd. "Why did they come in through the window when they could have come in by the door?" he asked.

We drove to the village of Jardiniah, southwest of Benghazi, and found the elders discussing their unexpected visitors. Eight men, we were told, had landed at 2:00 A.M. and been met by another, who had taken them in jeeps to the Al Khadra wheat project up the road. At the project, which seemed to have more satellite dishes than you might expect for a farm, and which, I later learned, was run by the first American to set up business in Libya after the country opened up in 2002, we found a group of young men who said, on searching the men's luggage, that they had found guns and explosives.

"We asked, 'why did you come?'" one of the men told me. "They said, 'we came to reconstruct Benghazi.' So we said, 'if you came to help, why come at this time of night? And why armed?'"

That night Libyan state TV played an audio recording of what appeared to be the British ambassador to Libya, Richard Northern, who was in London, calling the rebel leadership in Benghazi to ask for the men's release. Not only had British envoys been arrested, but the ambassador's attempt to free them had been bugged. "They thought they had clearance from the committee in Benghazi," said a senior official I spoke to in London. The British foreign secretary, William Hague, much discomfited, was left to tell Parliament that he had been advised that this was the safest way for the delegation to enter rebel-held Libya. Given that dozens of journalists had driven across the border from Egypt, it seemed like a poor explanation. The government maintained that they were diplomats and a security detail, although it was later reported that they were an MI6 agent and Special Forces officers. After two days the men were released to leave on the British warship HMS *Cumberland*, which had already docked at Benghazi's port several times to collect stranded foreigners and take them to Malta, and which presumably could have brought them to eastern Libya in the first place.

. . .

A few days later, things were looking more serious. Gaddafi's forces were advancing along the road from his hometown of Sirte toward the oil towns of Ras Lanuf and Brega, which the rebels had taken but seemed unable to hold. Every morning I would see the *shabab*—a gaggle of disorganized young fighters—assembling at the green arches, now covered in anti-Gaddafi grafitti, which marked the western gate of Ajdabia, the last town before the rebel capital of Benghazi. Burned-out tanks were parked on the roadside, their barrels still pointing toward the town. Gaddafi's forces had been repelled, but now they were coming back. The road westward was littered with the debris of burned-out cars, which the *shabab* said Gaddafi's forces had used to flee two weeks earlier. Camels moved, unbothered, across the thorny desert scrub on either side, and the *ghibli* whipped across the road. A few fighters had built berms in the sand and were attempting to outflank Gaddafi's forces, but most of the *shabab* just hurtled up and down the main road. There was no power for gas pumps, so at every garage young men were "fishing for gas"—dangling plastic bottles on poles into the reservoir belowground and transferring the liquid to jerricans to fuel their pickups. The gas station managers were long gone—fuel was free in the new Libya.

No one seemed to know who was in charge. Some said the commander was Gaddafi's former interior minister, Abdul Fattah Younes, who had defected to the rebel side, but others said it was Khalifa Heftar, the general who had commanded Libyan forces in the Chad war and then gone into exile in Virginia. Supporters of Fattah Younes said Khalifa Heftar was a CIA plant, while others suspected the former interior minister of still supporting Gaddafi. The *shabab* showed no sign of obeying anyone's orders, anyway. They had raided the weapons store at Ajdabia and welded mortar tubes and rocket launchers onto the backs of their vehicles, which they smeared with mud or sprayed with grafitti as camouflage. Each militia seemed to operate independently, and some fighters didn't seem to be part of any militia at all.

Idris Kadiki looked on in despair. With his penetrating green eyes and long tunic, he could have been mistaken for a member of the Taliban, but he was an oil engineer who had in recent years opened a couple of shops selling paint in Ajdabia and Benghazi. Idris was a Salafist, a follower of the strict Saudi-influenced form of Islam that demands a literal interpretation of the Koran. He wouldn't allow his photograph to be taken—that, he believed, was against Islam—but he spoke English well, because he had lived for several years in Middlesbrough in the north of England, and he had an ability to stand back and analyze the situation that was notably lacking in most fighters on the eastern front. Idris balanced his Kalashnikov, somewhat unwisely, barrel pointing down, onto his sandal-clad foot and watched his fellow rebels shouting, "Allahu Akbhar!" and firing into the air in excitement.

"They don't know what they're doing," he said. I had been asking fighters how they planned to retaliate against Gaddafi's encroaching forces, to which most had replied that God would protect them. Idris sighed. "God will not protect them if they can't protect themselves," he said. "We will lose this if they don't learn to fight properly, but they won't listen to anyone. They are stupid." Like so many I met in those days, Idris had a brother who had died in Abu Salim. He believed Gaddafi insulted Islam as well as ruled by fear, but he didn't see jihad as the answer. "I disagree with bin Laden," he said. "I disagree with everything he does, especially killing civilians. I don't like the Muslim Brotherhood either. I think they're completely wrong in the way they use religion for politics. I want democracy." I tried to probe his views on women—he would never shake hands in public but had no problem doing so when unobserved. His wife was at home looking after their three children, and he was clear that that was her role, and no more. We agreed to disagree, and the next day he brought me a pink-and-black checkered kaffiyeh scarf, shoving it at me awkwardly, slightly embarrassed about his gift and his conversations with such an un-Islamic female.

As they mused on whether or not to intervene, Western governments were looking closely at whether what people like Idris said was heartfelt or disingenuous. The east was the heartland of the LIFG, and while Western governments were impressed with Seif al-Islam's deradicalization program, they still worried that the revolution could let in Al Qaeda through the back door. They knew some LIFG members had joined Al Qaeda; they didn't know if they were influencing events. The reassurance they were looking for came from the tiny Gulf state of Qatar. As host to U.S. Central Command in the Gulf, Qatar was an ally of the West. It was scarcely a democracy, but Sheikh Hamad bin Khalifa al Thani was seen as a liberal, partly because he funded Al Jazeera, a TV news channel broadcasting in Arabic and English that frequently offended his more conservative neighbors. Al Jazeera had been the first Arab TV channel to interview Israelis, and the sheikh also allowed an Israeli Interests Section in Doha. But his government was a friend to Islamists too, and their views were also broadcast on Al Jazeera. The leaders of the Palestinian militant group Hamas and the anti-Israel Hizbollah were welcome in Doha. The Taliban had been there for talks. The sheikh and his government had gained a reputation for negotiating between Islamists and other Arab groups, and had successfully mediated an end to a political crisis in Lebanon in 2008.

Qatar was to play a critical role in Libya. The sheikh had been positioning his tiny country as the essential mediator in the Middle East, and this was his chance. The bigger countries had counted themselves out. Saudi Arabia, with its rigid system of religious government, was frequently mistrusted by Western governments and resented by Arabs. Egypt, the natural leader of the Arab world, had declined in importance under Mubarak and was now in turmoil. Sheikh Hamad believed that Qatar could promote a new model, in which Western interests and Islam could live side by side. Libya would be his testing ground.

Sheikh Ali al Salabi, the Libyan cleric who had led the deradicalization process started by Seif al-Islam, was based in Doha and in close contact with the government. His attempts to persuade Seif to announce a cease-fire and get his father to step down were failing. At the same time, his brother Ismail was leading one of the more effective militias in the east, the February 17th Brigade. With the Islamists so closely linked to the Qataris, Western governments felt more secure. The sheikh had another reason for favoring intervention against Gaddafi: His wife, Sheikha Mozah, had been brought up in Benghazi and sympathized with the Cyrenaicans. Qatar started to provide aid to the National Transitional Council in Benghazi, which was running out of cash because Libyan government accounts abroad had been frozen. The UAE joined the Qataris in providing support, and the regional body, the Gulf Cooperation Council, condemned Gaddafi, accusing him of genocide.

The Gulf Arabs were motivated partly by their dislike of Gaddafi and partly by their desire for more leverage over Western policy toward Bahrain. To Western eyes, the uprisings in Bahrain and Libya seemed similar, with protesters calling for democracy and freedom, but to Gulf Arab governments the two were entirely different. The Libyans were trying to get rid of an erratic leader who brought instability and shame upon the Arab world. The Bahraini demonstrators, they believed, were potentially opening the way for Iran to exert more influence in the region. Bahrain is a divided society. The majority are Shi'a, from the same branch of Islam as Iranians, but the ruling royal family is Sunni. Most of the demonstrators were Shi'a, protesting that they faced discrimination and lack of representation.

The Gulf royal families see Iran—Persian and Shi'a, rather than Arab and Sunni—with its nuclear ambitions and confrontational politics, as the main threat to the region. The Shi'a majority in Bahrain had long been regarded as a potential fifth column. As they came out on the streets, Gulf regimes began to fear that their discontent might infect Saudi Arabia's heavily suppressed Shi'a population in its oil-rich Eastern Province. The possibility that the House of Saud might crumble and the whole region slip out of their control was keeping kings, princes and sheikhs awake at night. The Gulf royals knew that if they helped the West support the revolt in Libya, it would be easier to suppress it in Bahrain. It wasn't a difficult argument to make. The U.S. Fifth Fleet is stationed in Bahrain, so the Americans had a vested interest in the status quo. The Bahraini protesters denied that they were allied to Iran, and said that they wanted democracy, just like the Libyans, but no one wanted to listen.

Qatar had an extra interest: Its phenomenal wealth is built on a natural gas field it shares with Iran. At $88,000 in income each per year, Qatar's 350,000 citizens enjoy the highest GDP in the world. Nearly a million of the peninsula's inhabitants are foreign workers—the citizens get a share of the money earned from gas and have no need to work unless they choose. Geology dictates that Qatar must have reasonable relations with Iran, but the last thing Sheikh Hamad wanted was a change in the regional balance of power.

Britain and France drafted a resolution for the UN Security Council, China and Russia resisted, and the Americans prevaricated. President Obama was reluctant; Defense Secretary Robert Gates was opposed to intervention, believing that a no-fly zone would drag the United States into a deeper war. He knew that they would have to disable Gaddafi's air defenses, which would require cruise missile strikes and drone attacks. This was the administration that was meant to extract U.S. forces from Iraq and Afghanistan not set out on more adventures. But two key people were pushing for something to be done, and for the United States to be part of it. Before her appointment as U.S. ambassador to the UN, Susan Rice had been involved in the campaign to get the Bush White House to act against the Sudanese government, which was murdering civilians in

Darfur. Samantha Power, an adviser in the National Security Council, had written a book exposing America's failure to stop genocide, most notoriously in Rwanda. They believed in intervention and persuaded the president and the secretary of state, Hillary Clinton, that they should go for it if they got broader Arab backing.

On March 12th, they got the diplomatic cover they needed. The Arab League, meeting in Cairo under its secretary general, Amr Moussa, called on the UN Security Council to impose a no-fly zone to stop Colonel Gaddafi from bombing the rebels from the air. Amr Moussa was only too aware of the significance of the move. Britain, France and the United States had made it clear that after Afghanistan and Iraq, the West would not intervene in a Muslim country in the Arab world without Arab League approval. Libya had been suspended from the pan-Arab body three weeks earlier. Moussa had his own reputation to consider. Everyone was speculating about when he would step down from his position to run for president in Egypt—he was the front-runner in the contest to replace the deposed Hosni Mubarak, and he wanted to present himself as a democrat on the side of freedom and the future. Gaddafi's regime, he said, had committed "serious crimes and great violations" and no longer had any legitimacy.

The following day, Gaddafi's forces shelled Ajdabia and massed west of the town. Idris Kadiki sent his wife, mother and three children to stay with relatives in Beyda, farther east, while he stayed to fight. A stream of refugees drove down the road toward Benghazi, as the ramshackle rebel militia vowed to fight on. Once Gaddafi had retaken Ajdabia, if he had enough forces, he could proceed on two fronts—east along the barely defended desert road to Tobruk and north along the coast to Benghazi. There was little to stop him. Gaddafi's forces had already retaken the town of Zawiyah, west of Tripoli, which had been held by rebels for twelve days, and were busy capturing those believed to have taken part in the uprising and killing anyone who refused to surrender. The trading port of

Misrata, which lay between the capital and Gaddafi's hometown of Sirte, was still under rebel control, but also under constant shelling. Besieged for months, it would endure the heaviest bombardment of the war, but at this point it seemed impossible that Misrata could hold out.

Secretary of State Clinton flew to Paris, where she met Mahmoud Jibril, a senior leader of the National Transitional Council who was going from capital to capital trying to muster support for armed intervention. She continued to Tunisia and Egypt, only too aware of how weak U.S. commitment to the Arab Spring would look if one week she was meeting democracy activists in Tunis and Cairo and the next Gaddafi's forces were killing similar activists in Benghazi. David Cameron was making the case to the British parliament. "Do we want a situation where a failed, pariah state festers on Europe's southern border, potentially threatening our security, pushing people across the Mediterranean and creating a more dangerous and uncertain world for Britain and for all our allies, as well as for the people of Libya?" he asked. France, Lebanon and the UK were ready with a draft UN Security Council resolution that would allow for a no-fly zone. Aware that Muslim countries would see any foreign troops as occupiers, it specified that no ground troops were to be sent.

By Wednesday, March 16th, Gaddafi's forces were inside Ajdabia. They fired tank shells into residential neighborhoods and hoisted the old solid green flag. The electricity was cut, and residents who had not fled cowered at home. An oil worker I met later told me that he was eating with his family on the ground floor of his house when a rocket came through the first-story wall. Everyone screamed and ran into the street; fortunately, he and his relatives escaped injury. At Ajdabia Hospital, doctors delivered babies by candlelight and patched up fighters from both sides as Gaddafi's forces tried to consolidate their hold on the town.

Hillary Clinton had returned to Paris to meet David Cameron and Nicolas Sarkozy. "We are well aware that the clock is ticking," she said. Many thought it was already too late—even if the UN passed a resolution,

Gaddafi was in position to move first. As the Security Council prepared to meet on the evening of the seventeenth, Libyan time, Seif al-Islam Gaddafi said, "In forty-eight hours, everything will be over." Colonel Gaddafi made a radio address to the people of Benghazi, telling them that the rebels were finished.

"They are wiped out," he said. "From tomorrow you will only find our people. You all go out and cleanse the city of Benghazi. A small problem has become an international issue. And they are voting on it tonight, because they are determined. But we are also determined. We will track them down, and search for them, alley by alley, road by road." It was *zenga zenga* all over again.

It was too late to flee. In Benghazi, shopkeepers pulled down their shutters—still painted Gaddafi green, but now covered in graffiti. The regime's fighters dropped two bombs near the airport, killing a shepherd and injuring twelve others. At night it was hard to tell if the crackle of gunfire was defiant celebration or skirmishes with the Gaddafi sleeper cells everyone feared had remained in the city. Young fighters with Kalashnikovs seemed to be the city's only defense. The regime had taken down the cell phone network, and no one quite knew what was going on, only that—spurred on by the rhetoric from Tripoli—the forces of the Brother Leader and his sons would show no mercy.

That evening the French and British put forward their draft Security Council resolution. The Russians countered with one that simply called for a cease-fire. The Americans came up with a draft that included not only a no-fly zone but for "all necessary measures" to protect civilians in Libya. A senior British official said, "We wondered why the Americans were adding more aggressive measures. Could it be a wrecking move?" It wasn't. Over the preceding weeks Clinton and Rice had worked the corridors of the UN and capitals of the world to secure the votes they needed. Arms were twisted, favors called in. Even the South Africans, who were allies of Gaddafi because of his role in the African Union and support for the anti-apartheid struggle, voted for the resolution. It passed 10 to 5, with Russia, China, Germany, India and Brazil abstaining.

Benghazi erupted with joy. A huge screen had been erected outside the courthouse so people could watch the UN session; the crowd cheered at every yes vote and threw shoes at the screen at every abstention. When the vote passed, celebratory gunfire mingled with fireworks in a euphoric and cacophonous display. Someone dressed up as Omar Mukhtar, the anticolonial hero, and rode a horse through the streets, followed by chanting teenagers. The resolution had given Gaddafi until midday Saturday to call off his troops and withdraw from Misrata and Zawiyah. He announced that he would cease fire to allow for talks, but the bombardment of Misrata never stopped. At 3:00 A.M. on the morning of Saturday, March 19th, Gaddafi's forces moved on Benghazi. They rocketed the town from the Ajdabia road to the southwest. There was firing in the city center— again, no one knew if it was rebels loosing off rounds or Gaddafi's sleeper cells being activated. Among the casualties, shot by a sniper, was Mohammed Nabbous, a young man who had established a TV station in Benghazi that had become a major source of news about the revolution. Other young men were captured and taken prisoner. After dawn, people looked up and saw a fireball plummeting from the sky, exploding as it hit the ground. They cheered and shouted, believing that the rebels had brought down one of Gaddafi's bombers, but it turned out they had hit one of the two planes they had managed to capture and fly themselves. Fighters with Kalashnikovs and rocket-propelled grenades manned barricades and tried to hold back the encroaching forces. Everyone had the same questions: Where is the UN? Did they pass this resolution for nothing? By dusk they had managed to push Gaddafi's forces back to the southern outskirts. Inside the city, they waited for deliverance.

It was the French who fired the first shot. That evening Rafale fighters bombed a convoy of Gaddafi's tanks and armored vehicles just outside Benghazi. Operation Odyssey Dawn had begun. A short while later 110 cruise missiles were launched from U.S. ships in the Gulf, targeting radar, communications, fuel storage and air defenses around Tripoli and Misrata, followed by air strikes from British Tornados. The tide of the war had turned. The next day rebel fighters removed the bodies of Gaddafi's tank drivers and gunners. By Monday I was watching children climbing over the burned-out hulks, gun barrels still pointing toward Benghazi. The accuracy of the missiles astounded the onlookers—several armored vehicles had been hollowed out and burned but the surrounding area was untouched. The residents of Benghazi, many of whom had boasted a few weeks earlier that they would prevail alone, spurning all foreign intervention, were waving French flags and shouting, "One two three, Sarkozy—merci!" A man with a superior knowledge of the French cabinet came up to me and said, "Thank you Sarkozy! And long live Alain Juppé!" Gaddafi's forces had been pushed back to Ajdabia. Qatar and the UAE also contributed aircraft—the six Mirages sent from Doha were almost its entire air force.

Intervention in one country pointed up the lack of intervention in another. A few days before the UN Security Council voted to stop Colonel Gaddafi's attacks on civilians in Libya, troops from Saudi Arabia and other Gulf countries including Qatar and the UAE drove over the causeway into Bahrain to put down the uprising there. British officials denied that the two issues were linked, but UAE officials hinted that their participation in the Libya campaign was conditional. The UAE and Qatar were instrumental in a military operation "to protect civilians" in Libya while supporting the government in Bahrain as it arrested, tortured and killed protesters in Manama. The Western powers murmured objections and looked the other way. "It's not comfortable for us," admitted a British official. "It doesn't look good as far as the outside world is concerned."

. . .

By the time NATO intervened, the city of Misrata, Libya's main trading port, east of Tripoli, had already endured a month of siege. At the height of the conflict an artillery round was coming in every six minutes. Thousands were killed and wounded and the buildings along Tripoli Street turned into burning shells, pockmarked and holed by tank fire and rockets. Trying to flee was sometimes more dangerous than staying. A local doctor, Ali Abu Fannas, and his wife were trying to reach her family home out of town when their car was rocked by a huge crash from behind. The car had been hit by a tank shell—their four children, sitting in the back, all lost their lives. In March, fishing boats full of weapons started to arrive from Benghazi, and the rebels would clear a few yards of snipers, then block the road with old shipping containers and sandbags to prevent Gaddafi's forces from bringing their tanks back in. Pushed down the road, the regime rained mortars and rockets onto Tripoli Street and the surrounding area.

Abdullah Abozeid's two sons, twenty-three-year-old Adan and twenty-six-year-old Tarek, both fought. "If the youth had consulted us, the older generation, we would have told them it was impossible, they should stay at home," he said, several months later, as we sat on the pale, jade-colored cushions that lined the reception room in his comfortable Misrata home, drinking thick, sweet Arabic coffee. A small, soft, round man, speaking carefully correct English, he stared into the distance, trying to make sense of what had happened. Some years earlier he had retired from his position as an aircraft engineer for Libyan Arab Airlines, depressed and embarrassed as he saw his country brought low in the eyes of the world. "I feel ashamed, because my generation was hopeless. No one thought the young people had this courage and wanted to die for their country." Certainly not in Misrata, where wealthy businessmen drove BMWs and spoiled youth might dabble in import/export but not expect to achieve anything of note in their lives. Yet the fighters of Misrata turned out to be the most tenacious and effective of all. Tarek, a lanky young man with a new beard who had just qualified as a pediatrician, started by working in the hospital but was soon on the front line. Injured in the back and the leg while fighting down Tripoli Street, a few days later he was fighting again. As the war in the east descended into a never-ending scrap over the tiny oil port of Brega, journalists got onto rickety fishing boats from Benghazi and ferries from Malta to reach Misrata. It was the most dangerous assignment of the conflict. On April 20th, the British photographer Tim Hetherington and his American colleague Chris Hondros were killed in a mortar attack on Tripoli Street. At least fifteen rebels and civilians lost their lives on the same day.

A private forty-five-bed clinic was turned into a casualty hospital, a white triage tent erected at the front. Hashem Dharat, a young medical student, worked for a while in the intensive care unit and then on ambulance duty, driving to the front line each morning. For twelve hours, without a flak jacket, he would patch up the injured and ferry them to the hospital. "Many lost arms and legs from mortars. I saw so many bullet wounds. My friend closed one guy's carotid artery with his fingers and saved his life," he recalled. Civilians and fighters alike would be brought in, a welter of mangled flesh, broken bones and blood. Doctors amputated legs smashed by shrapnel, staunched bleeding from bullet holes, bandaged head wounds, operating speedily with minimal anaesthetic. Some days there were fifty or sixty casualties, maybe half of them serious. Sometimes two or three were killed in the fighting, others thirty or more. The merchants who ran Misrata did their best to ensure that the hospital was supplied, but they ran out of analgesics, and the wards echoed with cries of pain from the living and "Allahu Akbhar!" from fighters and families mourning those who could not be saved.

Gaddafi's forces were shelling the port, as terrified African migrant workers tried to leave. Besieged on land east, west and south, there was no other way out. A family of seven Nigerians, five of them children, were killed by mortars and buried in a Christian graveyard created especially for them on the sand dunes overlooking the sea. Where was NATO? As long as the regime was still active within the city, NATO was afraid that its strikes might hit civilians, so it was left to the Misrata brigades to force Gaddafi's men out of the city. By the time British and French Special Forces units based in Benghazi started to organize regular tugboats full of Qatari weapons and ammunition to supply the Misrata fighters, toward the end of April, the most intense fighting was over.

Officially, the Special Forces weren't there, but their presence wasn't much of a secret. A dozen British and a similar contingent of French arrived in Benghazi in early April, according to a local man who worked as a translator for them. Planeloads of Qatari weapons had started arriving within a few days of the UN resolution. "The first few boxes we unloaded were medical supplies, but the weapons were underneath," he said. The Qataris sent an estimated twenty thousand tons of weapons, but not all of them went through the British and French pipeline. An unknown number went direct to the February 17th Brigade, under the command of Sheikh Ali al Salabi's brother, Ismail, which was fighting on the eastern front. The emir of the Libyan Islamic Fighting Group, Abdel Hakim Belhaj, another author of the book written by the jihadis who went through deradicalization, was involved with similar brigades.

After Gaddafi's forces were pushed out of Misrata, a large force regrouped at Dafniya, to the west, while others retreated south to Tawergha, where the residents continued to fight fiercely on Gaddafi's behalf, knowing that if he was defeated they would lose everything. Gaddafi's forces had encircled Misrata, but the fighters inside the city organized themselves into eastern, southern and western fronts to push them back. In June, Tarek Abozeid and his brother were fighting to the west, in Dafniya, when a tank shell hit their unit, injuring eleven fighters. The nerves in Tarek's left hand were damaged, while Adan caught shrapnel in his leg. It was a near miss. In the Abozeid family's neighborhood, forty-four young men lost their lives, maybe one in six of those who fought. NATO spotters were in Dafniya by then, and Apache helicopters attacked Gaddafi's tanks and other formations. Night by night his ability to attack was being eroded. The Misrata men fought on grimly. In Benghazi, people were now living an almost normal life, but Misrata had to keep fighting just to prevent Gaddafi's forces from reentering the town. Every day there were more casualties, more young lives lost. Western politicians started to mutter about "stalemate" and the possibility of dividing the country, which would have left Misrata to Gaddafi's mercies again. As the months went by the people of Misrata began to feel that they had fought and suffered more than any other town in Libya, that victory would be theirs alone, that their claim to power and glory would be the hardest won, and the most deserving.

On March 30th, a private jet took off from Djerba airport in Tunisia, heading for the small airport of Farnborough in the southeast of England. It was a discreet arrival for an important passenger. He had warned the British security service that he would be coming, and they had arranged his clearance to land. Musa Koussa, who had served Gaddafi as diplomat, spy chief and head of his international revolutionary center, had decided it was time to leave. He had slipped across the Ras al Jadir border into Tunisia the previous day and called his old friends in MI6 to ask for safe passage.

Dozens of Gaddafi's diplomats and a few of his ministers had abandoned him, but Musa Koussa was by far the most significant defector. The British government, which had publicly and privately been trying to convince its contacts that the game was up, wanted to make the most of the moment, but they knew this was delicate. Musa Koussa, before he became the point man for MI6 and the CIA, was believed to have been involved in

Lockerbie, UTA, the Yvonne Fletcher case, sending arms to the IRA and the assassination of Gaddafi's enemies in London. He was, as Libyans frequently told me, "Gaddafi's black box." Within a day the British press were calling for him to come clean, to spill the beans, to tell all, to face the music, to pay the price.

"Let me be clear, Musa Koussa is not being granted immunity. There is no deal of that kind," said Prime Minister David Cameron. The Foreign Office said their guest was being "debriefed." The clamor rose: If he had no immunity, would he be arrested, questioned by the police, face charges, put on trial? Of course not. He was a prize, not a suspect. Poised and elegant as usual in a pale gray suit, blue shirt and red tie, glasses halfway down his nose, he read from a script in Arabic as he made a single televised statement. He said nothing about his past nor the circumstances of his leaving Libya. "I know that what I did to resign will cause me problems, but I'm ready to make that sacrifice for the sake of my country," he said. "I personally have good relations with so many Britons. We worked together against terrorism and succeeded in dismantling weapons of mass destruction." He took no questions. A few days later the EU lifted sanctions against him, so he could travel freely. He left for Qatar, where he installed himself in the Four Seasons Hotel.

The British government was as coy about his departure as it had been about his arrival. They knew the ghosts of Lockerbie would not rest easy, that it would be impossible for him to stay in the UK and avoid legal challenges and media attacks. In Doha, Musa Koussa could have the protection he needed—against Gaddafi's people, against the National Transitional Council, against everyone who wanted to know the secrets only he knew of Colonel Gaddafi's doomed regime.

The thump of incoming mortars started just after dawn. Colonel Gaddafi's troops were firing toward the town of Nalut, high in the Nafousa

Mountains, west of Tripoli. This time the rebels didn't respond. It was mid-June, and three days earlier, when they had tried to push north from their mountain stronghold across the plain, they had been repulsed. At least eight fighters had been killed, their bodies borne aloft through the town as the survivors honored them by shooting into the air. The Amazigh, or Berbers, could guard their own mountain territory, it seemed, but not capture the plains below, where Gaddafi's forces had massed in the small towns of Ghazaya and Taluk. A message had come from rebel high command in Benghazi telling them not to try again, because their losses were too great.

In the Nafousa Mountains, instead of the images of Omar Mukhtar seen all over Cyrenaica, were pictures of Khalifa Ben Askar, a Berber of the same era, who had fought the French colonizers of Fezzan to the south and of Tunisia, as well as the Italians. Mussolini's forces had hanged him in 1920, eleven years before doing the same to Mukhtar. The rampant Barbary lion, a traditional symbol, had been reinvented for this new conflict, adorning stickers and decals with a red head and mane, black wings and green hindquarters and tail, carrying the tricolor flag in his front paws. Graffiti were not just in Arabic and English but in Amazigh, with its distinctive script. This was a revolt not just to get rid of Gaddafi but to reassert the pride of the Berbers, the original inhabitants of the region, who had settled there centuries before the Arabs. In Nalut, the ruins of their ancient mud-walled city were perched on the edge of a rocky outcrop to the north of the town, an emblem of a civilization that had been suppressed but not destroyed.

Accompanied by a fighter who had been a teacher a few months earlier, I drove to a lookout, passing half a dozen of Gaddafi's tanks that had been disabled in the early days of the uprising, now lying inert like giant dead cockroaches, left to rust on the rock-strewn hillside. Half a dozen men, the younger ones in baseball caps, the older ones swathed in loose brown cloth, were peering through a Soviet-era range finder onto the ochre plain before us. They sat on old iron bedsteads covered by thin mattresses, which had been hauled up the hill. I looked through the lens and could make out only a couple of pinpricks in the distance. Someone brewed tea under a tarpaulin. All the towns along the ridge—Nalut, Jadu, Zintan, Yefren—were now firmly in rebel hands, and they were closer to Tripoli than the fighters in Misrata to the east. The front line at Kiklah was only a hundred miles west of the capital. But they were unable to push their advantage. Askar Khalifa, the former teacher who was acting as my guide, looked at his fellow fighters. "We have a lot of courage but very few weapons," he said.

That was not strictly true. Four months into the rebellion, Qatari weapons were coming across the border from Tunisia and being flown in from Benghazi in ever greater numbers. Pushed a little, Askar agreed that they were getting help from "another country." He'd been primed not to tell me which, but it was no accident that the maroon and white Qatari flag was almost as popular as the Libyan tricolor around the Nafousa Mountains. In Zintan, some two hours' drive east toward Tripoli, reporters had caught sight of brand-new mortar-base plates, tubes and shells still in their vacuum packs, with the word QATAR stenciled onto the packaging. A few miles away they found new Milan antitank guided missiles. After the war was over, a briefing paper left on the abandoned desk of Colonel Abdullah al Sanussi, Gaddafi's brother-in-law, contained intelligence from what appears to have been a spy in rebel ranks, detailing how not only Qatar but also the UAE and Kuwait were bringing weapons to refugee camps in Tunisia, from where the rebels would smuggle them over the border.

The UN arms embargo extended to both sides in the conflict, so it was difficult for France and Britain to supply weapons, at least publicly. It might also be hard to argue that arming the rebels was within the mandate of "all necessary measures to protect civilians," but when the newspaper *Le Figaro* revealed that the French military had parachuted rifles, machine guns and rocket-propelled grenades onto a remote airstrip between Nalut and Zintan, the French government gave the equivalent of a Gallic shrug. The military spokesman in Paris argued that the weapons had been sent so that civilians could defend themselves. He said nothing about the twenty or so French Special Forces officers in Zintan training the rebels in how to use their new equipment.

Tunisia, the first country to overthrow its government in the Arab Spring, allowed its territory to be used as a conduit for arms, trainers, rebel forces and as a safe place where the rebels and their Arab and Western backers could plan. Men who wanted to fight would often leave Libya by the main Ras al Jadir border post, saying they were on family business or going for medical treatment. In the Tunisian beach resort of Djerba they would meet committees of rebels who would question each would-be fighter to gauge whether he was genuine or an infiltrator. "I would say, 'I'm not sure about this revolution,' and see how the guy reacted," said one recruiter I met. It didn't sound like a very secure method. Family and tribal connections were more important—every potential fighter was someone's brother or cousin. Instructors from Qatar and the UAE trained small groups of men in the Tunisian desert in fighting and spotting for NATO air strikes, while others underwent rapid instruction by Jordanian officers in the Nafousa Mountains. About one hundred Egyptian trainers were working in the east, and the Italians also had a small group of advisers working under cover inside Libya, while the Americans provided a covert team specializing in intelligence and electronic intercepts.

But while the rebels were becoming more professional as fighters, and learning to coordinate on the battlefield, the rivalry between Libya's different regions was growing. For years Gaddafi had pitted tribe against tribe, town against town. Now everyone believed that their group was the key to overthrowing Gaddafi, an issue that would cause even more problems after the war was won. Even within the Nafousa Mountains, the rivalry was intense. As a journalist, if you were with the boys from Zintan, you couldn't stay in Jadu—that was a separate territory. Every town had its own media committee. No wonder Libyans had never managed to overthrow Gaddafi before. But the men of the Nafousa Mountains, like those in Misrata, were much more competent as fighters than those we had seen in the east. As the summer wore on, and media commentators in the West wrote darkly about stalemate, the Amazigh and Arab mountain fighters began to coordinate with each other and with NATO. By July, the fighters had learned to wait for air strikes to soften up targets on the ground. Six weeks after I saw the Amazigh fighters in Nalut abandon their effort to capture Ghazaya and Taluk, they embarked on a far more serious assault: NATO air strikes hit Gaddafi's tanks and mortar positions at dawn, before ground forces moved down from the mountain to take the towns. It worked. They were on their way.

From the beginning, the NTC had said they would not divide Libya. The revolution had started in the east, but they knew that if they accepted Colonel Gaddafi's continued rule in the west, that would mean sacrificing those who had risen against him in the Nafousa Mountains, Misrata and Zawiyah. The fighters on the eastern front were blocked as they tried to move west from Ajdabia toward Colonel Gaddafi's hometown of Sirte, but that stretch of road was no longer strategically essential because they were winning elsewhere. Gaddafi's forces had been pushed back from Misrata on all fronts. The Nafousa Mountains were completely rebel-controlled. They had yet to conquer the towns along the coast road east from the Tunisian border, the isolated desert outposts of Fezzan, and Gaddafi's strongholds of Sirte and Bani Walid, but those could wait. What mattered now was seizing the biggest prize of all—the capital.

CHAPTER NINE

THE BATTLE FOR TRIPOLI

In a revolution, as in a novel, the most difficult part to
invent is the end.

—THE RECOLLECTIONS OF ALEXIS DE TOCQUEVILLE, 1896

Big apology to the world for the crimes of Gaddafi.

—GRAFFITI IN TRIPOLI

Sometimes, as the gunfire sputtered outside, Ahmed would close his eyes and think of Seattle. True, he had screwed things up by dropping out of college, but it was nonetheless a good life in America. He was thirty-four, a jeans-and-leather-jacket guy. Still no wife, no kids, no stability. He wondered if his family would mind if he married an American girl. He was good with computers, maybe he could go back to college, get a job in IT there. Then, as he opened his eyes, the present would come rushing in on him. He had work to do here in Tripoli.

Every few days he went to his friend's office. No one seemed to mind his presence. They would chat, then he would go to make coffee for himself and for all the men as they started their meeting in the room next door. He would sit at the computer, carefully leaving the door open a crack so he could hear what was being discussed. After checking thoroughly for bugs and malware, he would slip his flash drive into the USB port and start writing his report, his ears always open to what was happening on the other side of the wall. When he had finished he would open a hot mail-type e-mail account and copy the report into drafts, but never press send. He would remove the flash drive, making sure no trace of the document was left on the computer. After the meeting finished he would hang out for an hour or so, chatting with the guys, trying not to think of the flash drive burning a hole in his pocket. Time to go home.

In London Ahmed's brother-in-law would open up his e-mail and go into drafts, where Ahmed had left his report. He would read the report, compare it with others, then he would forward it with a covering note to his contacts.

Why did they never suspect? Why did they never question him? Every day it seemed more incredible. Officially Ahmed had no business in the office of his friend, who was one of Gaddafi's closest aides. Ahmed's family had left Libya for the United States after their properties, lands and businesses were confiscated in 1978, only returning in the 1990s. Nothing had been returned, and everyone knew they had a grudge against Gaddafi. Yet here was Ahmed sitting in the heart of the Libyan government military-planning machine, sending intelligence reports to NATO.

MI6, the CIA and French intelligence had assets like Ahmed all over Libya. As spies always do, they had been playing a double game. Even as Western intelligence agencies were returning Gaddafi's Islamist opponents to Libya through the program of extraordinary rendition, knowing full well the men were likely to be tortured in Gaddafi's jails, they were spying on their Libyan counterparts. Ahmed had been infiltrating the system for four years. In 2007, when he had been at his lowest, kicking around Tripoli with nothing to do, his brother-in-law in London had asked him to get to know some of those close to Gaddafi. He thought that maybe if he did, they might in the end return some of the family property, so he started to try and make himself useful to them. With his fluent English and knowledge of the West, he offered to help them set up companies overseas. He built on the paranoia in the system, gathering information on his contacts and subtly referring to such-and-such a deal or such-and-such a business, knowing full well that the guy sitting next to him had profited from corruption. When they grumbled about the way things were in Libya, he would praise Gaddafi. People began to wonder if he knew something they didn't, if maybe his connections were better than theirs. He homed in on his target, a senior official who was always at Gaddafi's side. Ahmed got to like him in a funny way. He was a patriot, at heart maybe more loyal to Libya than to Gaddafi, but bound by tribal and family ties. After a while everyone thought Ahmed was working for him, so they asked no questions.

Come February 17th, Ahmed told his mother he was going to fight. She gave him her blessing, but his father asked him not to pick up a weapon. "I was about to make a big choice," recalled Ahmed. He and his brothers knew that if they were found to be rebels, the whole family might be wiped out. His brothers changed their minds, and he realized that he could get a weapon much more powerful than a Kalashnikov—information. He told one person, his father. "He looked at me and said, do it. But whatever happens, don't get caught." For the benefit of the men close to his friend, the high-ranking official, Ahmed played the perpetual adolescent, obsessed with computers, unable to survive without playing games online and checking his e-mail. "I would play dumb," he said. "I think they thought I was brain dead." Then he started to work his other contacts to garner more intelligence.

In early March, Hussein, a friend from Misrata whose father had been killed in the 1984 coup attempt, approached him. They talked over spiced Arabic coffee made by Hussein's mother.

"What's in your mind?" asked Ahmed.

Tears welled up in Hussein's eyes. "My family's being killed and we're doing nothing," he said.

Ahmed looked at him. "How can we trust each other?" he asked.

"I know your brother-in-law. He can help us," said Hussein.

Ahmed was suspicious. "Are you a Gaddafi person trying to make me talk?" he asked. Gradually they began to discuss what they could do.

"I can provide weekly updates on weapons, missiles and the location of high-ranking officials," said Hussein. His father, a retired military officer, lived in the same neighborhood as Abdullah al Sanussi, Hannibal Gaddafi and other senior officials.

"Don't ever write anything down," said Ahmed. "Just talk."

By the time the UN Security Council voted for the no-fly zone in March, he had a network quietly gathering information. Troop movements, weapons stockpiles, locations where mercenaries were camping, he collated it all. He recruited more friends, some of whom knew people within the military, so he had more than one source on any piece of intelligence. They knew the phones were bugged, so they developed a code. "I need a coffee now" meant they had to meet immediately, there was something urgent. Using the word "Samsung" twice meant something was critical. "My computer is stuck" meant you were being watched. Ahmed would sit at home to draw and redraw maps until they were perfect, so NATO could match them with Google Earth to find the locations of targets. He knew Gaddafi's forces were trying to trick the Misrata rebels into thinking the airport was about to be attacked, when in fact their target was the seaport. He learned about the position of the Gaddafi lookouts trying to prevent weapons being smuggled to the fighters in Misrata by sea, so the British and French knew where their Apache helicopters should strike. He felt more alive than he ever had before. The stakes were so high, the cost of failure too terrible to contemplate.

The Libyan government invited journalists to stay at the $400-a-night Rixos Hotel. A sign pinned to the railings outside promised: "Exceptional and mesmerizing memories with a touch of elegance." In the chaos of the early days, reporters escaped government minders, interviewing protesters in Tripoli and even managing to get to Zawiyah, thirty miles to the west of the capital, during the twelve days it remained in rebel hands. Some days journalists were confined to their gilded prison, and late at night, just as they were falling asleep, a loudspeaker would sound in the rooms: "Journalists please assemble for a press conference." The spokesman, Moussa Ibrahim, a smooth media relations graduate of several British universities, would tell them that reports of rebel successes were exaggerated, that Libya was firmly under the Brother Leader's control, and any trouble was caused by a few drug-fueled Al Qaeda terrorists. Senior officials of the regime moved their families in—after all, the Rixos, with the international media in residence, was one place you could guarantee NATO would never bomb.

At night the skies rumbled as drones and reconnaissance planes circled overhead. Sometimes it was impossible to sleep, as NATO bombers dropped their loads around the city. Targeting intelligence came from spotters like Ahmed and dozens of others, as well as from images taken from satellites and drones. The UN mandate to "protect civilians" was stretched to the bursting point. They said they were targeting "command and control centers," but that was a catch-all phrase for any place or person NATO thought was central to the continued existence of the Gaddafi regime. One of Ahmed's raw intelligence reports from April lists the hotels and office blocks in central Tripoli where Gaddafi would go, never spending more than a few hours or a day in one place—he knew NATO wouldn't bomb the Red Castle in the medina of the old city, the Corinthia or Radisson Blu hotels or the Burj al Fathah tower, because they were likely to contain civilians. NATO leaders fudged the question of whether they were trying to assassinate Gaddafi, but there is little doubt that they were. "His most favored residency is still in the Gharghouer area, and most preferred because of the failed attempt by NATO," wrote Ahmed.

"NATO was given the correct area but wrong location at the time Gaddafi was there." He attached a careful pencil map of significant locations with annotations in small, neat, precise handwriting. "Location A and B are the homes of Gaddafi's sisters. Gaddafi was staying at these two locations at the time of the failed attempt on his life by NATO." Every sentry box where Gaddafi's guards stay is marked. In July, Ahmed noted that Abdullah Sanussi was frequently seen at the newly built and heavily guarded Sheraton Hotel. "It is believed that he constantly moves back and forth from this location and meets Gaddafi in normal, unoccupied homes. Meetings last no more than 15 or 20 minutes," he noted.

The rebels grew frustrated at NATO's caution. NATO leaders knew that a major mistake, in which they killed many civilians, would provide Gaddafi with a propaganda boost and weaken already equivocal public support back home for the campaign. They frequently delayed attacking a building for fear of hitting civilians, so by the time they were ready, the target—whether it was a regime member or a military unit—had long gone. If intelligence gleaned from cameras or sensors suggested that there were people inside a building who might be civilians, the strike was aborted. NATO hasn't said how many people were killed in their campaign, but a survey by the *New York Times* carried out after the revolution suggested that "at least 40 and perhaps more than 70" civilians were killed by seventy-seven hundred bombs or missiles. Britain's Royal United Services Institute estimates it could be as high as one hundred. Precision-guided missiles with a small blast radius, like the kind I had seen target the tanks outside Benghazi, meant there were fewer casualties than in Baghdad in 2003, or in Kosovo, where four hundred to five hundred civilians are thought to have been killed in a similar air campaign.

In early April NATO hit what they thought was a convoy of Gaddafi troops, but it turned out to be a group of rebels moving around the fluid front line. Their comrades buried them at the side of the road near Brega. The harsh desert wind blew the flag of the new Libya as the men were given a collective fighters' funeral—there was no time to bury each man individually or tell his family what happened. I arrived at the scene a few hours later. The victims must have been incinerated in a minute, burned oxygen cylinders the evidence that one vehicle was an ambulance. A fighter who had seen the vehicle told me that only bones and skulls remained of those who had died inside. The fighters, I was told, had been shooting into the air. "We blame the rebels and not NATO," said Idris Kadiki, the fighter with the piercing green eyes who looked like a jihadi. "The rebels are the ones who started shooting the plane; they shouldn't do such a bad thing. NATO just thinks someone is attacking them." The rebels, I thought, were remarkably forgiving. A strike on a house in Tripoli in June left four members of the same family dead—the bomb seems simply to have gone astray. In what seems to have been the worst case of a NATO strike killing civilians, doctors in Zliten, near Misrata, say thirty-four people were killed when NATO aircraft dropped five-hundred-pound laser-guided bombs on several houses in early August. NATO said it had attacked "military staging areas" and refused to acknowledge or investigate its mistake.

Every day, Libyan state TV reported that dozens of civilians were being killed by NATO attacks. Their estimates of numbers dead or injured varied—at one point they said forty-five hundred had been wounded and more than a thousand killed. The minders at the Rixos would sometimes take reporters to see damage at Bab al Aziziyah in the middle of the night, but it was hard to take their statistics seriously, because they couldn't prove them. On one occasion reporters were ushered into a hospital to see a comatose baby called Nasib, her mother weeping over her broken body. The minders said she was a victim of the previous night's air strikes, but one of the doctors quietly slipped a note into a reporter's hand. The baby, it said, had been injured in a car accident; it had nothing to do with the bombing.

In June, I spent a frustrating week in Tripoli. On the way in from the

Ras al Jadir border crossing the government bus sent to collect journalists turned right, detouring through the countryside instead of through Zawiyah. "Road works," said the minder, as we passed another tense checkpoint of soldiers and plainclothes militia, weapons cocked. Gas queues extended for more than a mile, and people would sit in line for days, but the minders wouldn't let us film the evidence that sanctions were having an effect. In the medina I slipped into a jewelry store.

"How is the situation?" I asked.

"You know," said the nervous elderly man behind the counter. "You know how it is. We cannot say."

It was the same everywhere—whispered conversations, stolen glances, fear, rumors and the distant sound of gunfire in the night. One morning the minders took a group of us to see a factory that manufactured oxygen cylinders for hospitals. No one had been hurt, but we were shown what looked like a control room that had been damaged. Outside, next to the beach, we saw a scrap yard for rusting tanks and armored vehicles. I asked a factory worker why he thought they had been targeted. He switched from English into French and, casting an anxious glance around to make sure we were not being overheard, pointed beyond a high wall to what looked like a huge warehouse with its roof torn off. "That's a barracks," he said. "The military come and go all the time and they have lots of vehicles there. It gets bombed all the time. I don't know why they hit our factory, but that's what they were aiming at."

One morning in March journalists having breakfast in the Rixos dining room heard the sound of screaming. A desperate young woman was calling for help. As the journalists tried to find out what she had to say, waiters and waitresses pulled knives, attacking her and the reporters. When it emerged that she was trying to tell the journalists that she had been raped by Colonel Gaddafi's militia, one of the minders pointed a gun at a cameraman's head and another smashed a camera to stop them from filming. Scuffles broke out as the journalists tried to shield the woman. By the time Gaddafi's men managed to drag her away to an unmarked car, she had shown her bruises and explained that she was Iman al Obeidi, a law student from Benghazi. Earlier that week, soldiers, hearing her eastern Libyan accent, had pulled her from the vehicle in which she was traveling and taken her to a barracks where, over three days, she was raped and sodomized by fifteen men. Feeling her life was ruined anyway, she decided the only thing she could do was let the outside world know her story. She managed to escape and went straight to the Rixos.

Rape had long been a weapon used against the mothers, sisters and daughters of those who defied Gaddafi. No one liked to talk about it. Everyone knew that if a man was arrested, his female relatives were at risk, and the threat was enough to make many men break down and confess to whatever their interrogators wanted. Sometimes the security forces would rape a woman in front of her husband. Afterward she might be rejected by her family, a double torture and misfortune.

Iman al Obeidi's story probably did more than anything else to bring what was happening in Libya to international attention. The images of a distressed woman, bruised and battered from rape, being silenced and dragged away by goons, galvanized world opinion. The price she paid was shame and trauma as both government and rebels tried to co-opt her suffering to their cause, to salvage their honor from her pain. Moussa Ibrahim, the government spokesman, accused her of being a prostitute, a drunk and mentally unstable, and the authorities tried to force her to go on television to say it was the rebels and not the government forces who had raped her. She refused. The initial attention gave her some protection—Gaddafi's son Saadi took up her case, arranging for her to be interviewed by CNN so she could give her story in more detail. Eventually, she escaped over the border to Tunisia, but by then everyone wanted a piece of her. By the time she got to Doha, under the supposed protection of the Qatari authorities, she was on the verge of nervous collapse, unable to trust anyone, reliving the nightmare of her attack and the international outcry that had followed. It wasn't over. The representative of the rebel National Transitional Council in Qatar decided she should be sent to Benghazi as some kind of trophy, living proof of Gaddafi's cruelty and the righteousness of their cause. When she resisted, they kidnapped her, bundling her into a plane in the middle of the night. After a few days and the intervention of U.S. secretary of state Hillary Clinton, she was allowed to leave for America, where she remained, safe but traumatized, an example not only of the horror inflicted by Gaddafi's forces but of the insensitivity of a rebel leadership who had seen rape not as a personal tragedy but as a way to bolster their legitimacy.

Iman al Obeidi's dramatic entry to the Rixos was the most jarring disruption to the picture of a tranquil Tripoli in full support of Gaddafi that the government minders had been trying to create. Gaddafi withdrew into a state of denial. He was shown on TV playing chess with the World Chess Federation president, Kirsan Ilyumzhinov, who once claimed to have been briefly abducted by space aliens and believed that the world could be saved from alien invasion if a billion people played chess. He and Gaddafi had become friends when Libya staged the world chess championships in Tripoli in 2004. Ilyumzhinov was taken around the Bab al Aziziyah compound to see the impact of the bombing before settling down to a game of chess, which he said he had diplomatically steered to a draw. Colonel Gaddafi, he said, was "an amateur who knows how the pieces move." By then even Russia had had enough of Gaddafi. President Medvedev's envoy told Ilyumzhinov to pass on a message: This is the endgame.

One day in May, the garbage began to sing. People walked past, some staring, others hurrying on. It was so loud, people driving past could hear. Curious, they slowed down—and then accelerated, fearful that Gaddafi's spies had spotted them, because the pile of black plastic bags on the street corner in the genteel suburb of Fashloum was singing the national anthem written at independence in 1951; it had been banned by Gaddafi and subsequently adopted as the theme tune of the uprising: "We will never go back to fetters, we have been liberated. And we have freed our homeland: Libya, Libya, Libya," sang the garbage.

It was a Free Generation Movement stunt. Nizar, the oral surgeon from Cardiff, and his sister, Mervat, had started a campaign of civil disobedience, an attempt to show the regime in nonviolent ways that the people were not with Gaddafi. They had recorded ten minutes of silence, followed by the anthem played multiple times, then uploaded the recording onto four sound systems, which they had placed in black plastic bags. On Thursday, the day everyone in Fashloum carried their garbage out on the street for collection, Niz put out bags like everyone else, quickly driving off. By the time the music started to play he was long gone, and no one could know who had brought which bag. Mervat felt nervous that morning. She found herself thinking back to when she was fifteen, coming into the living room as the TV was showing the hanging of Sadeq Shweidi, the young man accused of plotting against Gaddafi, who was finished off by the fanatical Gaddafi supporter Huda Ben Amr swinging on his legs. She could still hear him screaming. She banished the memory, got into her car and parked opposite one of the rubbish bags, carefully placing a small video camera inside a tissue box with a hole cut in it for the lens.

"It was amazing," she said. "I could see people were singing along. The shops put down their shutters. A kid shouted, 'It's in the trash,' and a truck came to pick it up, but someone shouted, 'Put it back!' so the man put it back again." Mervat reversed into a side street and adjusted the camera. People had not heard the anthem for forty-two years—playing it, even humming it, could get you sent to Abu Salim. Eventually the soldiers figured out where the music was coming from and picked up the rubbish bags, but by then the point had been made: Tripoli was not all with

Gaddafi, as he proclaimed. Opposition could spring up anywhere, and they could not control it. Mervat drove off.

That evening she showed her husband the video. "That's our car!" he said. "I recognize the dashboard. You filmed it, didn't you?" She confessed that she had. He knew that there was no way he could stop her now. "I had lost my fear," she said. "I think it was because I knew all those young men were paying with their lives, and I hadn't been able to do anything for forty-two years."

They posted the video on YouTube and sent it to Al Jazeera, CNN and the BBC. Making that possible had been one of the most nerve-racking things Niz had done. His cousin was an IT expert with a government department, so they hacked into the still-functioning government in-tranet, but soon realized that was too risky. They needed their own se-cure communication. No one was turning up for work these days, so they decided to "borrow" the satellite dish on the roof of his cousin's office. They thought of dressing in military uniforms. Or maybe overalls, like workmen. In the end, they walked in wearing their normal jeans and T-shirts, got in the elevator, went up to the roof, dismantled the dish and walked down the stairs with it. So far, so good—until they tried to squeeze a dish that was two yards in diameter into the back of their four-by-four parked outside. It wouldn't fit. Niz was sweating. They re-treated to the lobby with the dish. He called a friend with a truck. In ten minutes he was there, so they walked out onto the street for a second time, loaded the dish in the back, and drove to a house in a quiet suburb that they had picked for their headquarters. "We knew that if Gaddafi was successful in blocking our communication with the outside world, our usefulness would be reduced by half," said Niz. They also knew that if they were caught, they would be imprisoned, or worse. They moved headquar-ters four times, one step ahead—sometimes only half a step ahead—of the authorities.

The Free Generation Movement was the most inventive of the groups staging acts of defiance around Tripoli, but not the only ones. Banners with opposition slogans would frequently appear hanging from bridges, and Tripoli residents would look up and see balloons trailing revolutionary flags. One group sprayed cats in red, black and green dye, the colors of the revolution, only to see them shot by soldiers. Ever conscious of public opinion in the West, Niz and Mervat decided that neither children nor animals should be harmed in the making of their part of the revolution. They were assiduous in getting images out, believing, like Tawfik, the young man who had filmed the Green Book statues being destroyed in Tobruk, that letting the world know what they were doing was as important as doing it. The revolution would be televised.

In mid-June, word went around among the activists in Tripoli: Zero hour is approaching. On June 17th, everyone should come out of the mosque and demonstrate. Niz woke up and took a drive around to check the situation. He had never seen so many soldiers. They were everywhere—on the streets, on rooftops, on balconies. "You could sneeze and they'd shoot you," he said. At the Rixos, the journalists had got wind that something—we knew not what—was planned. Two reporters who snuck out early were hauled back by secret police who found them downtown. The rest of us were under hotel arrest until midafternoon, when the loudspeaker sounded through the lobby: "Journalists, please assemble and get on the buses." Our choice was another few hours drinking coffee and grumbling at the Rixos or being herded like goats to Green Square. We opted for the latter.

Most days, a dwindling coterie of enthusiasts would hang out by the medina, sitting and chatting until a TV camera arrived, whereupon they would start jumping up and down, waving green flags, yelling, "God! Muammar! Libya! That's all we need!" and haranguing any foreign reporters, especially if they came from France, the UK or America, the countries most responsible for the bombing. It was hard to know if they were true believers or paid extras in the fantasy film the regime's minders were staging for our benefit. That day the crowd was much larger and more belligerent than usual. Gaddafi's voice on a telephone line was broadcast over loudspeakers—he was by then rarely seen in public—shouting, "NATO will be defeated!" Families and young men in cars roared around the square. Just as at rebel rallies, young men, some uniformed, some not, shot wildly into the air, so we took shelter from falling bullets in the archways in front of the shops that surround the plaza. The mob grew angry with foreigners and surrounded an American TV crew, jostling the correspondent, shouting in her face, threatening her until she had to be rescued by the minders. I walked away and had coffee on the waterway promenade with other journalists. I couldn't tell the truth, because I didn't know what it was, but covering the rally somehow seemed like reporting an untruth. I had no idea what was going on, and no way of finding out.

Three months later, Niz and I compared notes about that day. By the time we were taken to Green Square, he and his group were back at home. They had emerged from the mosque straight into the barrels of the regime's guns. Soldiers were standing outside the doors, aiming directly at them. There was no way they could demonstrate—it would have been a massacre. It was a bad moment—the regime had its spies among the activist groups, and they knew what was being planned, so they could preempt it. "There were times when we felt alone," recalled Niz, "but we never considered stopping. I didn't know how long it would take, but I knew it could never go back to how it was before."

Gaddafi had proved his strength, but ten days later, anyone passing the huge billboard of his face opposite the Radisson Blu Hotel on the waterfront might begin to wonder if he really was invincible. Dressed in a gray Bedouin robe, his face in profile, he was wearing sunglasses and what looked like a soft fabric sun hat, the brim slightly turned up at the front.

The ubiquitous images of the Brother Leader were a form of intimidation, proof that wherever you turned you couldn't get away from him. But that morning something was wrong. A black line was creeping down Gaddafi's hat. Flames were emerging from just behind his sunglasses, and smoke was engulfing his face. People often looked away when they passed the poster, which is probably why Niz and his cousin had been unobserved when they climbed up the back of the billboard and hung a wire cage made of coat hangers, containing a plastic bottle of gas and a fuse made of string coated with a dried paste of water and the crushed tops of matches, over the top. They had been practicing at home for some days in a kind of revolutionary school chemistry experiment, to see how long it would take for the fuse to burn. They had ninety seconds to light it, clamber down, walk to the car they had parked under a tree and calmly drive off. Again, they were unobserved—and a few minutes later everyone could see Gaddafi gradually burn.

This time, the camera hidden in a tissue box was already running inside a parked car. They had thought it was too risky to have someone inside filming. The footage shows that by the time the security forces arrived, Gaddafi's face had been burned off. Soldiers took down the damaged billboard, leaving a blank space where the Guide's image had loomed over all who walked or drove by for so many years.

A quarter of a century earlier, after the National Front for the Salvation of Libya had failed to dislodge Gaddafi, Abdulmajid Biuk had put away his maps and intelligence notes and settled in Tampa, Florida. He was a senior member of the group but, like Wanise Elisawi and Huda Abuzeid's father, Ali, had despaired of overthrowing Gaddafi. In 2011, as the revolution unfolded, he rifled through his old suitcases and cupboards. "I pulled out all my files and found the information was still valid," he said. "Gaddafi's inner circle and the next closest were the same people." He had names and details of their families, and maps showing the location of their houses and offices. He e-mailed his old friends, including several who had been back to Libya. How much had changed? Not a lot, they said.

Abdulmajid flew to the Tunisian town of Djerba, where he met up with old friends and new revolutionaries. They established an operations room in a nondescript house and started to work up a plan. "We interviewed high-ranking military officers who defected," he said. "We checked with them the information we already had. We put up a big map that we'd had when I was with the NFSL in Algeria, and these guys confirmed which members of the regime lived where." They checked everything on Google Earth and began to draw up a list of key buildings, such as intelligence headquarters and arms dumps. They infiltrated the External Security Organization, and volunteers smuggled out flash drives with even more critical intelligence: the location of Gaddafi's operations rooms, military intelligence cells, barracks, *lijan thawriya,* police stations, safe houses, radars. The spies within the system listed the names and vehicle license plates of unit commanders and documented how they communicated with the head of intelligence, Abdullah al Sanussi, and with Seif al-Islam. They even managed to intercept the regime's communication channels and record conversations between key military and political leaders. NTC representatives arrived from Benghazi, and a businessman who they had named as envoy to the UAE arrived in Djerba to set up what became known as the stabilization team. In April, the groups working in Djerba nominated representatives for the Tripoli Committee, to coordinate the revolution in the capital. Tripoli was sometimes called the mermaid, so they adopted the code name Operation Mermaid Dawn.

NATO's help was critical. Undercover British agents had infiltrated Tripoli and planted radio equipment to help target air strikes. Intelligence from assets like Ahmed, deep inside the system, went first to NATO member security services and then to Djerba. In April and May, members of the NTC and the Tripoli Committee visited Paris to liaise with chiefs of staff of NATO countries and senior military officials from Qatar and the UAE. They even saw President Sarkozy at the Élysée Palace to update him on the plan.

They divided Tripoli into thirty-seven sectors. Each sector was divided further into neighborhoods and streets. Could you trust your neighbor? No one knew. To stop information from leaking out, or Gaddafi loyalists from infiltrating the rebels, those who wanted to join the revolution communicated only with a street coordinator, not with each other, in a classic cell structure. The wealthy merchants of Misrata were buying tons of weapons, as well as taking receipt of the Qatari weapons that the British Special Forces in Benghazi were shipping to Misrata by tugboat. The naval blockade imposed at the same time as the no-fly zone made it hard for Gaddafi's sailors to intercept the shipments, so boatloads of weapons sailed from Misrata to Tripoli and were landed and distributed late at night. Libyan exiles who wanted to fight also landed by sea, quietly rejoining their families in the suburbs. Many in Tripoli found an easier way of arming themselves—they bought rifles from Gaddafi's increasingly dispirited soldiers and police. It wasn't cheap—a Kalashnikov might cost as much as three thousand dollars—but there were plenty of weapons for sale.

A special unit was trained and armed. The Tripoli Brigade was made up mostly of exiles—hundreds of young men who had lived in America, Britain, Canada and the Gulf. They were doctors, dentists, students and the unemployed. Few had any military background, and some had never been to Libya before. They were the sons of families that had left for political or economic reasons, and many had thought they would never live in the land of their fathers, let alone fight for it. Now they were risking their lives for Libya. When the signal was given, they were to advance and seize the capital.

· · ·

Haunted by a memory from her childhood, Enas Dokali was desperate to do something. When she was five her parents took her to see her uncle Salem in Abu Salim prison. "I remember vividly that when they brought him out, he could hardly walk. It was because he had been beaten so badly on the legs," she said. It was 1990. Like so many other families, they took clothes and food to the prison gates even when told they couldn't visit. In 2010, the authorities gave them the death certificate, fourteen years after her uncle Salem was killed in the Abu Salim massacre. Enas's family was from the Warfalla, Libya's biggest tribe, which supported Colonel Gaddafi, but as Islamists they were opposed to the regime. Another relative, Mufta, was involved in a coup attempt in 1993. Enas watched his execution on state TV during Ramadan.

As rumors of an uprising spread in mid-February, Enas searched online until she found details of the proposed demonstrations. She wanted to protest, but she knew her family wouldn't agree to her going out on the streets where Gaddafi's forces were shooting into the crowds. She was in many ways a traditional, devout young Muslim woman—modestly dressed, with a long coat over her jeans and not a strand of hair escaping from her pale blue flowered head scarf. Every day she went to work as a computer programmer in the government planning department, where many of her colleagues were providing maps for the government forces— she felt alone, unable to say what she really thought among the loyalists in her office, but she observed what they were doing and realized that she could do something similar but for the rebels. Her appearance helped—in her long coat and head scarf she could walk around town, drawing little attention. She noted where military units were based and spotted important regime members going in and out of buildings. The sister of a friend was going back and forth to Tunisia, taking the information to other friends working with the rebels. Enas collected money and clothes to send to the fighters and coordinated shipments of weapons. She and her friends had no secure communications, so they used the cell phone network, talking in code: an important person was "Mr. Chips"; weapons and ammunition were "sandwiches"; videos were "underwear."

"I realize now that they were watching me for a long time," she said. "They knew something was going on, but they didn't know what. I noticed the same small white pickup following me, and I saw they took photographs." On July 31st, at 11:30 at night, armed men barged into the family house. "I couldn't tell you how many they were—too many to count," she recalled. "They grabbed me by the arm and pushed me into a car. I said, 'Get your hands off me, I'll get in alone.' I was expecting it. My mother collapsed." They took her laptop and money, but she had managed to get rid of her cell phone. Her brother was arrested with her, but after a mile or so they told him to get out of the car. She was on her own.

Enas thought she knew why she had been caught. The attempted assassination of Abdullah al Sanussi was the worst kept secret in Tripoli. Some of the rebels she was helping were part of the plot, and she knew in advance what they were trying to do. It seems that Sanussi had probably also been warned, because on July 21st, when they attacked the house where he had been staying, he wasn't there. She thought those who had arrested her wanted to get to the people who had tried to kill Sanussi. Surveillance had increased noticeably since that day, and worse than that, she had become suspicious of a member of the group. She couldn't say anything, but she didn't trust him; she was sure he had betrayed her.

The car stopped at a building in the Hey al Andalus downtown part of Tripoli. "I was scared, but I tried not to show it," she said. As they brought her into an office, the men who had arrested her tore off her head scarf. They said she wasn't a virgin, and they could do what they wanted with her. They tried to open up her clothes, so she crouched on the floor and screamed as loud as she could. "Every word I said, they laughed at me," she said. "They shone a torch over my body and said they would rape me, and take photographs of me naked and distribute them, so everyone could see. They were pushing my head down and saying I was a disgrace to the War-falla, punching and slapping me." Enas can't remember how long it went on, only that they were trying to get her to name neighbors, friends and family. They brought transcripts of the calls she had made, so there was no point in denying what she had been doing or what she knew. "I was just praying to God," she said. "I believe that whatever is written will happen, and I accept that. Even if it's rape."

In the end, she said, they backed off. It was Ramadan, so maybe they were hungry at the end of the day and just wanted to go off and eat. They taunted and threatened her, but they stopped short of rape. At dawn a female officer came in and blindfolded her. She was driven to another building and put in an office, where she slept on the floor. She cried, thinking of her mother's distress, but then collected herself—she knew she had to keep it together, somehow. Young men who had also been arrested were in the same building, so she slept between two female officers for her own protection. They interrogated her every day. Who was trying to kill Sanussi? Where are they? Sometimes they threatened her, at others they promised to protect her if she would go back into her group of rebels and spy for the regime. She tried to string them along, saying she would consider working for them. "They didn't want anything too bad to happen to me until they got the information," she said. "They started to be nicer to me." Her family had found out where she was and sent food; a neighbor who knew Seif al-Islam sent a message to her that they were trying to get her released, so maybe that also helped improve her treatment.

At night she listened to the crash and thump of NATO bombing. It was close and very loud. Sometimes the female officers would blindfold her and take her with them when they hid in a different building. They would sleep during the day and at night watch Al Jazeera or the new revolutionary TV station, Al Hurra, which was broadcasting from Qatar.

Sometimes they would take her up onto the roof, and she managed to get her bearings and realized she was not too far from home. She knew other prisoners were being treated far worse—she heard the screams and saw young men being beaten with rifle butts as they were dragged in. How much longer, she wondered, how much longer will I have to stay here?

At the end of July they came for Niz and Mervat. Thirty cars of plainclothes secret police and uniformed soldiers raided Mervat's mother-in-law's house. They found nothing incriminating, but the Free Generation Movement knew they had been found out. They cleared all their houses of paint, flags, printers and computers and dismantled the satellite dish. Niz and his cousin went into hiding. A few days later police arrested another cousin and brought him to Mervat and Niz's parents' house, where they found Mervat and her husband. Mervat never thought of herself as brave— she hated public speaking, and had never been an activist until the revolution—but the next day, when she was taken for interrogation, she knew she had to keep her nerve come what may.

"Where are your kids?" they asked. "Are you happy that we're going to be looking after them now?" Mervat said nothing.

"What do you know about the Free Generation Movement?"

She decided there was no point in pretending she had never heard of it, so she said she had seen their stuff on TV.

"You look familiar," said one of the interrogators. "Haven't I seen you on TV? I know your voice."

Her heart leaped. She had appeared on YouTube early on with two other women carrying a banner, their faces supposedly blacked out. Later she had given interviews to journalists they had smuggled to their house from the Rixos, with her face but not her voice disguised.

"No, I've never been on TV. I'm not an actress," she replied, acting better than she had ever needed to act before.

They produced the picture of her and the other women holding the banner.

"You're the one in the middle."

"What, me? No."

And so it went on. They played "good cop, bad cop," but Mervat got the impression that the good cop really supported the revolution. He never called her a rat, and he told her to drink the juice and eat cake he offered so she didn't lose track of what she was saying. After nine hours the bad cop tried to take her to a cell, but his colleague persuaded him to let her go home, saying they could always call her in again for further questioning. She breathed deeply. She had got away with it, at least for now.

In mid-August I traveled back to the Nafousa Mountains. In the east the rebels were still blocked, but in the west it was a different story. The training and influx of weapons had transformed their fortunes. I went to Zintan, where the fighters were preparing for their assault on Tripoli. There was nowhere to stay, and it was hard to find gas, food or a driver and a vehicle—it was Ramadan, so no one was eating or drinking during the day, preferring to sleep in daylight hours, waking up at sunset to break their fast with the *iftar* meal. The TV team I was with ended up staying in a private house, surviving off crackers and Laughing Cow processed cheese, eventually finding a group of rebels who agreed to escort us toward Tripoli. We passed a group of donkeys in a field. "Hah!" said the driver, mustering his few words of English. "Gaddafi family!"

Driving north toward Zawiyah, dozens of cars were coming the other way, laden with mattresses, pots and pans and the occasional fridge. Families were bribing the soldiers on Gaddafi's checkpoints to let them out of the city. Some had stood in line for three days or more to fill up with gas—the only fuel available was smuggled over the border from Tunisia at huge cost. Rebels within the city were staging nightly raids on government checkpoints and spraying anti-Gaddafi graffiti under cover of darkness. "Now the Gaddafi soldiers are afraid," said a man who was driving his family out. His daughter put it more poetically. "In Tripoli there is no silence in the night," she said.

There was street fighting in Zawiyah, thirty miles west of Tripoli, which had been in rebel hands for twelve days back in February. The rebels retook it on August 19th, cutting off Tripoli from the Tunisian border. Assuming he was still in Tripoli, Gaddafi was now surrounded. I arrived in Zawiyah the following morning to a scene of devastation. Tank shells and mortar rounds had destroyed the buildings around the main square, and uniforms discarded by Gaddafi soldiers lay among the rubble and shattered glass. The square was almost deserted—retreating forces were firing Grad rockets, several of which had landed just a few minutes earlier near where people had been celebrating. The rebels showed me the bodies of four black men, lying in alleyways, who they said they were African mercenaries who had been fighting for Colonel Gaddafi. A putrid smell rose from the corpses; they had been there for several days. An old man pulled me into the square to see where the mosque had stood until March, when Gaddafi's forces demolished it to eliminate a center of resistance. The bodies of those killed in the fighting back then had been buried just outside. Gaddafi's men had concreted over the graves, a gesture to deny respect for the dead and send the message that anyone who opposed the regime would be obliterated.

Zero hour was approaching. NATO dropped leaflets over Tripoli telling Gaddafi's forces it was time to give up. The Americans sent extra drones in for reconnaissance, and the pace of the bombing was stepped up. With most major towns now in rebel hands, they could concentrate on the capital. Several hundred trained men who had infiltrated the capital as sleeper cells were ready to go. August 19th saw the most important defection since Musa Koussa: Abdul Salam Jalloud, Gaddafi's right-hand man in 1969, the most senior member of his Revolutionary Council, fled the capital. The rebels helped him and his family escape to Zintan, and then on to Tunisia, from where he went to Rome and eventually Qatar. After the fall of Zawiyah, NATO chiefs suggested it was time to pause and regroup, but the Tripoli Committee said there was no stopping the momentum. More than that, there was a date and a time that would have meaning for Libyans: the twentieth hour of the twentieth day of Ramadan, the anniversary of the Muslim conquest of Mecca in A.D. 680. In 2011, it also happened to be the twentieth of August, exactly six months since they had first rebelled in the capital on February 20th.

Ahmed struggled to remain calm, but he knew that Gaddafi's spies had infiltrated the rebels. He realized they must have hacked into rebel communications. They always seemed to know beforehand what was going to happen, because, he realized, they had information on others like him who were giving targeting coordinates to NATO. He reported the arrival of several thousand mercenaries from Chad and Sudan, who he said were assisting on military roadblocks. Empty schools and houses were occupied by Gaddafi's troops. He grew increasingly edgy, not least because a senior official he had cultivated told him that Gaddafi was planning to use chemical weapons if he lost Tripoli. "He said Gaddafi will order the use of mustard gas and three other types that are unknown," he wrote in his intelligence report. The following day, another source told him that gas masks had been distributed to troops on the front line. Documents from the Department of Chemical Protection found in an abandoned military base after the revolution bear out Ahmed's information. Dated between April and July, they chronicle the ordering and delivery to Sirte and to Khamis's Thirty-second Brigade of chemical weapons protection suits, napalm and pressure fillers for pressurizing gaseous chemical weapons into warheads. Gaddafi never used his stocks of chemical weapons, but the evidence suggests that that was his intention. Late on the afternoon of August 20th, neighborhood coordinators told the Tripoli cells, "We're going to have soup tonight." That was the code phrase. After the imams had spoken, when everyone was in their homes eating the *iftar* meal, Operation Mermaid Dawn would begin. "O Allah, on this day, open for me the doors of the heavens, and lock the doors of Hell from me, help me to recite the Koran, O the One who sends down tranquility into the hearts of believers," said the imams, reciting the traditional *shura* for the twentieth day of Ramadan, before the cry of "Allahu Akbhar!" sounded from the minarets. Mustafa Abdel Jalil, the interim president of the NTC, gave a speech broadcast on Al Hurra, the rebel TV station based in Doha. "The noose is tightening," he said. "You have to rise to the event," and everyone knew what he meant.

"Six months earlier, on February twentieth, everyone headed for the city center," said Abdelmajid Biuk, who was part of the coordinating team in Djerba. "This time, people were to stay in their own localities and only spread out after they had secured them." Tajoura, Fashloum, Souk-al-Jouma, Ben Ashur—across the capital men came out on the streets with guns and what they called *gelatinas*, grenades made from fishing explosive. Boys went into the streets and whistled, drawing out Gaddafi's soldiers, who were promptly ambushed. The secrecy of the cell structure had worked. "I thought I would be the only one on my street with a gun," said a man I met a few days later. "But when I came out I found fifty of my neighbors had guns. Everyone had got them from people they knew in the army."

Razia Sholeh, the protocol officer in the Foreign Ministry, ate the *iftar* meal with her husband, Salah, before he rushed back to the ministry, where he also worked. As the uprising erupted across the streets of the capital, she heard the gunfire and worried about him. Salah was close to Seif, and she knew he would be loyal to the last. He called to say it was too dangerous to drive home, and he would see her in the morning. That was the last she heard from him. A few days later a journalist told her he had seen Salah at the Rixos the next day—regime guards were still holding reporters in the hotel, refusing to let them out into the city to witness it falling to the rebels. Razia waited, alone with their one-year-old son, but there was no more news. Salah's cell phone was dead. "I think he must be with the Guide," she told me later. "I can't believe the Guide would abandon Tripoli like that. They must both be out there on the ground somewhere."

One of the rebels' key assets was General Mohammed Eshkal, a relative of Gaddafi's from his Gadaffa tribe, whose brigade guarded Bab al Aziziyah and much of central Tripoli. In 1985, during a period of plotting and unrest within the inner circle, Gaddafi had ordered the execution of his brother, Colonel Hassan Eshkal. General Eshkal had quietly nursed his grievance for more than a quarter of a century. He had tried to join the rebels several months earlier, but they told him to stay in place until the time came. This was that time. Some say he ordered his men to lay down their weapons, others that he just disappeared and left them leaderless. Either way, the bulk of Gaddafi's forces in the capital took off their uniforms, revealing the jeans and T-shirts they had been wearing just in case, and vanished into the night, leaving just a few scores of loyalists and African mercenaries.

Mervat Mhani was on her balcony listening to the *muezzin* from the mosque and the gunfire. "I had thought of going into hiding after my arrest," she said. "I had buried my phone. But I didn't want to be cooped up. I wanted to be in the middle of it. I believe in destiny—whatever is written will happen." She whistled and ululated, the traditional cry of Libyan women at times of tumult or grief. "I had never done that before," she said. Nizar, hiding in a safe house on the outskirts of town, listened to Mustafa Abdel Jalil's speech, and then heard cries of "Allahu Akbhar!" He and his cousin went by bicycle to the center of town. "Mecca fell peacefully," he thought, hoping that the date was auspicious. "The Apaches were smashing a path along the coastal road, and I will never forget the thunderous noises," he recalled. "Grad rockets and mortar shells were whizzing and whistling over our heads as Gaddafi was lashing out at Tajoura and Ein Zara—the gateway from the East and, along with Fashloum and Souk-al-Jouma, the most active districts of Tripoli." Near Aisha Gaddafi's house, he heard rebels who had entered the mosque calling for soldiers to put down their weapons. "It's over, let us break fast together tonight," he heard them say. "The regime has fallen." It was not so easy. Snipers were shooting from the roofs, and the rebels shot back with Kalashnikovs and rocket-propelled grenades, before storming Aisha's compound. She was long gone, but the battle continued for hours before people from the neighborhood stormed in.

It should have been the moment Nizar and Mervat could rejoice. But just as they were feeling they could breathe again, news filtered through that their cousin Suleiman was missing. Their uncle spoke to a doctor at the main hospital. "I have hundreds of dead in the morgue," he said. "Most of them are Suleiman's age." He was twenty. "His mother knew," recalled Mervat, talking to me a few weeks later. "She kept saying he was dead." Mervat began to cry. "He was so young," she sobbed. "He hasn't lived his life." After three days, Suleiman's body was found in the morgue. He had been shot in the head. "I know it's a cliché, but it's real," said Nizar. "Nothing could make you prouder than to know he sacrificed his life for freedom. On his Facebook page back in February he wrote: 'This is it—ultimate sacrifice or victory. I would accept the ultimate sacrifice if it meant freedom.'"

Enas Dokali could hear the imams preaching from the mosques. "They were saying, 'Pray for us, God bring us victory,'" she recalled. "I kept asking the prison guards what was happening, but they didn't know. They were scared." As she sat in the office where she had been imprisoned, she could hear crossfire outside and the sound of a grenade exploding within the compound where she was being held. At dawn on the twenty-first, her captors put her in a car and took her to Abu Salim. "They shoved me into a room of files and old clothes with a stinking, bloodied carpet," she said. "There were ropes in there. It was obviously a place where people had died." They opened the window, so she could at least breathe some fresh air, and brought her a mattress. After a while she heard voices and realized there were other female prisoners in neighboring cells, but she couldn't communicate. For two days and two nights, she was on her own, hearing gunfire outside, not knowing what was going on. Abu Salim, a stronghold of Gaddafi supporters, was the last neighborhood to fall to the rebels. On the morning of the twenty-third, as she was washing, Enas heard a banging on her door and someone shouting, "Open up!" "I can't!" she replied. "It's locked from the outside! And I haven't got my head scarf on—wait!" Within a few minutes the door was broken down, and she was confronted with a man she had never seen before, who was bleeding from the mouth. "Go!" he shouted. "You're free!" He started to curse Gaddafi as he realized there were half a dozen female prisoners in the block. Enas was rooted to the spot, unable to understand what was happening. "Run, run!" he kept saying, and in the end, she did just that.

A few weeks later, retelling her story, it was the only moment where she looked as if she might break down. "I could tell from the accent that he was from Misrata, but I never got his name," she said. "He set me free. I want to see him again and thank him, but I don't know who he was." The women prisoners all ran together, until a family who lived near the prison took them in, along with dozens of male prisoners who had also been released by the fighters. "Some had been inside for twenty or thirty years," said Enas. "They had never seen the light of day. The family kept telling them to go inside the house, because they might be shot, but they just wanted to be in the sun for a few minutes. There was one old man wearing a diaper—he'd been there for years."

Enas called her brother, who came to collect her. "My mother didn't believe nothing had happened to me," she said. "My father said that when I was arrested he gave me to God for safekeeping."

The Tripoli Brigade and rebel units from Zintan swept up the road from Zawiyah on the night of the twenty-first, storming the headquarters of the Thirty-second Brigade, which was led by Gaddafi's son Khamis, twenty miles west of the capital, and clearing a way into the center. I drove into Tripoli at dawn the following morning. As the fighters careered down Gargaresh, one of the main shopping and residential arteries, leaning out of the windows of their pickups, flashing V for victory signs, antiaircraft weapons mounted on the back, the people of Tripoli came out onto balconies and into the streets to cheer. An old man knelt in the road and wept. "These are all my sons," he sobbed. "This is my country, this is my house, this is my street. And all of us are free." A carload of cheering young men drove past. "*Caio*, Gaddafi!" they shouted. "Gaddafi, bye-bye!" A group of fighters in a shop doorway played revolutionary music on a ghetto blaster and danced with their weapons. I asked an old woman with a craggy face and traditional blue Bedouin tattoos on her cheeks what should happen to Gaddafi, and she drew her finger across her neck in a gesture of throat slitting. But it wasn't over. Advancing on foot, past a mosque, I heard gunfire and ducked into a side street. Farther on there were snipers, the remnants of Gaddafi's forces, some in vehicles, others hiding in apartment blocks. A young man with an Irish accent—he had studied medicine in Dublin— told me they had caught nine or ten mercenaries that morning. For about half an hour I crouched by a wall, waiting for the shooting to finish. This was a day when people would lose their lives because they thought it was safe.

The NTC had announced the capture of Seif al-Islam on Sunday night. But on Monday evening, as great volleys of celebratory gunfire echoed through the city, he turned up at the Rixos Hotel, where some journalists were still staying. He had never been apprehended, but whether the misinformation was deliberate or accidental remained unclear. He took reporters to Bab al Aziziyah, where he stood in the back of a pickup, dressed in a khaki green T-shirt, waving his arms in the air in triumph in front of a crowd of loyalists waving posters of his father. "We are here. This is our country!" he shouted. "These are our people, and we live here, and we will die here. And we are going to win, because the people are with us. Look at them, look at them, in the streets—everywhere!" By morning he had disappeared. It had been his last public appearance as a free man.

The next day the fighters overran Bab al Aziziyah. Black smoke rose from the compound and the sound of heavy weapons boomed across town. I met Mukhtar Nagasa, the dentist from Bath who had loved Gaddafi so much as a boy. He and friends from Zintan had walked into Saadi Gaddafi's house on the northern side of the compound. With his dark beard and fatigues he looked like a rebel commander, but he had only started fighting in the last few weeks of the war. "I had no training," he said. "Just what I'd learned in school about how to handle a Kalashnikov." He hadn't needed any military prowess that day—by midafternoon there was no further resistance in Bab al Aziziyah. The Gaddafi family had fled, their supporters running with them or disappearing anonymously back into the city. On his cell phone, Mukhtar showed me snapshots of himself and his friends posing in front of a mural of old Tripoli in Saadi's house. He was carrying a framed line drawing of a young girl that he had taken as a souvenir. Suddenly he was embarrassed that I might think he was a looter. "It's to remind me of the moment, but I'll give it back after everything settles," he said. "I promise you."

The fighters from Misrata and a contingent led by Abdel Hakim Belhaj, the leader of the Libyan Islamic Fighting Group who had undergone the deradicalization program in Abu Salim, entered Bab al Aziziyah at the same time. By then the greatest danger was uncoordinated units shooting each other. They made straight for the house that had been bombed by the Americans, which Gaddafi had kept as a shrine to his own victimhood, the statue of his golden fist grasping the silver aircraft standing in front. I thought back to 2003, in Baghdad, when I watched Iraqis, assisted by an American tank equipped with a steel cable, pull down the statue of Saddam Hussein in Firdous Square. It was the U.S. Marines who choreographed that event, but the pictures broadcast around the world nonetheless came to represent the moment the Iraqi dictator met his downfall. The Libyans had no such assistance, and moreover technology meant that everyone could film or photograph his own part in history. Live TV pictures showed fighters filming on their cell phones as they tore up posters of Gaddafi in front of the statue. They climbed up the fist and swung off the plane's tail, posing not just for TV cameras but for each other, on the most potent symbol of Gaddafi's power.

The days rushed past in a welter of intense heat and arbitrary gunfire. Temperatures reached 95 degrees Fahrenheit, but when outside it was too insecure to take off my heavy flak jacket. Snipers remained in some buildings—one shot three rounds directly into the room at the Corinthia Hotel where I was editing a TV story, the bullets smashing the window and ricocheting from the ceiling and the walls, narrowly missing the producer and cameraman. Everyone had a story to tell. A young man I interviewed broke down as he told me that he and two other brothers had been arrested just before Tripoli fell and imprisoned in a warehouse attached to Yarmouk, one of several military bases used by the Khamis Brigade. On August 23rd, while the rebels were taking Bab al Aziziyah, Khamis's forces threw grenades and fired into the warehouse. As flames engulfed the building, he ran, losing in the chaos the brothers who had also been imprisoned. When rebel fighters found the warehouse the following day it was still smoldering, and inside were the charred bodies of some forty-five men who had been shot to death or died in the blaze.

Anger and excitement combined as Libyans entered the Gaddafi family compounds and houses to explore the secret network of tunnels and marvel at the luxury in which the family had lived. Someone cleared away the bodies of soldiers and mercenaries lying where they had fallen in gun battles on the roundabout just outside Bab al Aziziyah. The fighters from Zintan and Misrata became the heroes of the day, riding around in their armored pickups, tanned and muscled from their months of fighting, firing into the air in delight and celebration. Ahmed began to breathe more easily. Gaddafi had not used chemical weapons, and—although his loyalists were still fighting from his hometown of Sirte—it seemed that the moment might have passed.

That year Eid al Fitr, the day that marks the end of Ramadan, fell on August 31st. At dawn, thousands of people crammed into Green Square, now renamed Martyrs' Square, a great murmur rising from the kneeling crowd as they rose and bent down and rose again in prayer. Afterward, some started to sing and dance, waving the new flag. As I walked through the crowd, people thrust trays of sweets at me. Gaddafi had always decreed the date of Eid, irrespective of what the imams in Mecca judged to be the correct phase of the moon. "This is the first time in my life I feel free and can pray freely without any restriction from Gaddafi's regime," said one man. "I need a hundred, a thousand, a million words to say what I feel," said a middle-aged woman in a blue head scarf gripping my arm. On the roof of Tripoli Castle, the fortress that overlooks the square, a man in what looked like a Mexican sombrero was waving an oversized flag. Someone had pasted cartoons around a lamppost, images of Gaddafi as a rat, a vampire or a monkey. He was no longer the Guide, he was Abu Shafshufa, "Old Frizzy Head," an object of derision, not fear. A group of young women, wearing tunics and trousers, pale-colored head scarfs pinned modestly around their faces, were gathered around giggling—they had never seen Gaddafi caricatured before.

On panels erected at the foot of the fortress, people had started to post pictures of those who had died in the uprising in Tripoli and over the preceding six months. No one knew how many had been killed, nor how many were missing. And the fighting wasn't over—Gaddafi's forces still controlled his hometown of Sirte, and scores of young men had gone to fight there, and in the strongholds of Sabha and Bani Walid. But Operation Mermaid Dawn had succeeded. The forty-two-year rule of Muammar Gaddafi was over.

CHAPTER TEN

AFTER THE REVOLUTION

They wept and quarreled: freedom was so wild.

—W. H. AUDEN, "SONNETS FROM CHINA II"

No retribution, no taking matters into your own hands and no oppression. I hope that the revolution will not stumble because of any of these things.

—MUSTAFA ABDEL JALIL, LIBYAN INTERIM PRESIDENT,

SEPTEMBER 2011

Huda Abuzeid, whose father, Ali, had been murdered in London, went to see Gaddafi's body before it was put on public display in Misrata. She had returned to Libya to take part in the revolution and was working for a minister in the interim government, who asked her to accompany him. She was in turmoil during the three-hour drive from Tripoli, as she imagined seeing the body of the man who had destroyed her family and dominated their lives for so long. They were ushered into a room, and there he was, laid out, face bruised, hair matted, his body battered and bloodied. She stared. "In the end I felt nothing," she told me the next day. "He seemed so small, and I found myself thinking that he was just a man, nothing more." She paused to gather her thoughts, and began to cry. "Then I realized that the last time I saw a body in a state like that was when I saw my father." Huda, like other Libyans, had hoped that coming face-to-face with the evidence of Gaddafi's death would bring closure, but it just conjured painful memories. Even in death, he had a hold over them.

The last gasp of the war, after Tripoli fell, had become more ragged and desperate by the day. The fighters, who could no longer be called rebels because they controlled the capital, besieged Gaddafi's stronghold of Bani Walid and launched a series of attacks on Sirte, his hometown. By the final week, more men were being killed and injured from "friendly fire" than from genuine battles, as scores of uncoordinated brigades from Tobruk, Benghazi, Tripoli and Misrata piled in, firing wildly and destroying as much of Sirte as possible. Gaddafi and his remaining followers had been cornered, with no water or electricity. They were now the rats, scurrying down alleyways, lurking in culverts, hiding underground. The sober men of the National Transitional Council, in Benghazi and Tripoli, were trying to establish a government and convince the world that they were a responsible and legitimate authority, but the fighters lived a different reality. This was their chance for revenge.

I drove east from Misrata to Sirte to see what was left of Gaddafi's dream city, on which he had lavished millions. He had created a place of white-washed villas, concrete apartment blocks and monumental government buildings decorated with murals glorifying himself, now defaced or destroyed. The Ouagadougou Conference Center, an imposing green-and-white-striped, curved structure where Gaddafi had announced his United States of Africa vision in 1999, was still standing, but the windows were smashed and mortars had drilled huge charred holes in the walls. Some of Gaddafi's men had fought for weeks from inside the compound; debris and bullet casings littered the road outside. An old man, bearded and stooped, carrying a white sack across his shoulder, was walking past. His name was Suleiman, he said, and he had only just realized that all his neighbors had left. "They never asked, where is Suleiman?" he said. "I woke up and they had all gone." In his youth he had worked as a day laborer. He wasn't one of the privileged residents who had lived in the luxury villas Gaddafi built for his tribesmen and others who showed him loyalty. He had no idea where he was going, nor how he would get there, a senile old man caught up in a conflict of which he had no understanding.

Now that the fighting was over, other Sirte residents were coming back to see what had happened to their properties. Some buildings were still smoldering, flames licking around the window frames, black smoke rising. In the Al Madar area, which had endured some of the heaviest fighting, three goats were browsing among the shell casings, spent bullets, rubble and twisted metal. An office chair had ended up in the middle of the road. The blackened hulks of what had been shops and apartments, holes blown through the concrete walls, doors swinging open, rose from streets flooded by rain or burst water mains. Someone had scrawled on a wall: "Libya will be free and the dogs will be gone." In Sirte, those who said they were fighting for a better Libya had created a desolation and called it peace. A heavy-set man who looked as if he had not shaved for several days drove up in a blue pickup piled high with blankets. "Why are they going inside our houses and destroying everything?" he asked. "We are civilians and we fled the bombardment. Gaddafi is dead. We are 120,000 people in Sirte. What are we going to do? Where do they expect us to go?" A smartly dressed commander tried to restrain one of the packs of looters riffling through the deserted buildings, but no one was listening. The fighters saw the residents of Sirte as Gaddafi's people, and they had no intention of letting them return to the lives they had enjoyed before the conflict.

In the garden of the Mahari Hotel on the seafront, human rights investigators found the decomposing bodies of fifty-three men, some with their hands tied behind their backs, others with bandages around injuries. Spent cartridges of AK-47 and FN-1 rifles were scattered around the blood-stained lawn, bullet holes in the ground suggesting that the men had been shot where their bodies were lying. Graffiti sprayed in red and black on the hotel walls named the Misrata brigades that had been occupying the area for the past two weeks: Tiger, Jaguar, Lion, Support and Citadel. Residents who were about to bury the bodies identified four of the dead as local officials loyal to Gaddafi, and said that several of the others were patients who had recently been released from the hospital. Human rights groups said some three hundred people were killed in Sirte in revenge attacks by fighters who were by now half crazed with exhaustion, adrenalin and fury. No one was in control, no one was stopping the violence that was not only diminishing hopes of reconciliation, but making Libya increasingly difficult to govern.

I drove on to Benghazi, another six hours along the straight desert road, through towns I had approached from the other direction with the rebels back in March, in the early days of the uprising. I found myself remembering lines from Keith Douglas, the World War II poet who fought along this road in 1942:

> Up there, the immensely long road goes by
> to Tripoli: the wind and dust reach
> the secrets of the whole
> poor town whose masks would still deceive a passer-by;
> faces with sightless doors
> for eyes, with cracks like tears
> oozing at corners. A dead tank alone
> leans where the gossips stood.

Wind and dust blew through Nowfilia and Bin Jawad, the small towns that marked the farthest point the eastern brigades had reached before Gaddafi's forces pushed them back in March. The houses were shuttered— it seemed that no one had dared come back yet. The rows of white villas where the oil workers lived in Ras Lanuf were deserted but undamaged, like an American suburb in a nuclear holocaust movie, where the people disappear but the buildings remain intact. I remembered a family I had watched leaving in a battered car back in March, when the rebels had made Ras Lanuf their base as they tried to push west. A few camels meandered along the roadside among torn car tires and the occasional rusting pickup, but much of the debris of war had been carted away. Just west of Brega a crumpled TV tower poked from rubble—it had been hit by a NATO strike. Two dozen burned-out tanks and armored personnel carriers were parked near where the green arch at Ajdabia's western gate had stood, before the fighters who used to gather there demolished it, because it made such an easy target. Someone had hung a banner from two of the tank turrets that said: THE MARTYRS OF AJDABIA. Crowds had come out to welcome the fighters home from Sirte, waving flags, honking horns and cheering. By the time I got to Benghazi, the road was clogged with cars full of excited families, the children dressed in green, red and black, leaning out of the windows waving V signs, as fighters shot into the air with their Kalashnikovs and the occasional heavy machine gun. It was over. They had won.

Sunday, October 23rd, was Liberation Day. The National Transitional Council had decided to hold the celebration in Benghazi as a tribute to the role the people of Libya's second city had played in the revolution. The square where they had demonstrated on February 17th was filled with singing, cheering, flag-waving crowds. One young woman wore a floppy top hat in the revolutionary colors. A little girl was brandishing a glove puppet of Gaddafi. They threw perfumed water over the fighters, and danced. A stall sold black sneakers decorated with a picture of Gaddafi's head on the body of a rat and the words *zenga zenga* printed on either side of the shoe. An elderly woman insisted that I take a picture of her holding up a poster of her son, who had died in the fighting; others gathered round, showing me photographs of husbands and brothers, the martyrs who would go down in Libyan history. The deputy head of the NTC, the Benghazi lawyer Abdul Hafez Ghoga, made the declaration of liberation, saying, "Raise your head high. You are a free Libyan," and the people in the square echoed: "You are a free Libyan."

Mustafa Abdel Jalil, the former justice minister who had become the interim president of the NTC, got up to speak. Small and diffident, quietly spoken, balding and dressed in a gray suit and a gray tie, he was as different from Colonel Gaddafi as you could get. Libyans respected him because they believed he had tried to stand up to Gaddafi and had deserted him at the earliest opportunity. "I call on everyone for forgiveness, tolerance and reconciliation. We must get rid of hatred and envy from our souls," he said. Then he deviated from the text his speechwriters had provided. Libyan law, he said, would now be based on the *sharia*. For example, the law Gaddafi introduced banning polygamy would be rescinded. "Is that what we fought for?" asked Huda Abuzeid when I saw her a few hours later. "So Libyan men can marry four wives?" Islamists might have been happy with the proposal, but Huda was not the only one to protest. Many Libyans wanted Libya to be prosperous and liberal, a place where people would practice Islam but not be confined by the edicts of a government that saw the *sharia* as the sole basis of law. Western governments that had backed the revolution were also startled by Jalil's speech. The next day he was forced to qualify what he said. "Libyans are Muslims, but we are moderate Muslims," he said.

What did that mean? The outcome of the debate would define the kind of country the revolution had created.

Just outside Benghazi, in a dusty, gravel-covered compound belonging to a Turkish construction company, among cement mixers and bags of aggregate, I came across some of the losers of the Libyan Revolution. Six thousand Tawergha—men, women and children—who had been driven out of their town by the Misrata brigades were camped in warehouses and workers' quarters. Dark-skinned, swathed in brightly colored robes and veils, the women sat cradling their children on carpets laid on the concrete warehouse floor. They looked like refugees in Darfur or Niger, the familiar victims of famine and war in Africa. The Tawergha had allied themselves to Gaddafi, and the allegation that their men had carried out a campaign of rape in Misrata ensured that they would not be forgiven. When the war turned the rebels' way, in mid-August, the Tawergha had fled their town. The Misrata brigades stormed in, ransacking and burning houses, scrawling "Misrata's slaves" on the walls, ensuring that the inhabitants understood there would be no compromise: The Tawergha could never return.

The women told me they had fled Tawergha nine days before Tripoli fell, walking for forty miles before finding trucks, which had taken them to Jufra, deep in the desert, where they had found shelter in an unused factory. The Misrata brigades had pursued them, forcing them to leave Jufra, and now they were dependent on the kindness of the Benghazi brigades, who had said they could stay here, at least for the moment. "Our men were in the Libyan army, but they were only obeying orders," said a middle-aged woman. "Our life was good before. All I want is peace again." The men were hanging out around the old workers' quarters, where families of eight or ten were crammed into small rooms designed for two people. "We watched TV and were told we were winning," one explained. "We thought Benghazi had been destroyed. The TV said that to make us stay on Gaddafi's side."

Mohammed al Hadi Mohammed, a man in his midthirties who said he had been unemployed, told me that several hundred Misrata fighters in pickups with DEATH BRIGADE emblazoned on the side had pursued them to a military base in Jufra, where the fighters took the old men to one side and forced the younger ones to kneel with their hands on their heads. The fighters searched the young men and found car keys in Mohammed's pocket. In his car they came across what he described to me as "a bit of green cloth"—presumably a Gaddafi flag, or the remnants of one. Half a dozen fighters set upon him, hitting him on the head and back with their rifle butts and bayonets until he passed out. This had happened two weeks previously; he lifted his shirt to show me the scars. His twenty-five-year-old nephew, Issam, had gone to buy food for the family, he said, and on his return, the fighters made him run laps. Then they shot him dead. Issam's mother emerged from the next room onto the muddy pathway where we were talking. "Issam wasn't in the military," she said. "He had just got a job as a nurse at Tawergha hospital. I don't know why they killed him." More people came up to tell their stories. The Misrata brigades would shout insults, accusing them of being traitors and mercenaries, they said. A young man told me how one of his friends had been beaten and told to identify who among them had been in the army. Under duress, he had pointed arbitrarily at a dozen or so men, who were taken away, never to be seen again. Day after day it went on, until one of the Jufra brigades turned up. "They saved us," said one of the Tawergha. "They gave us security." But in the end, the local brigades couldn't prevail over the men from Misrata, so they arranged for fighters from Benghazi to come and collect the refugees. "What caused the problem was the behavior of Tawergha people in Misrata," said one man. "They got out of hand. But it's not right to blame all of us."

As we left, I asked the young man from Benghazi who had been translating for me what he thought about the Tawergha. He snorted. "What did they expect?" he said. "It's war. They killed people. They raped people. Of course they got beaten, and some were executed." I said I knew that some Tawergha had done bad things, but I wondered if there was an issue of racism here as well. I had heard that lighter-skinned Libyans like him sometimes referred to black Libyans as *abed*, meaning slaves. He looked at me in astonishment. "I've got black friends, and when I call them *abed*, they don't mind," he said.

Back in Tripoli, Mukhtar Nagasa had taken it upon himself to try to reconcile people. Although Zintan had gone over to the rebel side at the beginning, Zintanis, he explained, had not been on bad terms with Gaddafi's tribe, so they could act as a bridge. It wasn't easy. Whenever I met Mukhtar, his phone rang constantly with people asking him to intercede in disputes. He went to Bani Walid to try to persuade Gaddafi supporters to accept the revolution. "We have to reach out," he said. "We need to focus on this over the next six months or we'll have a problem in ten years' time." He took me to a friend's farm where a Zintan brigade was stationed, among them a former guard of Gaddafi's who had defected in March, and a Tawergha man who had fought with the rebels. Both were under the protection of the Zintanis; neither dared leave the compound. "It's crazy," said Mukhtar. "These people are on our side, but they don't dare walk in the street." He took a seven-year-old boy who was distantly related to the Gaddafi family on a trip with his nephew into the city center. "His mum hadn't let him out of the house for two months, and when he saw the anti-Gaddafi graffiti he covered his eyes, he was so shocked," said Mukhtar. "I'm really worried about those kids, because when they go back to school, the other kids will curse them."

Some of those who had backed the revolution were getting frustrated. Asma Imtiar, a young dentist from Sirte who had been treating the rebels' teeth for free as her contribution, tried to organize an ambulance to go to her hometown but found it difficult to get any support from the interim authorities. "People from Sirte and Tawergha still think Muammar Gaddafi is the best," she said. "We need to convince them that the revolution is for them too. Our problem is that we have this instinct for revenge—we each have Gaddafi inside us. Muammar killed us, and we think the solution is more killing."

Relations between allies were deteriorating too. It started back in July, before Tripoli fell, when Major General Fattah Younes, the commander of the rebel army in the east, was assassinated. His position had been disputed from the start. Not only had he been Gaddafi's minister of the interior, but also one of the army officers closest to the Brother Leader. Although he resigned early on, after Gaddafi's *zenga zenga* speech, saying that he had ordered his men not to shoot at protesters in Benghazi, many rebels didn't trust him. Unlike Mustafa Abdel Jalil, who resigned around the same time, he had had no public disagreements with Gaddafi. As far as anyone knew, he had been utterly loyal to the Brother Leader.

Nonetheless, by April, Fattah Younes seemed to be broadly accepted as the commander of the military in the east, pushing to one side Colonel Khalifa Heftar. But the suspicion never went away. The *shabab* militia resented his attempts to send them back from the front line, reducing theirs to a support role while his professional soldiers did the fighting. Word got out that he had been to Rome to meet a general who was still on Gaddafi's side. Fattah Younes's supporters said he'd been trying to persuade the general to join the revolution; his detractors said he'd been consorting with, maybe even giving intelligence to, the enemy. By July, the Misrata rebels were forcing Gaddafi's men back west toward Tripoli. The Nafousa Mountain fighters were closing in on the capital from the other side. Yet in the east, the front line remained stubbornly at Brega. The muttering grew louder. Why were Fattah Younes's men making so little progress? Whose side was he on?

I met Mutassim Fattah Younes, the general's youngest son, in Benghazi in October. On July 28th, he said, his father was in Ajdabia with a dozen bodyguards—he had dispatched to the front line the Special Forces brigade that normally stayed with him. Late at night some eighty vehicles full of fighters with heavy weapons arrived at his father's headquarters, demanding that he accompany them to Benghazi. They had an arrest warrant signed by the then interim deputy prime minister, Ali Essawi. The general phoned the NTC leader Mustafa Abdel Jalil, but his cell phone was switched off. He called one of the most senior men in the general's Obeidi tribe, who went to Jalil's house, only to be told that Jalil was sleeping and couldn't be disturbed. There was not a lot of choice—he had to go. The road to Benghazi was clear, and no one stopped the convoy on the checkpoints. The general's land cruiser was driven into the Garyounis military base, but the car with his aides inside was shut out. Something was badly wrong, but by the time his Special Forces brigade arrived to surround the base it was too late. "The vehicle with my father and his two aides in it had been driven out of the back gate," said Mutassim. "They were taken to the Obeida ibn Jarrah base."

The general must have known then that his fate was sealed. The Obeida ibn Jarrah, named after a companion of the Prophet, were a militia of Islamist fighters, many of whom had been in Abu Salim prison. Their brothers and cousins had been killed in the massacre. Some were survivors of the battles around Beyda and Derna in 1995 and 1996. They had gone through no deradicalization process. To them Fattah Younes would always be an enemy. Two Egyptian workers at the base later testified that militiamen opened the doors to the vehicle containing Fattah Younes and his men and opened fire. All were killed.

The investigation into his murder drifted on, with no resolution. Neither Mustafa Abdel Jalil nor anyone else in the interim authorities wanted to antagonize the Islamists by demanding that they hand over the killers. Even though the group in whose custody he was killed had been identified, there were many unanswered questions. What were the names of the individuals who killed him? Would they be brought to trial? Where were they? No one seemed able or willing to explain why the order for his arrest had been issued, nor the connection between those who had seized him in Ajdabia and those who killed him in Benghazi. This was Libya, where no one in a position of authority had any experience of transparency or the rule of law, where awkward questions were dealt with in secret or not at all. Jalil announced that he had sacked the government, including Essawi, but they carried on working and no replacements were announced. There was even confusion about General Fattah Younes's replacement. Some said it was his old rival, General Khalifa Heftar, others that it was his colleague from Tobruk, General Suleiman Mahmoud Obeidi. No official announcement was made, as if somehow ambiguity and confusion was the best option.

Nothing appeased the family. Mutassim Fattah Younes told me he was still a supporter of the revolution, but he wasn't going to accept blood money, nor let his father's death be forgotten. "We, the family, will find out what happened, even if it takes the rest of our lives," he said. "But we will do it by law. If we get nowhere with the NTC, we'll take it to the International Criminal Court in The Hague." A huge poster of Fattah Younes was hung near the wall of the North Courthouse where the Abu Salim families put the photographs of the men they had lost in the prison massacre. He loomed over them in his khaki uniform, with his sunglasses and white hair, an emblem of the perils of a revolution in a country where political murder had gone unpunished for so long there were no credible structures to bring killers to account, and where no leader had the confidence or the authority to hold together those who had united for freedom, and were now tearing themselves apart.

By October, the conquering heroes from Zintan and Misrata were losing some of their luster in the eyes of Tripoli residents. At first it was lighthearted. The Zintan boys were reluctant to go home, not least because they were having fun roaring around the capital in pickups with heavy machine-guns mounted on the back, cheered on by young women who treated them as pop stars. In cosmopolitan Tripoli, girls would come out on the street, keen to have their photographs taken with the heroes of the revolution. In conservative Zintan, a young man had little opportunity to meet any women other than a cousin or the daughter of a family friend who his mother might have decided was a suitable match. But the Zintanis, seen by more sophisticated Tripolitans as country bumpkins, got a reputation for stealing. Fair or unfair, it became the joke of the town. At Eid al Adha in early November, when families bought sheep to slaughter, the joke was: "Why are the sheep naked this year? Because the Zintanis have stolen the wool." An elephant disappeared from the zoo—the poor creature probably died of starvation—and everyone said the Zintanis had taken it. One evening Mukhtar took me home to meet his wife and mother-in-law. As we entered the house, two small boys ran past, shouting at him. I asked what they were saying. "They're asking, 'Where's the elephant?'" he replied.

The jokes became less funny. The fighters' armored pickups clogged the Tripoli traffic, and they often ignored checkpoints set up by neighborhood committees. Everyone was getting fed up with their habit of "happy shooting," loosing off into the air whenever there was something to celebrate, or just when they felt like it. People were getting killed by falling bullets, and there was a growing sense of anarchy on the streets. I called Mukhtar one day and found he had gone back to Zintan for a funeral. A young cousin of his, Khaled, had been driving with a friend, who had shot into the air when stopped at a checkpoint. The men on guard berated the Zintan boys for their ill discipline, but as they drove off, the friend fired into the air again. Angered by the Zintanis' behavior, the checkpoint guards fired at the vehicle, injuring the friend in the leg and killing Khaled with two bullets to the head. Mukhtar was trying to stop his cousin's friends from wreaking revenge. "I lied," he said. "I told them we'd got the guy who did it, and he's being held at the airport."

One night in October I was kept awake by persistent gunfire until the early hours—it didn't sound like happy shooting, but a battle. The next day I learned that two people had been killed and seven injured when fighters from Zintan tried to enter the Central Hospital to kill a man they had shot and injured for some reason earlier in the day. When doctors refused to let them enter, one pulled a pistol. Hundreds of Zintan fighters then turned up, followed by members of the Tripoli Brigade whose job it was to secure the city. The battle continued until dawn.

Underneath the rivalry was a deeper divide, foreshadowed by the murder of General Fattah Younes. The Zintan leaders were suspicious of the Tripoli Brigade, because it was led by Abdel Hakim Belhaj, the leader of the Libyan Islamic Fighting Group, which had changed its name to the Libyan Islamic Movement. Its February 17th Brigade fought in the east, under the command of Ismail Salabi, the brother of Sheikh Ali al Salabi, the cleric based in Doha. Belhaj—who had been rendered back to Tripoli from the Far East with Sami al Saadi in 2004, and had gone through the same deradicalization process in prison—came to the fore when he made a speech in front of the golden fist statue the day Bab al Aziziyah was taken. Other commanders complained that they had no idea how he was appointed leader of the Tripoli Brigade, but their suspicions were aroused in September, when he attended a meeting of militia leaders trying to sort out a unified command, accompanied by Major General Hamad Ben Ali al-Attiyah, chief of staff of the Qatari armed forces. The Qataris, it emerged, had funneled some of their weapons through the NTC, but other consignments had gone directly to the Libyan Islamic Movement brigades.

Secular members of the interim government feared that Belhaj was still receiving weapons from the Qataris. "To any country, I repeat, please do not give any funds or weapons to any Libyan faction without the approval of the NTC," said Ali Tarhuni, the oil and finance minister, an economist who had lived in the United States for nearly forty years and returned in March. No one could accuse Tarhuni of cooperating with Gaddafi, but several other leaders, including interim Prime Minister Mahmoud Jibril and President Mustafa Abdel Jalil, had held positions under the old regime, which made them easy targets for Belhaj and the other Islamists, who urged them to stand down. The political lines of the new Libya were being set. A group called Etelaf, meaning Union, had established itself in Benghazi and Tripoli to—as they put it—protect the revolution. They put flyers round mosques, accusing Jibril of nepotism, but Etelaf's real, unstated, complaint was that he was secular. Etelaf was a pressure group, but it seemed to be positioning itself as a political party, ready to bid for power when the moment came.

Following the killing of Osama bin Laden in May 2011, Abu Yahyia al Libi, one of the LIFG members who remained in Afghanistan, had become second in command of Al Qaeda. "At this crossroads you have found your-selves, you either choose a secular regime that pleases the greedy croco-diles of the West, and for them to use it as a means to fulfill their goals, or you take a strong position and establish the religion of Allah," he said in a video message addressed to Libyans and distributed on jihadi Web sites in late 2011. Al Qaeda's new leader, the Egyptian Ayman al Zawahiri, was one of its most extreme. Would the Egyptian and the Libyan now turn their attention to the power vacuums in their home countries? A franchise known as Al Qaeda in the Mahgreb was already active in Mali and Mauri-tania. What was to stop it from extending its reach across the border into the vast desert of Fezzan and garnering further support in the old jihadi stronghold of Derna, in eastern Libya?

I asked Sami al Saadi what kind of Libya he and his Islamist colleagues envisaged.

"I want a liberal country, where people can say what they think with-out fear or threat," he said. "There is no compulsion in Islam."

"Do you support *sharia* punishments like cutting the hands of thieves?"

"If the majority want those punishments, I would respect the majority opinion."

"Is that what they want?"

"Maybe."

"Do you want Libya to be like Afghanistan under the Taliban?"

"Libya is not Afghanistan."

"So which country might be a model?"

"I would like Libya to be like Turkey."

I felt I would never be able to penetrate what Sami really believed. Libyans constantly told me that they were conservative or moderate

Muslims, but these labels were undefined and untested. Under Gaddafi, Islamists were banned but had organized nonetheless, so the Muslim Brotherhood and the Libyan Islamic Movement existed as putative political groupings. The liberal opposition had been in exile, and secular Libyans inside the country had on the whole turned their faces away from politics. There were dozens of people who might want to stand for election on a liberal ticket, and almost as many fledgling parties. No umbrella group like Etelaf was emerging. In Tunisia and Egypt, Islamist candidates in the first elections after the uprisings won, because they got their message out, and many voters felt that to vote against them was to vote against Islam. It seemed inevitable that in Libya too the Islamists would be the best organized and the strongest. But if Islamists won initial elections, would they keep their word about building democracy?

As I turned these questions over, I found myself wanting to ask Tarek Ben Halim, the banker who had tried to work with Seif al Gaddafi, what he thought. He was the first Libyan I had met, eight years before the revolution, and we had often debated his article of faith that democracy was the answer to the problems of the Arab world. But Tarek had died of a brain tumor in 2009, at the age of fifty-five. He had dreamed of democracy in his homeland for so many years, yet he never got to see the Arab Spring with all of its promise and danger.

Shortly after dawn on August 29th, a convoy of Mercedes-Benz sedans slipped across the border into Algeria. Inside were Gaddafi's wife, Safia, plus their daughter Aisha, sons Mohammed and Hannibal and their families. Hana Gaddafi may have also been there. They had to get to a hospital fast—Aisha was at the point of going into labor. She gave birth to a baby girl the following day. Her husband and two of her children had reportedly been killed in the NATO bombing alongside the Gaddafi's sixth son, Seif al-Arab, but like so much information about the Gaddafi family, it was impossible to confirm. The Algerian government mistrusted the NTC, because Islamists like Belhaj had previously been linked to jihadis who fought in Algeria's civil war in the 1990s. They said they would give the Gaddafi family asylum for "strictly humanitarian reasons," and confined them to a luxury villa fifteen miles west of Algiers.

Through September, Colonel Gaddafi, holed up in Sirte, made occasional phone calls to Al Rai, a little-known TV station broadcasting from the Syrian capital, Damascus. He described those who had overthrown him as "germs and rats" and blamed France, Italy and the UK for his fate. Then he said it was impossible to overthrow him, because he had given up his position in 1977 when he created the Jamahiriya, the state of the masses. "The political regime in Libya is the people's regime, where the power is for the people practiced by all Libyans, men and women, in people's conferences and committees," he said. "This magnificent regime cannot be toppled." In his time of desperation, Muammar Gaddafi clung to the belief that he was simultaneously a beloved leader and a mere bystander, that he had bequeathed to Libyans a system of government, not a void where the state should be.

The Algerian government said the Gaddafi family could remain on the condition that they kept silent, but after the traditional forty-day mourning period, Aisha sent a message to the Libyan people via Al Rai. "My father has not left, he is always among us," she said. "Don't forget the orders of your father urging you to continue fighting, even if you no longer hear his voice." In December her lawyer put out a statement calling on the International Criminal Court to investigate the killing of her father and her brother Mutassim. "The images of this savagery were broadcast throughout the world, causing my client severe emotional distress," he wrote. Khamis, the seventh son and head of the Thirty-second Brigade, was killed in a NATO air strike the day Aisha and the rest fled. He had been reported dead several times before, but this time it was true. After forty days, Al Rai put out a message mourning his death. That left Seif al-Islam and Saadi.

In late August, Saadi put out feelers to see if he might negotiate a deal. In an interview with the TV station Al Arabiya, without revealing his location, he said that he and his father would lay down their arms. Abdel Hakim Belhaj said he had spoken to Saadi, and he wanted to surrender. But it seems that even if the NTC had been willing to talk, Mutassim, Seif al-Islam and their father didn't agree. A few days later Saadi fled south into the Sahara, crossing into Niger in a nine-vehicle convoy, accompanied by three generals and an Australian bodyguard. Niger, which had benefited from Gaddafi's largesse but which remained one of the poorest countries on earth, was not Saadi's first choice. The Mexican government later said it had foiled a plot to smuggle him to Punta Mita, a luxury resort on the Pacific coast much frequented by film stars, where he planned a new existence under the name Daniel Bejar. The group of Canadians and Mexicans planning Operation Guest were arrested. Saadi would have to stay in Niger, where the government offered him asylum in exchange for silence.

Seif al-Islam, like his father, saw no distinction between family and country. "Every Libyan is Muammar Gaddafi, every Libyan is Seif al-Islam," he said on Al Rai. The son who had wanted reform and change had become as hard line as his old enemy, his younger brother Mutassim. "I say go to hell, you rats and NATO behind you. This is our country, we live in it, and we die in it and we are continuing the struggle. I'm in Libya, alive, free and intend to go to the very end and exact revenge." Within a few weeks, he was trying to follow Saadi into exile in Niger. Only the Tuareg knew the desert well enough to find their way across the unmarked border, so one of Seif's entourage asked a nomad if he could help "someone important" get across. Immediately suspicious, the Tuareg alerted a brigade from Zintan that was in the area. In the early hours the fighters stopped two land cruisers. A tall, bearded figure swathed in sand-colored cloth got out. "My name is Abdul Salam," he said. It was no good. Facial hair and a turban couldn't disguise one of the most well-known faces in Libya. They arrested him without a struggle and flew him to Zintan.

The manner of his capture made a stark contrast with that of his father. Video taken by the fighters shows him sitting on the plane, looking out of the window, still in his robes. His right hand is roughly bandaged—he later said that he had lost the top joints in a NATO air strike outside Bani Walid, but Libyans believe the rebels cut off his fingers as punishment for wagging them in the speech he gave at the beginning of the revolution. Pictures taken after the plane landed in Zintan show hundreds of people climbing all over it, sitting on the wings and tail, shouting, but somehow the fighters got Seif out unharmed and put him in an anonymous concrete house, the location of which was kept secret so that no one would attack him. Two representatives of the International Committee of the Red Cross and a Ukrainian doctor who worked in a Zintan hospital saw him later that day. They said the fingers needed amputation, because gangrene was setting in, but otherwise they pronounced him well if a little frightened.

He doesn't sound frightened in a video recorded the next day. Easing himself into an armchair, wincing in pain, presumably from the injury to his fingers, he lectures the men around him, referring to NATO members as "infidels" and telling the Zintan fighters that they have made a huge mistake in trusting the people of Benghazi, Misrata and the Nafousa Mountains. His harshest warning is about Belhaj and Ali al Salabi, the Islamists he worked with on the deradicalization program. "I swear to God I did too much good to those two guys, and they paid me back with betrayal," he says. "I assure you that Abdel Hakim Belhaj and Ali al Salabi will not bring any good to the country nor to the Libyan people." It is a mirror image of his February 20th speech. Then, dressed in a sober black suit and tie, a clean-shaven Seif wagged his right index finger and warned the Libyan people that Al Qaeda would take over and "rivers of blood" would flow. Now he wagged his uninjured left index finger. "Never deny that on the day Seif al-Islam was taken prisoner, he warned all of you," he said.

The commander of the brigade that caught Seif al-Islam, Osama Juwali, was appointed defense minister when the NTC announced a new government the following week. It was a reward for Seif's orderly capture, and also an acknowledgment of the importance the high-profile prisoner gave Zintan—the fighters may have been right when they said they could better protect him in their small town, but he was also a useful bargaining chip in power struggles with other cities. The bigger question was, What would happen to him next? Most Libyans wanted him tried in Libya and then executed, after what they saw as an inevitable guilty verdict, whatever the charges might be. Luis Moreno-Ocampo, the prosecutor of the International Criminal Court, who visited Tripoli a few days later, agreed that it might be possible to put him on trial there, but that judges from The Hague would have to be involved. Libya had lawyers and judges, but it had no functioning legal system because the courts had been subjugated to Gaddafi's committees and secret police. It was another void left by Gaddafi that could take months or years to fill.

Huda Abuzeid was among those trying to make order out of chaos, getting a Finance Ministry up and running, trying to persuade those who had suddenly been thrust into power to communicate what they were doing. As a woman and an exile, she sometimes found it hard to make her voice heard. There were days when she wanted to pack it all in and go back to London, but then she would be in a room full of people, or out on the street, and realize that for the first time in her life everyone around her was speaking Arabic the way her family spoke it. She was overwhelmed by a feeling of coming home. "I never had any sense of Libya pre 17th of Feb; it was a place that just symbolized so much pain and loss that I could hardly bear to think about it," she wrote on Facebook. "I hadn't been there since I was a toddler, but since I returned nine months ago I find every time I leave that I miss it. I recognize the people, and traits which are out of place elsewhere suddenly make sense. That ache I never understood is suddenly less so in the company of relatives I never had a chance to know. It's hard to take London out of a girl, but I love being a Libyan in a country full of Libyans."

After the failure of the attempted overthrow on Gaddafi in 1984 and the years in Abu Salim, Wanise Elisawi also finally felt that now was his chance to do something. During the revolution he had been part of a security committee in Benghazi, ensuring that Gaddafi's people didn't mount a counterrevolution and trying to stop revenge attacks. "Sometimes I too had the feeling that I wanted to kill someone," he told me. "But I could control it, because we were winning." Now he was a bureaucrat in charge of "electronic government," establishing an online system for visas, identity cards and all the paraphernalia of a normal country. He moved between an office in Benghazi and one in Tripoli, staffed by young men and women who had studied computing and were developing the requisite systems. It was hard to get anything organized. "We did everything backward," he said. "We finished the revolution and then created these offices, but really we needed to get prepared first." He blamed Gaddafi for destroying the organs of state but could see that Mustafa Abdel Jalil was struggling to replace the old ways with something that could work. "He's a good, clean person and lawful, but truly he's not a good decision maker," he said.

Jalil was initially popular because most Libyans agreed with Wanise that he was a man of principle, but it was frequently unclear what, if anything, he did. The NTC was struggling to assert its authority. It was made up primarily of academics, lawyers and other professionals from the east, plus representatives from the rest of the country, some of whose names remained unpublished even after Gaddafi had been toppled. As a self-appointed body, its legitimacy had been in question from the start, but while the fighting continued most Libyans were willing to let it champion their cause overseas—which it did very effectively—and worry about politics later. The question of how to disarm the militias went unresolved, and while basic services were maintained, voluntary neighborhood groups were filling in where local government should have been. The first interim prime minister, Mahmoud Jibril, was widely criticized, because he was rarely in the country, and he had worked for Seif al Gaddafi, which made him vulnerable to the Islamists' whispering campaign. After Liberation Day, the NTC elected a sixty-one-year-old professor of electrical engineering, Abdulrahim al-Keib, as the new interim prime minister, to govern until elections in June 2012. The first question Libyans asked was: Abdulrahim who? No one knew him, because he had left Libya for the United States in 1976 and had most recently been teaching in the United Arab Emirates. Asked to explain their choice, NTC members said he was "quiet and friendly." Exile ensured that he had no history with Gaddafi, but he was a dual Libyan/American citizen. There was no law against that, but then, there was no law against anything.

The NTC had at least set out a clear political path. Within eight months of the official declaration of liberation, elections for a new national assembly would be held. That body should write a constitution in preparation for general elections within twenty months. The constitution would be critical, because it would define whether men and women would be equal, whether the law would be based exclusively on *sharia* and what checks and balances there would be to prevent the rise of another Gaddafi. Unlike Tunisia or Egypt, Libya had never had even an approximation of democracy—political parties were abolished by King Idris after just one election with a limited franchise in 1952. "We don't have the infrastructure or even a database," said Salwa Bughaigis, who I had met back in February when she had been involved with the NTC in Benghazi. She returned from observing Tunisia's October elections alarmed at how much there was to do. "Getting freedom doesn't mean reaching democracy. We haven't even started to prepare people, and time is so short." Libya had no electoral law, no election commission, no safeguards against rigging and no experience in how to establish the mechanisms needed. Salwa had grown frustrated with the NTC, because she felt, as a woman, her voice was not being heard. "My sister Iman and I were very effective in the beginning, but the men didn't believe that women could play a role at this time. They didn't think we had the strength, background or ability." By December, Salwa and some twenty thousand Benghazi residents had established tented protest camps to draw attention to lack of transparency on the part of the NTC and the new government. What decisions had been made? By whom? What was the process? Who was consulted? Those running Libya had no experience of governing, let alone governing in a transparent and democratic manner.

In Misrata, they were creating their own myth, in which no other Libyans featured. Much to the annoyance of brigades from other towns, the Misrata fighters had removed the golden fist statue from Bab al Aziziyah and placed it on Tripoli Street, alongside a model of an eagle with a three-yard wingspan holding a Gaddafi doll in its talons, several burned-out tanks and thousands of spent shell casings. Loud revolutionary music played as Misrata residents came to have their photographs taken alongside the memorabilia. The sole exhibit to be stolen from the Tripoli Museum during the conflict was the possessions of Ramadan Al-Swehli, Misrata's answer to Omar Mukhtar, who had fought against the Italians. Rather than leave his memory to stand in the capital among the other national heroes of the anticolonial struggle, the fighters of Misrata had brought it back to the town.

The people of Misrata created two museums of the revolution. In a building behind the golden fist statue, row upon row of photographs of those who had lost their lives in the siege were pasted on the walls, plus the ID cards of Africans they said were mercenaries. When I visited it was packed with families. The other museum, in an abandoned municipal building, featured wooden models of various weapons, children's paintings of the battle for Misrata and a photocopy of Gaddafi's death certificate. They had made replicas like dolls' houses of the destroyed buildings along Tripoli Street. Someone had wired-up a smoke machine, so you could press a button and white puffs would blow out of the charred windows of the model insurance building. Misrata was coming down from a massive adrenalin high. Twenty-six-year-old Tarek Abozeid, who had been injured fighting on the front line, was contemplating a return to life as a hospital doctor. "Normal routine is so boring," he said, his long legs stretched out in front of him, as he sat on the cushions lining the family living room. "We've grown used to dealing with life and death. It was the best time of my life, because the guys I fought with are the best people I ever met."

On the sand dunes overlooking the Mediterranean, they had created a cemetery for the Gaddafi soldiers who had died. Seven hundred graves marked by plain concrete tombstones were arranged in neat rows. Photographs had been taken of every body before burial, so relatives would be able to identify them. Some already had names inscribed; others were given a mark to indicate that they were still unknown. I asked about mercenaries. "They didn't deserve burial," said the young man who was showing me around. Several hundred men suspected of being foreign fighters or Tawergha were still being held by the Misrata brigades in unofficial prisons around the town. They had no intention of allowing any central body to take control of them—these were Misrata's prisoners, and they would do with them as they pleased. Disturbing reports of torture and killings emerged. In Misrata, the new ways were not dissimilar to the old ways.

In Benghazi, I tracked down Tawfik, the young man whose images of the Green Book statues being toppled in Tobruk had alerted the world to the revolution in Libya. After Ramadan and the fall of Tripoli, he had gone to fight in Sirte with the Omar Mukhtar Brigade, composed of, he said, "me and about 150 of my cousins." His face was darkened by the sun, and he seemed much older, more solid and strong, a man not a youth. He had narrowly escaped death when the vehicle in which he was traveling was hit by a rocket-propelled grenade. One of his comrades had lost a leg, the other an arm. "When you're on the front line, you don't think about death," he said. "A friend from Benghazi was shot between the eyes right next to me, and I carried his body to the ambulance, and I didn't feel anything." He said he had received no training before going to fight. "Just, pull this, push this, and shoot." I said that was probably why the battle for Sirte took so long and there had been so many casualties. "I'm always careful," he said. "But we never retreated without a reason." He was planning to return to university in Tobruk, but he would defer his scholarship to the United States for a few years. "We're all needed here," he said. He grinned. "I knew deep in my soul that we would win. In Tobruk, we breathed freedom for one month, and then we couldn't let go."

One morning, in between the fall of Tripoli and the death of Gaddafi I had coffee with Razia Sholeh, the young woman who had been part of the family entourage. She had chosen a deserted café in a shopping center where no one was likely to overhear our conversation. "I don't know why they tell so many lies about the Guide," she mused. "They say he liked little girls. But I spent four years traveling with him, and I never saw anything like that." She was giving me the same answers she had given the new authorities the five times they had interrogated her. "They are polite with me, but they always ask the same questions about the Guide's private life—I don't know why." They kept asking where her husband was too, and she didn't have an answer to that question either. She hadn't seen him since the *iftar* meal on August 20th, the evening of the uprising. "I think he must be with the Guide," she said. I asked where that might be. "I don't know," she said.

Razia lurched backward and forward in her mind, at one moment talking of how to adapt to the new reality, at another refusing to accept reality at all. "Do you think the Guide will come back?" she asked. I said I didn't. She was silent for a moment. "I agree. It's too late," she said. Then her brown eyes flashed and widened. "But it's not finished," she said. "No one can say he isn't strong! He took his weapons, and he's got his people with him." Three days earlier, she said, a storm had whipped up along the coast, and that made people think Gaddafi was coming back. "They all put up green flags," she said.

Every day brought her more proof that life had been better under Gaddafi, and that the future was dark. "I don't understand why the people of Misrata did this," she said. "They were rich! I don't believe they did it for freedom. They've destroyed everything." We drove through the chaotic traffic of downtown Tripoli, avoiding head-on collisions by a whisker at every junction and turning sharply left or right, perilously close to vehicles hurtling up on either side. "There's no law any longer," she complained, as if she had never seen bad driving before. "I am a Muslim, an Arab and a Libyan," she said. "I have to tell you that democracy cannot work here. It's not possible with Arabs. Gaddafi did a lot for Libya." She was especially scornful of those who had supported Gaddafi in the past and abandoned him when the wind changed, and of those of her colleagues who pretended not to know her when they saw her on the street. "What's the difference? These are the same people! Is that democracy?"

The week after Gaddafi's death, Razia fled to Tunis to stay with friends while she worked out her next move. "I cried about the way the Guide was killed," she said, as we drank tea in a downtown hotel. "I couldn't sleep. Every time I closed my eyes I would see him." There was still no word of

Salah. She showed me his picture: a man in his thirties with a plump face and the trace of a mustache, posing with their son, both wearing the traditional *jird*. Salah's name was on a wanted list issued by the NTC, which was trying to track down those closest to Gaddafi for questioning. "I'm sure he's still alive," she said. "I have that feeling. But for me it would be better if he were dead than if the rebels put him in prison." She shook her head. "There's no justice here anymore," she said.

Razia had been around the morgues and hospitals before leaving Tripoli. Thousands of families on both sides of the war were still looking for missing relatives. Mervat Mhani founded an organization called Mafqood, which means, simply, Missing, and set up a Web site where people could register the names of family members they had lost. She put the word out on Facebook, Twitter and by leaflet, and by December she had six hundred names. "I don't ask if they're Gaddafi supporters or not," she said, but many of the families were looking for young men who had been fighting for Gaddafi in Sirte or Misrata, so she knew. It was the three days that her aunt and uncle spent looking for her cousin Suleiman that inspired her. "Not knowing was more painful than finding him dead in the morgue," she said. She and a group of volunteers trudged around hospitals and morgues taking photographs and matching them with pictures families had posted on the Web site. "Sometimes the bodies were so destroyed or decomposed the only identification was a belt, or a mark on the forehead," she said. Soon people were calling her not just about those who had gone missing during the revolution but during the four decades of Gaddafi's rule. "There are women whose husbands disappeared in the nineties," she said. It was work that could take a lifetime, tracing not just the well-known victims, like those who had been killed at Abu Salim, but thousands of unknown cases, of people who didn't matter, whose families had never dared say anything, who had lived in silence for forty-two years.

Mervat's brother Niz went back to his job as a surgeon in Cardiff. In the middle of the revolution he had been appointed to a more senior position in the hospital. "I did the interview on Skype," he said. "I didn't explain that we'd stolen the satellite dish from one of Gaddafi's offices." We met outside the Royal Festival Hall, overlooking the Thames on an unseasonably sunny autumn afternoon, a few days after he had returned to Britain. He was struggling to adjust. "It seems so strange," he said, looking at the mothers with babies, the students starting the new term, the middle-aged middle-class women on a day visit to London to see the exhibitions. "All these people are thinking about something else. I will never do anything as important as I did in those seven months. What we did will be talked about for generations." He thought of his cousin who had died just as the revolution triumphed. "They will talk about people like Suleiman long after we are all dead."

Mervat believed that Libyan women couldn't now be held back. "We are way stronger than Libyan men," she said. "We don't need to ask anyone's permission. We're involved whether they like it or not." Yet there was only one woman on the NTC and two in the government, and the Islamists were carefully not making their views on women's participation known. "The men say that women don't have the experience to go into politics," said Mervat, "but they don't have the experience either! We've all been living under dictatorship."

Enas Dokali decided to go public about her experiences in prison, giving interviews to Arabic TV stations, only to find that for every person who sympathized with her experience there was another who blamed her. "Some people say I took money to go on TV, and that I'm running after fame. Others don't believe I wasn't raped," she said. "But just because you're arrested you shouldn't feel shame. Even women who *were* raped should say so; they shouldn't be ashamed."

In the medina, Mohammed Mustafa Saudi was bashing out brass trays as he had done for nearly five decades, since before Gaddafi came to power. His most popular designs were now maps of the country embossed with the revolutionary flag and commemorative trays for the families of the martyrs. He laughed about the old days, when he would have to charge thirty dinars for a twenty-dinar tray if it had Gaddafi's face on it. "It was supposed to be more precious!" he chuckled. "With this revolution I feel as if I've been reborn." He was sixty-four now, and his priority was his eight children and eleven grandchildren. "You look at other Arab countries, and they've progressed, but Libya hasn't changed," he said. "I just want the government to serve the country, and not to steal."

One afternoon in October I went to the Tripoli Festival, a family event in a marquee near the harbor. Dozens of stalls were selling revolutionary merchandise, everything in red-black-green, from baseball caps and mugs to feathered hair barrettes and iced cakes. Two women with pink bunny ears were face-painting, giving the children red butterfly wings over their eyes with a green-and-black stripe down their noses. One stall had glossy Photoshopped images of the Gaddafi family—Muammar covered in blood with a speech balloon saying, "I'm a hyena, and I'm going to eat you," with Seif al-Islam next to him saying, "I'm the hyena's son," and the Guide styled as the Iron Maiden figure, long hair flying to one side, his body and guitar as skeletons. I got into conversation with two seventeen-year-old boys. "This is good, because Tripoli is so boring," they explained. The perennial cry of the teenager was understandable, because the Libyan capital had no clubs or youth centers, nothing for young people to do. "The girls want shopping malls like they have in Dubai, so they have somewhere to hang out," they said. And the boys? "We want shopping malls too, so we can hang out with the girls! We meet on Facebook, but then there's nowhere to go."

Libyans, I thought, had such differing aspirations for their country. A few days earlier a small group of young men had attacked Sufi shrines around Tripoli. Sufis pray over the graves of saints, which Salafis and other hard-line Sunnis see as idolatrous. In one incident a dozen armed, bearded men wearing military uniforms arrived in pickup trucks mounted with heavy weapons and stormed into a mosque, where they burned relics and exhumed the remains of two imams. In the midst of the joy and chaos of revolution, destroying graves that had been there for centuries was their priority.

Every day some group or other would hold a demonstration in Martyrs' Square or outside a ministry. There were myriad causes, and protest was the chosen method of making your wishes known, fueled by the fear that if you didn't get your way now, maybe you never would. It was as if Libyans thought that Gaddafi might come back, that they would lose the freedom they had fought for if they didn't exercise it to the maximum all the time. Some protested about too many Gaddafi-era employees working in this or that department, others about sending the militias back to their hometowns; there were demonstrations for and against the Islamists. The new Libya was a blank canvas on which any group might paint its own design. After four decades, everyone was in a hurry, apart from those who were supposed to be restoring order and creating government, who held endless meetings, the outcomes of which they failed to convey to those protesting outside.

That year, the rains came early—Libyans said they had never known the winter to start so soon. The road to the Tunisian border was awash, and cars moved slowly, over their hubcaps with water. People said it proved that God was happy—he was rewarding Libyans for getting rid of Gaddafi. Waves crashed onto the beach around the island that Saadi had used as the jumping-off point for his adventures with Jet Skis and speedboats. One night I leaned out of my hotel window in Tripoli and watched jagged bolts of lightning zigzagging between the buildings as thunder cracked and roared, drowning out the honking car horns and happy shooting that had erupted on the street below. Between Bin Jawad and Brega, where the eastern rebels had fought so desperately and to such little effect, clumps of green emerged through the sand. The *ghibli* was long over, the dust subsided, the sand settled. Somewhere out there, Gaddafi lay in his unmarked grave, anonymity thrust upon a man who had courted notoriety all his life. The people of Libya had to learn to look beyond his legacy. The north wind, the *bahri,* whipped across the seaboard in furious gusts, bringing longed-for cool air and torrential rain that drained slowly into rivulets, tracing new patterns through the damp sand of the desert.

EPILOGUE

Omran Shabaan died in Paris on September 25, 2012. The man who had spotted Muammar Gaddafi in the culvert in Sirte, and who had shown me the dictator's Cuban-heeled boots and golden pistol, met a fate scarcely less brutal. In July, he went as part of a group of fighters from his hometown of Misrata to Bani Walid, ninety miles to the southwest, to negotiate the release of two local journalists who were being held hostage. Nearly a year after the overthrow of Gaddafi, the people of Bani Walid still refused to accept the revolution, which had rekindled their decades-old feud with Misrata; there were skirmishes and raids, and both sides seized and held men from the other town. Elders were hoping that prisoner swaps would calm things down, but Shabaan was shot in the lower back and kidnapped. His father told journalists that his captors would ring and leave messages. "If you want Omran back, tell us where Gaddafi is buried," said one.

Shabaan's family said he was beaten and tortured for two months before the speaker of Libya's newly elected parliament, Mohammed Magarief, eventually persuaded the fighters of Bani Walid to release him. It was too late. Emaciated and unconscious, he was flown to France, where he died in hospital.

Thousands surged to Misrata airport to greet Shabaan's body when it was brought home for burial. They gathered at a football stadium for funeral prayers. Grief was augmented by anger, not just with the men of Bani Walid but with Libya's weak and incompetent leaders, who had allowed the last redoubt of Gaddafi's support to rule itself though a council that was still loyal to the deposed dictator. Yet the Misrata fighters had taken equal advantage of the authorities' failure to impose the rule of law.

Nearly a year after the official declaration of liberation, few Libyans had laid down the weapons they had taken up to overthrow Gaddafi. Misrata, Zintan, and Benghazi chafed at rule from Tripoli, preferring to govern themselves as city-states protected by their own young men. Each town had its own military council and none paid much attention to the fledgling Ministry of Defense in the capital.

Militia proliferated across the country. The National Transitional Council decided that, being powerless to make the fighters join a formal national army or police force, they would provide umbrella groups to license the brigades. The Interior Ministry announced the formation of the Supreme Security Committee for militia who fancied becoming policemen. Those who came under the Libyan Shield Forces were nominally the National Army, which frequently meant that militia simply added a new decal to their armored vehicles. A warriors' commission was formed to pay fighters in the hope that the lure of money would make them register, but all it did was encourage young men who had not fought in the revolution to create new brigades and demand salaries.

Drug smugglers found that the cover of being a militia enabled them to continue their trade. Others were more interested in revenge or seizing property. In July, I met General Salem Abu Shrida, a sheikh from eastern Libya, who had retired from Gaddafi's army some years before the revolution. Sitting on a white plastic chair, leaning forward with hands crossed on his traditional walking cane, he was receiving visitors under an awning outside his comfortable house in central Tripoli. This was a mourning tent, erected for friends and relatives to pay respects on the death of a family member. As he told me the story, the old man began to cry. One evening the previous week, his eldest son, Abdu Salam, had been kidnapped by armed men from Zawiya, where the family had bought a farm some years earlier. When he set out to find his son the next day, he too was kidnapped, taken to a house near their farmstead, tied to a chair, and beaten. They interrogated him about his links to Gaddafi but that, he said, was not the main issue.

"We had bought the farm with our own money," he insisted. "It was not given to us by Gaddafi. But they wanted it." After a night of being beaten and forced to sleep in a bathroom, he signed away the farm, hoping to save his and his son's lives. The next day the kidnappers dumped him on the road but when he reached home he got the bad news: Abdu Salam's body had been found lying in a hospital morgue, his feet, chest, back, and face covered in blood and bruises. He showed me the hospital death certificate—cause of death: torture.

General Abu Shrida said he knew the gang who had killed his son, and as we were talking a call came saying that the suspects had been arrested by men from the SSC. He had little faith they would end up in court, or that he would see justice.

"There is no future," he said, wiping his eyes. "There is just blood and tribes. It's not easy to forget."

Other Libyans were putting their faith in the first multiparty elections since 1952, to be held the following week. In June, a Muslim Brotherhood candidate had been elected president in Egypt. The moderate Islamist party Ennahda had won elections in Tunisia. In Washington and London, analysts were saying that an Islamist wave sweeping across North Africa was the inevitable outcome of the Arab Spring. Libya would be no exception. More than half the seats in the national assembly would be allocated to individuals, but Libyans and foreigners alike were talking about the new political parties contesting the remainder. The Muslim Brotherhood styled itself as the Justice and Construction Party. Sami al Saadi, who had been in the jihadi Libyan Islamic Fighting Group and had later been rendered back to Libya with the help of the CIA and MI6, formed his

own party with two candidates for election, himself and a friend. His former colleague Abdel Hakim Belhaj founded a much bigger party, with
purple-themed posters that were conspicuously better produced and more
professional than anyone else's because—Libyans muttered—he had the
backing of Qatar.

I flew east to Benghazi and drove onto Derna, which the U.S. diplomat
Chris Stevens had visited in 2008 to find out why so many of its young
men had gone to fight as jihadis in Iraq. Derna was always cited as an
Islamist stronghold. Black Al Qaeda–style flags fluttered over a few buildings on the edge of town. At the mosque overlooking the central square a
group of middle-aged academics gathered to explain what was going on.

"These people with the black flag—you can count them on the fingers
of one hand," said one. "They come at night and in a hurry because no one
likes them." The jihadis had killed an official, he said, but he was more
worried about the Muslim Brotherhood. "They will use democracy to get
their goals and then pull up the ladder," he warned. Some easterners were
boycotting the election because they resented rule from Tripoli and
wanted historical Cyrenaica either to split off and become an independent
state, or at least to have more seats in the new assembly. Outside the
mosque a few men were holding a demonstration. "The west of Libya has
stolen our revolution," said an old man. Some of the youths were tearing
down election posters when a young woman wearing a head scarf appeared
and started shouting at them. She was a candidate, she said.

"I'm very sad to see my people with this mentality," she told me.
"Libya is free but we want elections and a new government. It's OK, this
is freedom, but they shouldn't tear down posters. We want to settle down
and rebuild the country." As she argued with the men, I thought how
remarkable it was that just eighteen months earlier only one face looked
down from billboards and walls, and just one view was allowed in Libya.
Now every surface was plastered with faces: men in suits, men in tradi-

tional *jird* and *fez*, women both head-scarfed and bare-headed. And you could have a political argument in the street.

On election day, I went to the polling station with Wanise Elisawi, who had spent nineteen years in Abu Salim prison and been an eyewitness to the massacre. He wanted every moment to be filmed—checking the voter list, picking up the ballot papers, going behind the screen, getting his forefinger inked to prove he had cast his vote. On the brink of tears, he held up his purple finger for the camera. "I never lost hope," he said. "Not even when I was in prison being tortured. This is a historic day for me."

The results confounded those who had predicted so confidently that Libyans would vote for Islamists. The largest number of votes went to a party led by Mahmoud Jibril, a Westernized technocrat who had once served as an economic adviser to Gaddafi, but who had been the international face of the revolution, flying around the world drumming up foreign support. The Muslim Brotherhood did poorly, as did parties led by Sami al Saadi and Belhaj. Libya was defying expectations again. Oil exports were back up to prerevolution levels and foreign companies started to think seriously about investing. Now there would be a government with legitimacy and a mandate to move Libya forward. At least, that was the hope.

Across the Sahara, the revolution in Libya was having unintended consequences. When Gaddafi was killed, hundreds of Tuareg, whom he had armed, fled through the desert, crossing the border into Niger and then into Mali. The Tuareg had been on the losing side in the war in Libya, but they decided to take advantage of the weapons they had salvaged. Ignoring a peace accord they had signed with the Malian government after a previous uprising, they announced they would create an independent Tuareg state called Azawad in northern Mali.

Mali was celebrated as one of the more democratic countries in West Africa—it had held several elections and was a great favorite with Western donors. Yet the north of the country had been unstable for a decade. In 2002, jihadis who had been fighting the Algerian government were defeated and moved south to take up residence in the ungoverned spaces of Mali's northern deserts, calling themselves Al Qaeda in the Islamic Mahgreb (AQIM). They made money from drug smuggling and ransoms from kidnapping tourists. European governments were ready to pay high prices for citizens adventurous (or foolish) enough to stray beyond the picturesque mud-walled mosques of Timbuktu. When the Tuareg started fighting for independence in early 2012, the jihadis joined in.

Malian soldiers, many of whom had not been paid or given rations, fled. Tuareg commanders switched sides and joined the rebels. Furious that they had not been provided with the means to resist the rebellion, junior officers staged a coup in the capital, Bamako, and the president fled. Overnight Mali went from model democracy to failed state. On April 1, a convoy of Tuareg and Islamist fighters drove into Timbuktu in six dozen commandeered vehicles that the U.S. government had given to the Malian army as part of an antiterrorism program. Both the black Al Qaeda flag and the red, green, black, and yellow flag of Azawad fluttered over the fabled city.

The Tuareg proved to be disorganized and at times brutal rulers. They careered around in four-wheel-drive vehicles looting and pillaging and on occasion abducting women and girls to rape. Many non-Tuareg fled the region, heading south to the relative safety of Bamako. Tuareg living in the south fled over the border to Burkina Faso, because other Malians were persecuting them for bringing the country to ruin. Mali was disintegrating, and half a million of its citizens were on the run. The marriage of convenience between the Islamists and the Tuareg broke down and in the fight that followed, the Islamists prevailed. It was a chain reaction: the defeat of Gaddafi had forced the Tuareg to flee, which had sparked the rebellion in northern Mali, which had led to a group linked to Al Qaeda taking control of an area the size of France, including the cities of Gao, Kidal, and Timbuktu and three international airports.

"NATO has a moral responsibility for what's happened in this country because we are paying the consequences of their actions in Libya," said Tiebile Drame, a former Malian foreign minister. "It's not fair to wash their hands of what's happened here."

Yet NATO governments seemed content to let Mali drift. The UN did not pass a resolution authorizing intervention until September, and then it farmed the problem out to West African states.

In a refugee camp in Mauritania, I talked to Tuareg who had fled Timbuktu.

"We're frightened because there's no government we can trust to protect us from the armed groups," said one. The Islamists put a couple accused of adultery into a hole and stoned them to death. They took jackhammers to Timbuktu's ancient Sufi shrines, decrying them as idolatrous. They held summary trials and amputated the hands of alleged thieves. "We're scared of everyone. You can't even go out to buy food, because your life is at risk," said a woman tending a malnourished baby. In Bamako, a Malian journalist showed me cell phone footage of a teenage boy in Timbuktu being whipped for smoking. "See the man with the whip?" he said. "He's from Pakistan." Northern Mali was attracting jihadis from around the world who threatened to use northern Mali as base for terror attacks. "When we've conquered France, we'll come to the USA, we'll come to London and conquer the whole world. The banner of Mohammed (peace be upon his head) will be raised from where the sun rises to where it sets," snarled one of their military commanders.

History was moving in unforeseen ways. Gaddafi's recruitment of the Tuareg and NATO's support for the revolution had left an unpredictable legacy.

. . .

Back in Libya the excitement and pride engendered by a successful election was fading. Despite its democratic legitimacy, the new General National Council was as weak as the transitional body it had replaced. The first sign of how serious this could be came within a few days when the shrine in front of the mosque I had visited in Derna was blown up by the Salafists. At the end of August, gangs of armed and bearded men in jeeps and bulldozers attacked Sufi shrines in Zliten and Tripoli. Fighters from the SSC not only failed to stop the demolition but held back those trying to protect the mosques. The SSC had been infiltrated by Islamists. From her apartment with its balcony overlooking Tripoli harbor, Huda Abuzeid, who had come back to Libya from London to join the revolution after the murder of her father, watched in dismay as the Salafists destroyed the Al Sha'ab shrine, right in the center of the capital. Her anger and frustration at the authorities was shared by others who came out on the streets the following day to demonstrate. Watching from the medina in Tripoli, Mohamed Mustafa Saudi, the metal worker, shook his head. "They are chopping the hands off thieves before they have even stolen anything," he said. "It's hard to fix all that is now wrong, to put law and order in the country." The minister of interior resigned for a day but then reinstated himself on the grounds that the attackers were armed so could not be confronted. "If all shrines in Libya are destroyed so we can avoid the death of one person, then that is a price we are ready to pay," he said.

It was a signal to the Islamist brigades: whatever they did, no one would stop them.

The American diplomat Chris Stevens had returned to Libya during the revolution the previous year, setting up an office in Benghazi. After the fall of Gaddafi, he was appointed ambassador and moved to Tripoli. An Arabic speaker with a great love of Arab culture, he was an enthusiast for the revolution, numbering senior Libyan politicians and civil society activists among his friends. On September 11, the twelfth anniversary of the attack on the Twin Towers in New York, he was visiting the consulate in Benghazi.

What happened that night not only shook Libya, but became an issue in the 2012 U.S. elections. That week, anti-American demonstrators were holding protests across the Muslim world in response to an obscure and laughably bad film made in California, that portrayed Mohammed as an idiot, a pedophile, and worse. It gained notoriety when the Egyptian Salafist TV station Al Nas broadcast extracts as evidence that America was anti-Islam. In Cairo, Islamabad, and other places where people could not distinguish between U.S. government policy and the activities of a prejudiced fringe, Islamist political parties whipped up the mob.

During the day Ambassador Stevens held meetings inside the consulate rather than venturing out. Security was tight because of the demonstrations and the date. Around 8:30 P.M. he escorted his last guest, the Turkish consul, to the gate. Just over an hour later, armed militiamen in jeeps turned up. A local journalist I spoke to the next morning described the scene. "They fired a rocket propelled grenade and then fighting started," he said. "The national army tried to stop them but they went in and burnt the embassy compound." The militia, he said, were from Ansar al Sharia ("Partisans of Islamic Law"), a local Islamist brigade with members in Benghazi and Derna. The leaders were well-known, and they flew flags with the brigade's insignia. A crowd gathered. The armed men said they were attacking the consulate because the film had been made by Americans. "They said we shouldn't have these people in our land," said the journalist. "There were hundreds of them."

Guards inside the compound heard cries of "Allahu Akbar!" outside. As the attack started, staff at the consulate operations center radioed for help and informed the State Department in Washington that they were under attack. The ambassador's close protection officer took him to a "safe room" with no window or door to the outside, in one of the three villas within the compound. Five armed Americans and three Libyans from the February 17th militia—one of those that had been licensed by the authorities—were tasked with guarding the consulate, but they were outnumbered and outgunned. The attackers put up a ladder and poured over the nine-foot-high wall, carrying cans of diesel that they sprinkled around the villa before setting it alight.

Eventually, a six-man U.S. quick reaction security team plus sixteen Libyan fighters arrived. Amid the shouting, the smoke and flames and continued firing no one seemed to know where the ambassador had gone, but the rest of the Americans were bundled into armored vehicles and driven away. They took with them the body of a State Department official, Sean Smith, who had been overcome by smoke. The reinforcements had come from a supposedly secret CIA complex known as "the annex" and that was where they now headed. In the early hours it came under sustained attack—one report suggests that fifteen rocket propelled grenades and a mortar were fired within two minutes. This was no demonstration that got out of hand—it was a carefully planned, targeted assault on a building that turned out to be neither safe nor secret. Two Navy Seals died trying to defend the annex before the remaining Americans were flown to Tripoli.

Back at the consulate, looters and onlookers were combing through the wreckage. Video footage shows a crowd of men entering the smoldering building and dragging out a man in dark trousers and a light-colored shirt. He's unconscious, or is he dead? "Alive! Alive! Allahu Akbar!" shouts one. They drove him to Benghazi Medical Center, where doctors tried without success to revive him. At 2:30 A.M. the dead man with the soot-covered face was identified: it was Chris Stevens, the U.S. ambassador. He had died of smoke inhalation.

In Washington, the State Department was in shock. Secretary of State Hillary Clinton fought back tears as she announced the four deaths. No American ambassador had been killed since 1979. Only five ambassadors had been killed in U.S. diplomatic history. Worse than that, Libya was not an enemy country but a place where the U.S. government had helped to topple a dictator. President Obama had supported the revolution. Was this his reward? Recriminations were swift. "It is our responsibility and the responsibility of the president to use America's great power to shape history, not to lead from behind, leaving our destiny at the mercy of events. Unfortunately, that's exactly where we find ourselves in the Middle East under President Obama," said Mitt Romney, Obama's Republican rival.

Romney saw the tragedy of Benghazi as evidence of Obama's passivity in the face of a renewed terrorist threat. Republican Congressmen accused the Obama administration of failing to provide adequate security—after all, convoys carrying the UN representative and the British ambassador had been targeted some months earlier, and on occasion people had lobbed "gelatinas," small devices made from explosives used for fishing, into the U.S. compound. The administration seemed confused about the sequence of events, at first suggesting the attack had been spontaneous, the result of a demonstration which was "hijacked by Islamists." Later Hillary Clinton linked the attackers to AQIM, the jihadis operating in northern Mali, saying a call between the two had been intercepted at the time of the attack.

Al Qaeda central, based now in the tribal areas of Pakistan, was also cited. On his death, Osama bin Laden had been replaced by an Egyptian, Ayman al Zawahiri, who in turn appointed a former member of the Libyan Islamic Fighting Group, Abu Yahyia al Libi, as his deputy. Al Libi was killed in an American drone strike in June. On September 10, al Zawahiri called for Libyans to avenge his deputy's death. Some believed the attack on the consulate was that revenge. The U.S. administration was reluctant to provide details. The annex, it seems, was an important CIA hub for monitoring jihadi activity. It had been destroyed by the very men the officers inside were trying to monitor and defeat.

Libyans who had supported the revolution and voted for moderate leaders watched aghast. In the days that followed they came out onto the streets of Benghazi and Tripoli with banners: THUGS AND KILLERS DON'T

REPRESENT BENGHAZI NOR ISLAM, CHRIS STEVENS WAS A FRIEND TO ALL LIBYANS, NO TO TERRORISM. Nizar and Mervant Mhani of the Free Generation Movement started online campaigns. Huda joined protests in Tripoli. Mukhtar Nagasa, the dentist from Zintan, wrote on his Facebook page: "I am no longer proud to be a Libyan." Ten days later, an estimated thirty thousand people came onto the streets of Benghazi determined to act. At dusk, the women and children returned home and the men, some of whom were armed, marched to the headquarters of Ansar Al Sharia. At first they argued with the zealots. Then they attacked. Eleven people were killed in the melee but by the morning, Ansar al Sharia had been driven out of town. The crowd marched on the headquarters of two other brigades that had not been implicated in the attack but were regarded as Islamist. They also fled. The following day, two black flag brigades in Derna announced that they too were disbanding.

Those who had started the revolution were reclaiming it, but the authorities continued to let them down. By October, only a handful of arrests had been made and the leader of Ansar al Sharia was back wandering freely round Benghazi, drinking strawberry frappe with a *New York Times* journalist in a hotel. The first prime minister after the election had been forced to step down and a new one appointed—there was still no effective government. It was hard for the British and American governments who had supported the revolution to trumpet Libya as a success story.

Seif al Gaddafi spent the year after his capture in detention in Zintan. A new high-security prison was under construction for him in Tripoli, but as the Libyan government and the International Criminal Court tussled over who would put him on trial, it was not clear whether the Zintanis would ever let him go. The other surviving members of the Gaddafi family remained under gilded house arrest, Saadi in Niger, Aisha and the others in Algeria. In March, Abdullah al Sanussi, Muammar Gaddafi's brother-in-law, the man who had overseen the Abu Salim massacre, was detained at Nouakchott airport in Mauritania. He had flown in from Morocco on a fake Malian passport. France, which had already found him guilty in absentia of bombing the UTA plane in 1989, wanted him to serve his sentence there. The ICC and Libya both made claims, and in September he was handed over to the authorities in Tripoli.

The demise of the Gaddafi clan did nothing to deter loyalists in Bani Walid. Most of the town's eighty thousand residents were from the Warfalla, Libya's biggest tribe, which had been the bedrock of Gaddafi's support. As long as the Misrata tribes were fighting the Warfalla, Libya would never be stable. After the death of Omran Shabaan, the government gave the Gaddafi loyalists in Bani Walid ten days to surrender. Nothing happened. Eventually Libyan Shield Forces, including Misrata militia, surrounded the town and attacked. The fighting was vicious; no one announced the number of casualties. Refugees fled in cars and on foot as soldiers went house to house searching for members of Khamis Gaddafi's 32 Brigade and other holdouts. On October 24, a week before the festival of Eid al Adha, and almost exactly one year after the killing of Muammar Gaddafi, the Libyan chief of staff, General Yusuf Mangoush, declared Bani Walid liberated.

There were few celebrations. In Tripoli, youths did not shoot in the air or hurtle around in their jeeps waving the revolutionary flag. The country had moved into a new phase. After a lifetime of living with too much authority, Libyans were now experiencing the uncertainty of living with not enough. It would take a decade to build a functioning state, and they had wasted much of the first year. After the killing of the U.S. ambassador international support was wavering. Families bought sheep to slaughter and gathered for the traditional feast, but there was none of the euphoria of last year's Eid. The fall of Bani Walid completed the revolution, but Libyans had yet to decide what to do with the freedom for which they had fought.

ACKNOWLEDGMENTS

I would like to thank my editors at Channel 4 News—Dorothy Byrne, Jim Gray, Martin Fewell and Ben de Pear—for giving me the time to write this book. Sarah Corp and I fell in love with Libya together, and I could not have asked for a better producer. Thank you also to camera operators Graham Heslop, Philippa Collins, Alastair Thomson, Ken McCallum, Jason Farrington and Paddy Wells and to my C4N colleagues Nevine Mabro, Jonathan Miller, Jonathan Rugman, Richard McElroy and Claire Sinka. Noman Benotman and Ashur Shamis were endlessly patient with my questions. Abdul Twebti was a tenacious researcher and Molly Tarhuni kindly reviewed the manuscript. I am grateful to Peter Bouckaert of Human Rights Watch, Susan Glen, Christopher Michael Brown, Martin Fletcher and Lucy Young for the photographs and to Giuma Atigha for permission to translate and quote from his memoir. For advice, help and much more, thank you to Jon Lee Anderson, Ray Bonner, Alistair Burt, Michael Clarke, John Corp, Chris Finn, Bubaker Habib, Pete Irons, Hassan Morajea, Cynthia Oakes, Jane Perlez, Scott Peterson and Shariff Shalabi. Thanks also to my agents, Felicity Bryan and George Lucas, and to Scott Moyers and Emily Graff, my editors at Penguin. Finally, thank you to my father, Cyril Hilsum, and my partner, Tim Lambon, for their support and encouragement.

NOTES ON SOURCES

This book is based on my reporting for Channel 4 News and the stories of Libyans I met, mainly during four trips I made to Libya in 2011. I have changed three names, on request. I am also indebted to scholars, writers, analysts and other journalists whose work I have consulted.

For background on the Gaddafi era and what preceded it I referred to *A History of Modern Libya* by Dirk Vandewalle (Cambridge, UK: Cambridge University Press, 2006) and *Libya: Continuity and Change* by Ronald Bruce St. John (London: Routledge, 2011). David Blundy and Andrew Lycett's 1987 book, *Qaddafi and the Libyan Revolution*, published by Weidenfeld and Nicolson (London), is excellent on the early years, as is John K. Cooley's *Libyan Sandstorm: The Complete Account of Qaddafi's Revolution*, published by Holt, Rinehart and Winston (New York) in 1982. For details on Gaddafi's arms purchases I turned to "Arming Libya: Transfers of Conventional Weapons Past and Present," by Derek Lutterbeck in *Contemporary Security Policy* 30, no. 3 (2009): 505–28.

In Chapter Four, I quote from *Memories of Prison and Exile*, by Giuma Atigha, which was published in Arabic by Dar Al Rowad (Cairo) in 2012. For information on the Muslim Brotherhood and the Libyan Islamic Fighting Group I referred to Camille Tawil's 2010 book, *Brothers in Arms: The Story of Al-Qai'ida and the Arab Jihadists*, published by Saqi (London), and *The Muslim Brotherhood: The Burden of Tradition* by Alison Pargeter, also published by Saqi (London) in 2010. Two academic articles were especially useful: Yehudit Ronen, "Qadhafi and Militant Islamism: Unprecedented Conflict," *Middle Eastern Studies* 38, no. 4 (October 2002): 1–16, and George Joffe, "Islamic Opposition in Libya," *Third World Quarterly* 10, no.

2 (April 1988): 615–31, as well as a report of the International Institute for Counter Terrorism, *The De-radicalization Process of Terrorist Organizations: The Libyan Case,* published in August 2010.

For Chapter Five, on Gaddafi's involvement in terrorism, I drew on Patrick Seale's 1992 book, *Abu Nidal: A Gun for Hire,* published by Hutchinson (London), and two books on the IRA: Ed Moloney's *A Secret History of the IRA* (London: Penguin, 2002) and *Bandit Country: The IRA and South Armagh* by Toby Harnden, published in 1999 by Hodder and Stoughton (London).

For Chapter Six, on Africa, two academic articles were especially useful: "Bush Path to Destruction: The Origin and Character of the Revolutionary United Front of Sierra Leone," by Ibrahim Abdullah, in *The Journal of Modern African Studies* 36, no. 2 (1988): 203–35, and "Qadhafi's Comeback: Libya and Sub-Saharan Africa in the 1990s" by Asteris Huliaras, in *African Affairs* 100 (2001): 5–25. I also referred to *The Mask of Anarchy: The Destruction of Liberia and the Religious Dimension of an African Civil War* by Stephen Ellis, which was published by Hurst and Company (London) in 1999.

For analysis of the events of 2011, I consulted reports by Human Rights Watch and Amnesty International, as well as two reports by the International Crisis Group: "Popular Protest in North Africa and the Middle East: Making Sense of Libya" (June 2011) and "Holding Libya Together: Security Challenges after Qadhafi" (December 2011), and Hugh Roberts's essay "Who Said Gaddafi Had to Go?" in the *London Review of Books,* November 17, 2011. For background on the military campaign, I referred to "Accidental Heroes: Britain, France and the Libya Operation," a report by the Royal United Services Institute (September 2011).

POETRY QUOTATIONS

Chapter Two

W. H. Auden, "Epitaph on a Tyrant," *Collected Shorter Poems 1927–1957,* Faber, 1966.

CHAPTER FOUR

James Fenton, "Blood and Lead," *Out of Danger*, Penguin, 1993.

CHAPTER TEN

W. H. Auden, "Sonnets from China II," *Collected Shorter Poems 1927–1957*, Faber, 1966.
Keith Douglas, "Mersa," *Complete Poems*, Faber, 1998.

INDEX